Crazy About Christmas

What People Are Saying ...

* Someone ought to call MyLinda Butterworth *Mother Christmas,* she has got so many great ideas and stories and oh, the recipes are so tasty. This is a great book! More than just a book for Christmas, I can use the recipes and crafts all year long."

    Kye Yeaman, Marriage and Family Therapist

* It is more than a recipe book or a storybook or even a activity book to keep the kids occupied. It is all three wrapped into one. With stories, activities and recipes for **all** of the days of Christmas. An advent calendar with a twist. DESTINED TO BE A PERENNIAL FAVORITE!

    Heartland Review.

* Popular with busy families who want to find ways to build traditions with their children. Individuals who want to find new ways to celebrate the holiday. Teachers for all the stories and activities they can use in their classrooms.

    Linda S. Day award-winning author of *Grandma's Magic Scissors*

* MyLinda Butterworth has created a kind of advent calendar that parents can use to create Christmas traditions with their children, individuals can share seasonal camaraderies with friends, and teachers can draw upon for classroom activities. The recipes are delicious, the crafts-based activities are totally entertaining, the stories are inspiring and engaging. This book is a welcome addition to any family, school or community library Christmas celebration ideas and references collection.

    Midwest Book Review

* This book is absolutely delightful! I can spend hours just reading the stories and experimenting with the recipes. It is pure fun and enjoyment for all ages. A must for every household.

    Orlando Sentinel

* A wealth of information and holiday excitement! This delightful book is stuffed full of wonderful ideas and delicious easy to prepare recipes. It is a **must have** for all teachers and mothers of young children. I LOVED IT!

    Carol Elaine Powell author of *Along the Way*

What People Are Saying ...

* "Don't count the calories! Just count on lots of fun and great food!"   Paula Kalinoski

* "The complete and ultimate guide for Christmas for kids of all ages. My tip of the day: Buy this book, it will be the only Christmas book you will need this year!"

  Bob O'Brien, Consumer Advocate,

* What a wonderful tool this book is for teacher. It saves the teachers time by providing an activity to go with the story. With so many stories and activities, my teachers are set for the whole Christmas season and receive a bonus of yummy recipes too."

  Cheryl Bottom, director of University Carillon Preschool

* It's Christmas in a nutshell. This magical work picks you up and delivers you right into the middle of the most heartwarming holiday season of the year. You will love what you feel as you read *Crazy about Christmas* and as you taste--literally and figuratively--the joys of each day! You will cherish this for years to come to this special one-of-a-kind creation.

  Linda S. Humphrey *Daily Post Athenian.com*

* I got this book to find some simple family time ideas and we have been reading the stories every night. We love it. I believe this will become our family's newest holiday tradition.   Jenny Dong

* With the world in turmoil, it is nice to have a book that thinks of family first. *Crazy About Christmas* lets us find simple ways to spend time with our family and to make the most of this crazy season. There are new stories, old legends, and traditional stories; assorted crafts and activities for every day including a Christmas Carol game, and some holiday jokes, not to mention all those delicious recipes. With 45 days of fun, food, activities, and stories your family won't lack for things to do or eat.

  Chris Carr - *Finding Family Time*

Crazy About Christmas

45 Days of Fun, Food, Stories, and Activities

written and compiled by

MyLinda Butterworth

Day to Day Books  *Lake Shore, Maryland*

Crazy About Christmas: Celebrating 45 Days of Fun, Food, Stories, and Activities
© 2022 MyLinda Butterworth

All rights reserved. No part of this publication may be reproduced, stored in a retrieval system or transmitted in any form by any means electronic, mechanical, photocopying, recording or otherwise, except brief extracts for the purpose of review, without the permission of the publisher and copyright owner. She grants the owner of this book the right to make copies of the patterns for their own individual and classroom use. She also grants storytellers permission to tell her stories as long as proper attribution is given. If large quantities of copies are desired please contact the publisher for permission.

Cover and Book Design: MyLinda Butterworth
Cover Photo from AdobeStock Photo

Paperback: ISBN-10:   1-890905-73-9
Paperback: ISBN-13:   978-1-890905-73-6
Hardcover: ISBN-10   1-890905-72-0
Hardcover: ISBN-13   978-1-890905-72-9
eBook: ISBN 10 -   1-890905-74-7
eBook: ISBN 13 -   978-1-890905-74-3

Printed in the United States of America
10 9 8 7 6 5 4 3 2 1

Library of Congress Control Number: 2020946828

Published by Day to Day Books a division of Day to Day Enterprises, Port St John, Florida
Visit us on the web at http://www.daytodayenterprises.com or
contact us at books@daytodayenterprises.com

All efforts have been made to give attribution to the authors and photographers used in this book. If we missed you please contact us.

I will honour Christmas in my heart,
and try to keep it all the year.
I will live in the Past, the Present, and the Future.
The Spirits of all Three shall strive within me.
I will not shut out the lessons that they teach!
Charles Dickens

Other books by MyLinda Butterworth

Just 24 Days Till Christmas
For Health's Sake: A Cancer Survivor's Cookbook
The Monster Run
Crazy for Christmas Holiday Planner

Coming in 2026 -
45th Anniversary Edition: For Health's Sake

Frogazoom with Linda S. Day
Springtime with Magic Scissors with Linda S. Day
Summer Sizzles with Magic Scissors with Linda S. Day
Autumn Adventures with Magic Scissors with Linda S. Day
Winter Fun with Magic Scissors with Linda S. Day

Storytelling CD
Just So Wild: Animal Stories from Around the World

Dedicated to the best gift around
The presence of my family wrapped in love.

Thank You and Merry Christmas!

I just wanted to say thank you for taking the time to read my book.
I hope you enjoyed it.

I love hearing your reaction as it helps me as I create my next book.

Please leave me a helpful review at Amazon, Barnes and Nobles, or
Good Reads letting me know what you thought of this book.
Your comments help me in creating better books for you.

As my way of saying thanks I will send you my
Embracing Togetherness for the Holidays Journal
if you email me a screen shot of your review to
CrazyAboutChristmasBook@gmail.com

Thanks Again!

My Linda Butterworth

Table of Contents

Introduction		xiii
November 23	Mullah Nasreddin and the Feast	1
	Jigsaw Puzzle	3
	Creamy Coconut Curry	4
November 24	The Clever Baker	5
	Indoor Fairy Garden	7
	Irish Dairy Cake	9
November 25	The Violin's Song	11
	Musical Chairs	13
	Brigadeiro	14
November 26	The Three Skaters	15
	Sock Snowman	20
	Ontbijtkoek or Peperkoek	21
November 27	**Luda, The Reindeer Maiden**	**23**
	Handprint Reindeer Shirt	26
	Harvest-Nut Granola	28
November 28	The Gingerbread Bees	29
	Chief Cookie Baker Apron	33
	Gingerbread Cookies	35
November 29	The Story of Childe Charity	37
	Tug Dog Toy	43
	Tasty Dog Treats	44
November 30	The Young King and the Stones	45
	Word Rocks	49
	Savory Cheese Coins	50
December 1	The ABC's of Christmas	51
	Scrabble Ornaments	53
	Taco Stack-Ups	54
December 2	In the Great Walled Country	55
	Gift Tags	60
	Hot Chocolate Sticks	61
December 3	A Kidnapped Santa Claus	63
	Crystal Coal Garden	71
	Strawberry Santa	72

December 4	A Letter from Santa Claus	73
	Handsy Santa	75
	Carrot-Apple Cake	78
	Pecan Cream Cheese Frosting:	78
December 5	Teach the Children	79
	Clay Pot Santa	82
	Idaho Style Cinnamon Rolls	84
December 6	Today is St. Nicholas Day,	86
	Little Piccola	87
	Cinnamon Stick Santa	90
	Lebkuchen Bars	91
December 7	Why the Evergreens are Forever Green	93
	Rustic Wood Slat Tree	94
	White Christmas Chili	95
December 8	The Tailor Of Gloucester	97
	Candy Cane Mice	102
	Chocolate Cherry Mice	104
December 9	The Legend of the Christmas Robin	105
	Bird Bath/Feeder	108
	Hummingbird Cake	109
	Cream Cheese Frosting	109
December 10	The Miracle	111
	Holiday Coasters	113
	Savory Toasted Cheese with Noodles	114
December 11	The Stranger Child	115
	Holiday Pillow Cases	117
	Spicy Sausage and Bean Soup	118
December 12	The Wooden Shoes of Little Wolff	119
	Spinning Whirligig Toy	122
	Gingerdoodles	123
December 13	A Sweet Reminder	125
	Candy Cane Vase	129
	Winter-Mint Crunch	130
December 14	The Christmas Fairy of Strasburg	131
	Christmas Fairy	134
	Cranberry Raspberry Jam	135

December 15	The Nutcracker and the Mouse King	137
	Holiday Cone Boxes	140
	Spiced Candied Pecans	142
December 16	The Worker in Sandalwood	143
	Christmas Card Boxes	148
	Pumpkin Pie Fudge	150
December 17	The Most Beautiful Thing	151
	Kissmas Trees	153
	Hot Fudge Pudding Cake	155
December 18	Christmas Humor	157
	Cookie Cutter Gift Bags	161
	Glazed Popcorn	162
December 19	The Legend Of The White Gifts	163
	White Elephant Exchange	165
	Finger Food Party Night	
	Mistletoe Punch	166
	Herb and Garlic Cheese	167
	Ham Pinwheels	167
	Amazing Crustless Quiche	168
	Chicken Nut Puffs	169
	Streusel Linzer Squares	170
December 20	The First Christmas Rose	171
	Stained Glass Jars	174
	Sand Art Brownies	176
December 21	The Star	177
	Dishtowel Angel	180
	Cream Puffs	181
December 22	Two Babes in a Manger	183
	Fruity Playdough	185
	Gingerbread Muffins	186
December 23	A Christmas Orange	187
	Pomander Ball	189
	Caramelized Orange Flan	190
December 24	A Different Kind of Christmas	191
	Stained Glass Manger	194
	Bacon Baklava	196

December 25	The Story of Christmas	199
	The Christmas Carol Game II	202
	Christmas Feast	
	Overnight Eggnog French Toast	211
	Sweet Potato Casserole	212
	Cheesy Potatoes	213
	Broccoli Cauliflower Salad	214
	90 Minute Dinner Rolls	215
	Pumpkin Pie Crunch Cake	216
December 26	Letter of Thanks	217
	Thank-You Cards	221
	Turkey Pot Pie	222
December 27	The Christmas Cuckoo	223
	Embossed Foil Art	229
	Barley Cream with Fruit	230
December 28	Offero, The Legend of St. Christopher	231
	The Quest for Stories	234
	Humble Pie	237
December 29	The Legend of the Snow Maiden	239
	Snowflake	241
	Homemade Marshmallows	243
December 30	The White Dwarf	245
	Cascading Star Mobile	247
	Snowdrop Pecan Pie	248
December 31	A Happy New Year	249
	Personalized Calendar	251
	Party Chow Snack Mix	252
January 1	The Fairy's New Year Gift	253
	Personalized Journal	255
	Lentil, Kielbasa, and Garlic Stew	258
January 2	Where Love Is, There God Is Also	259
	Ojo de Dios or God's Eye	269
	Soft Pretzels	271

January 3	The Elves and the Shoemaker	273
	Pine Cone Elves	275
	Bacon Cheddar Potato Pancakes	276
January 4	Three Trees	277
	Classic Tangram Puzzle	279
	Appetizer Tree Board	282
January 5	Le Befana the Giver of Gifts	283
	Aroma Therapy Candles	286
	Herbes de Provence	287
	Season Salt	287
January 6	The Magi in the West and Their Search for the Christ	289
	Fizzy Bath Bombs	296
	Quick and Easy King Cake	297
Works Cited		298
Index		299
About the Author		307

Want More Places to See Our Books or Follow Me on Social Media
Check out These Resources:

For Stories, Tongue Twisters and Alliterations follow me on YouTube;
https://www.youtube.com/@totallystories

Follow Me on Instagram for stories and food
https://www.instagram.com/totallystories/

Follow me on X
https://x.com/totallystories

Follow me on TikTok
h**ttps://www.tiktok.com/@totallystories8**

For All Things Story check out:
www.TotallyStories.com

Introduction

Christmas is a gift, one that keeps giving all season long. At this time of year people have open hearts and are willing to submit to a spirit of thanksgiving, kindness, giving, and love. People are more willing to forgive, to repair relationships and give freely and what is so intriguing is that most of them do not even recognize that this is due impart to the light of Christ working in their lives and in their hearts. There is a universal joy that encompasses the world and I enjoy seeing the sparkle in people's eyes and the smile on the faces of the children as they count down the days till Christmas. I cannot discount that the season has gotten far too commercial for me. I cringe when the ornaments and the trees start coming out before we even get to Halloween. I remember when you wouldn't see any decorations until after Thanksgiving, some may say I am old fashioned in my thoughts but I think each holiday deserves their own time to shine.

Christmas is my favorite time of year. I look forward to it with the anticipation of a child. The very first book I wrote was *Just 24 Days Till Christmas* with the idea that this holiday is an opportunity to spend time with family and reconnect like no other single time of the year. I wanted this book to encourage family time by providing stories, activities and food that could be shared for each of the 24 days leading to Christmas. A couple years after the release of my book I got a letter from a reader reminding me that Christmas does not end on December 25th but also includes the 12 days of Christmas which extend the holiday season all the way to January 6th and she was right. It has taken me far too many years to write this new book, but today I can say that this book celebrates the full season of Christmas starting the day after Thanksgiving all the way through to January 6th and is full of new and old stories, lots of crafts, activities, and of course...food. That brings the count up to 45 days of holiday celebrating depending on the actual date of Thanksgiving, so all you need to do is pick a day that you want to start and have fun.

My hopes and dreams are the same as my first book that it will help you find new ways to spend time with your family and friends, create new traditions and enjoy the old ones. This is a crazy old world and sometimes we just need to slow down and smell the gingerbread and enjoy the gift that Christmas is in your life and share it with those you care about

Crazy About Christmas

A 17th-century miniature of Nasreddin, currently in the Topkapı Palace Museum Library

November 23

Mullah Nasreddin and the Feast
A Tale of the Middle East
As told by MyLinda Butterworth

Mullah Nasreddin was sometimes a wise man and sometimes a fool. I will leave it up to you which he is in this story, but he is always watchful and kind. You see, it happened to be on a fine fall day when he was traveling home from a trip that he heard there was to be a great feast in town and that all were invited to attend, and since Nasreddin loved food, it is something he was not going to miss. As he passed through the town gates, he observed two children chasing after a drove of goats, trying to get them into the pen without any luck. In fact, it was going very badly, for they were knocking over laundry and eating vegetables out of baskets; they were creating quite a scene.

Nasreddin sat on his faithful donkey for a moment trying to figure out how he could help when he had a brilliant idea. He slowly climbed off his donkey and had the children bring him a basket. He then produced a round of bread which he broke into small pieces and put in the basket. Then he handed each child a handful of bread pieces and told them to quietly offer them to the goats to coax them home. He then began making a path of bread back to the pen where he placed the rest of the bread in a pile. The bread path worked like a charm, and before you knew it, all of the goats were back in the pen, but one who before going in knocked poor Nasreddin over and took the last piece of bread he had from his hand. The children helped Nasreddin up and thanked him for his help.

It was now late. Nasreddin had dust all over his clothes, but he wanted to get to the feast sooner than later, so he dusted himself off and approached the feast hall. Standing at the door of the feast hall was a rather large guard who looked at Nasreddin with disdain, for he did not look or smell good. The visiting prince had proclaimed that all were welcomed to the feast regardless of their station in life. Nasreddin was led into the banquet hall and sat at a table in the back of the room where few would see or smell him. The smell of the food wafting through the room was delightful, and he could hardly wait for the plate of food to make it to him… but when it got there, only crumbs were left. After this happened a couple of times, he decided to go home but not before noticing that all the best food was going to the well-dressed people in the room and the prince was at the head table.

Nasreddin left quickly, went home, had a scented bath drawn for himself, and requested his best clothes be brought to him straight away. When his bath was over, he put on his best coat and turban and went straight back to the feast hall. Nasreddin strutted up to the guard who thought he was someone important and bowed to him. He then escorted his elegantly dressed guest to the head table, where he sat him close to the visiting prince.

Crazy About Christmas

Before long, servants brought large platters of spiced meats, seasoned vegetables, breads, fruits, nuts, sweetmeats, and other delicacies were put before him, and a large glass of wine was poured for him. Before Nasreddin began to fill his plate with food, he looked out over the hall and saw people from all walks of life and varying stations of importance. Some people he recognized and some he did not, but nobody knew who he was in his fancy clothes, and many people smiled and waved at him as if he was someone of great importance.

Nasreddin spent a few minutes talking politely with the prince about trivial things and then began putting food on his plate. While this was the normal thing to do, what he did next was completely unexpected. He grabbed a piece of eggplant and smeared it on his beautiful coat, then he took a handful of spiced lamb and put it into the cuff of his coat. He put nuts and dates into the pockets of his trousers. He took a string of sausages and wrapped them around his neck like a scarf. Everyone in the room stopped and stared in amazement as Nasreddin continued to feed his coat. They didn't know what to say or think. Finally, Nasreddin took his glass of wine and poured it into one of the folds of his turban. At this point, the prince could no longer be silent and said, "My elegant friend, why are you putting this fine food all over your beautiful clothes?" Nasreddin stopped feeding his coat, rose, bowing slightly to the prince in respect, and said, "When I first arrived, I was dusty and smelly. When the platters of food came by, they were empty, and I went hungry. So, I went home and dressed in my very best clothes, which got me treated like royalty. I figured since it was the coat that had gotten me such a prime seat at the table, perhaps I should feed it first."

With that, the prince laughed and laughed and realized that if you are going to invite the whole town to feast with you, perhaps you should feed them all the same regardless of their appearance…and in the future, that is exactly what he did.

Many people claim Nasreddin as their own, i.e., Turks, Afghans, Iranians, even China, and Italy, to mention a few. Nasreddin's stories are best known throughout the Middle East and are usually told as a joke followed by a moral. These stories have been shared since the early 12th century.

November 23

Jigsaw Puzzle
Craft/Activity

MATERIALS

Cereal box or foam board
Photograph, drawing, magazine clipping
Spray adhesive or glue
Scissors or craft knife

image comes from a 17th century Hodja miniature

DIRECTIONS

1. Choose a photo or other image you want to be on your puzzle. Best to use one with lots of colors so it isn't to hard to put together.
2. Cut the box the a little larger than your image.
3. Place newspapers down on your workspace and spray the back of the box. Then carefully place your photo or image and carefully smooth out the air bubbles. If you decide to use glue, cover the box with glue then squeegee it so it covers evenly. Place picture on top and smooth out the air bubbles. Place something heavy on top and let dry completely before cutting out the pieces.
4. Trim off excess cardboard.
5. Turn your picture over and either freehand draw or trace a puzzle design on the cardboard. Don't make them too intricate or they will be too hard to cut out. You can find additional puzzle designs online by searching for jigsaw puzzle templates.
6. Carefully cut out your puzzle pieces by using a craft knife or some very sharp small scissors.
7. Put the puzzle together.

Creamy Coconut Curry

When you have had your fill of turkey sandwiches try taking those leftovers and making some creamy curry using your leftover turkey and vegetables.

INGREDIENTS:

2	cups cooked turkey or chicken, cut into bite sized pieces
1	cup chopped onion
1/4	cup oil
1/2	cup water
1	(13.5 oz can) coconut milk
1/4	cup tomato paste
2	teaspoons curry powder
1	teaspoon garlic powder
1	teaspoon ground ginger
2	teaspoons garam masala*
2	teaspoons sugar, optional
1/4	teaspoon salt
	Cooked rice, for serving

INSTRUCTIONS

1. In a large pot or high-sided skillet, heat oil on medium heat. Add onion and cook until translucent, 6 to 8 minutes.
2. Add spices and cook until fragrant, about 1 minute. Add tomato paste and cook until darkened slightly, 1-2 minutes more, be careful not to scorch it.
3. Add coconut milk and water and bring to a simmer.
4. Add turkey pieces, salt, sugar and let simmer until meat is warmed through, about 5-6 minutes.
5. Serve over hot rice with some naan or crispy bread
6. Optional serving ideas squeeze a little lime juice over curry and garnish with chopped fresh mint and cilantro.

* If you don't have garam masala you can add this spice blend instead: 1/2 teaspoon ground cumin, 1/4 teaspoon ground coriander, 1/4 teaspoon ground cardamom, 1/4 teaspoon ground black pepper 1/4 teaspoon ground cinnamon, a pinch ground cloves and ground nutmeg.

The Clever Baker
A Celtic Tale

Annie was a baker – the best in all Scotland. Shortbreads and buns and cakes-she made them all. And they were so delicious that no one ever left a crumb behind, on a table or floor.

Now this was fine for everyone but the fairies, who depended on those crumbs, and who had never had so much as a tiny taste of one of Annie's famous cakes. So one bright morning, the Fairy King decided to do something about that. He hid himself among the wild flowers by the side of the road, and when Annie passed on her way to market, he sprinkled fairy dust in her eyes to make her fall fast asleep.

When Annie awoke, she was no longer on the road, but deep in fairyland, face to face with the Fairy King.

"Annie!" the King commanded. "Everyone has tasted your wonderful cakes. Everyone, but us! So from now on, you will stay here in fairyland and bake for us every day."

"Oh dear," thought Annie. But she didn't show that she was worried, or even scared, for she was a clever woman. No, she set her mind at once, to making a plan for her escape.

"Very well," she said. "But if I am to bake you a cake. I will need ingredients-flour and milk, eggs and sugar and butter."

"Fetch them at once!" commanded the Fairy King. So off the fairies flew, to Annie's house. And back they flew, in a flash, with everything she needed.

"Oh dear," Annie sighed, shaking her head and still without a plan. "If I am to bake a cake. I will also need my tools-my pots and pans and pitchers and bowls and spoons."

"Fetch them quickly!" the Fairy King commanded again. But when the fairies returned, they were in such a hurry that they stumbled and sent the pots and pans crashing and clanking across the floor.

"OOH! OWW!" cried the Fairy King, jamming his hands against his ears. "You know very well that I cannot stand loud noises!"

And, at that moment, Annie had her plan.

She broke the eggs and poured the milk and mixed in the flour and butter. But when she stirred the batter, she made the spoon clatter-clackety, clackety, clack—against the side of the bowl.

The Fairy King winced at the noise, but Annie could see that it was not loud enough. And so she said, "Oh dear, I am used to having my little yellow cat beside me when I bake. I cannot make my best cake unless he is here."

So the Fairy King commanded and the fairies went, and came back at once with the cat.

Annie put the cat under the table and, as she mixed the batter, she trod, ever so gently on the cat's tail.

And so the spoon went, Clackety, clackety, clack!

And the cat went, "Yow! Yow! Yow!"

And the Fairy King looked even more uncomfortable.

"Oh dear," said Annie again. "It's still not right. I'm also used to having my big brown dog beside me when I bake. I don't suppose…?"

"Yes, yes," sighed the Fairy King. "Anything for a taste of that cake."

And the fairies were sent for the dog.

Annie put him next to the cat, and he soon began to bark.

And so the spoon went, "Clackety, clackety, clack!"

And the cat went, "Yow! Yow! Yow!"

And the dog went, "Woof! Woof! Woof!"

And the Fairy King stuck a fairy finger in each ear.

"Just one more thing," said Annie. "I am worried about my little baby. And I cannot do my best work when I am worried."

"All right, all right," moaned the Fairy King.

And he sent off his fairies one more time.

The baby was asleep when she arrived, but as soon as she heard all the noise she awoke with a cry.

And so the spoon went, "Clackety, clackety, clack!"

And the cat went, "Yow! Yow! Yow!"

And the dog went, "Woof! Woof! Woof!"

And the baby went, "Wah! Wah! Wah!"

And the Fairy King put his hands over his ears and shouted, "Enough! Enough! Enough!"

And everything went quiet.

"Even the best cake in the world is not worth all this racket," he cried. "Take your baby, woman, and your dog and your cat and your noisy spoon. Go back to your own world and leave us in peace!"

Annie smiled. "I'll do better than that," she said. "If you promise to leave me be, I'll put a special little cake for you and your people by the fairy mound each day."

"That's a bargain," smiled the Fairy King, and Annie and all that belonged to her were returned to her kitchen in a flash.

And every day, from then on, Annie left a cake by the fairy mound. And the Fairy King not only left her alone; each day he left her a little bag of gold, where the cake had been. And they were all very happy for the rest of their days.

November 24

Indoor Fairy Garden
Craft

The magical world of fairies is all about imagination, cute little houses surrounded by tiny furniture, tea cups, plants, and other fairy garden accessories. You can keep it simple or you can go crazy.

The fairy garden I made is fairly simple. It has a small house, table and chairs, a small pond and assorted trees and flowers which I put in a small tray I got at the dollar store.

MATERIALS LIST:.
pebbles   dirt (either potted or dig it yourself)   tiny clay pots
assorted artificial or dried flowers   small birdhouse   dried moss
marbles or glass beads   seashell pieces   twigs/stick
hot glue or Tacky® Glue   Craft paint/brushes

1. To start you need a container to design your indoor fairy garden, I used a small tray and filled the bottom with a light layer of pebbles, this gives it some stability. Then place a layer of potting soil or dirt over the top, don't fill it all the way to the top if you are going to use dry moss like I did.

2. I used a small birdhouse which I got at a dollar store, there are several styles to choose from. Next you will want to use some craft paint to paint it whatever color you want.

3. To make the door I collected some twigs and cut them a little longer than the opening in my birdhouse. Cut one twig first the length you need to cover the opening or the height you want the door. Now cut as

 Crazy About Christmas

many more as you will need for the whole door. Then cut two short pieces to go across to hold the frame together (see illustration to the right). I glued the sticks right onto the birdhouse with a drop of glue at the top and bottom. Fit the sticks close to each other and then glue the two smaller pieces across to hold the door frame together.

4. Being that this is a birdhouse, I chose to use a large glass stone to glue over the opening with hot glue to make a window, you can of course leave it open.

5. For the roof I used dried moss, you could also make shingles out of a pine cone (pull it apart first). To do this cut two pieces of moss the size of each roof side and glue them on with hot glue or Tacky glue. Your house is finished.

6. This garden has a small pond which I made using a broken flower pot with glass rocks and marbles flowing out. Like I said things I found around the house. Set the pot where you want it and then set your marbles in a circle or if you want make it a stream instead. I lined the pond with small stones.

7. Place your house where you want it in your garden and now it is time to decorate. I used the dried moss for grass and cut it to the appropriate size. For the table I used a small clay pot for the base and a wooden circle for the top which I hot glued together. For the chairs I used tiny clay pots. Then I used some pieces of dried flowers and pieces of other plastic flowers for the trees. Because you have rocks for drainage and dirt you could put in real plants.

8. Fairy gardens are personal to the individual creating them. If you have fairies you want to put in them or miniature pets all of that works. You will find items you can purchase at craft stores or at the dollar store to put in your fairy garden or create your own with found things or clay. You can put your garden in a large flower pot, a tray, or even in a tea cup, you are limited only by your imagination. Consider using an a theme like for the holidays with twinkling lights or in spring with lots of live flowers, I have even seen a fairy garden for pets. Inside or Outside the fairies will love them.

Note: While this fairy garden was crafted for indoors, you can create one outside as well in a large clay pot, planter box, on the ground near a tree, or in your flower garden.

November 24

Irish Dairy Cake
An Authentic Irish Pound Cake

INGREDIENTS

- 1½ cups butter, softened (3 sticks)
- 3 cups white sugar
- 6 eggs at room temperature
- 1 (8 ounce) package cream cheese, softened
- 1 teaspoon vanilla extract
- 3 cups all-purpose flour, sifted

INSTRUCTIONS

1. Preheat oven to 300°F and grease and flour a 10-inch Bundt® or tube pan.
2. In a bowl cream together the butter and sugar until completely smooth.
3. At the eggs one at a time beating each egg until fully incorporated before adding the next one.
4. Add the softened cream cheese and vanilla extract and mix thoroughly
5. Add the flour to the wet mixture about a half a cup at a time, mixing all the flour has been added and the batter is smooth and velvety. Pour batter into prepared pan. Rap the pan on the counter a couple of times to remove air bubbles.
6. Bake cake in the preheated oven until top is golden brown, about 1 1/2 hours. Insert a long wooden pick in center 5-10 minutes before the end if it comes out clean it's done.
7. Allow cake to cool for 10-15 minutes on a wire rack in the pan. Remove from pan, and cool completely on wire rack.
8. Can be sliced and served as is, glazed or served with fruits and whipped cream, dusted with powdered sugar or even toasted and served with butter and jam.

OPTION 1: To make cupcakes: Line cupcake pans with 24 paper liners and bake at 350°F for 23 minutes. For a bit of variety fill cupcake liners about 1/3 full and drop a 1/2 teaspoon of jam in the center and then add more batter to cover to about 3/4 full. Once cooled you can glaze or put a little buttercream frosting on top.

OPTION 2: A standard pound cake is generally vanilla in flavor but don't be afraid to try other flavor, like almond, orange, lemon, rum ...

We can *always*
make a difference to someone,
no matter what role we play.
—Lindsey Stirling—

November 25

The Violin's Song
A Tale of Brazil

Once upon a time there lived a young boy named Rafe who was all alone in the world but for the things his parents had left him -- a plot of land, a big orange cat and a few orange trees. But living alone left Rafe sad, so he decided he must move on to see the rest of the world. He sold the land and the orange trees, and with that money he bought a violin. He wanted to play the songs his parents once sang to him.

Day and night he practiced his violin, and soon he played it so well and with such emotion that his cat wept at the sound of the sad songs.

"Come," Rafe said to the cat. "Let us go into the world and find some work."

He set off toward the palace, taking along his violin, of course. At the palace he asked the king for work. But the king shook his head. He did not need any more musicians or servants or guards or shepherds.

"I need only someone to fight the giants," he said, referring to his kingdom's enormous enemy. "But you are obviously not fit for that sort of job." And with that the king sent Rafe away.

Rafe walked into the forest, and there he began to play his violin. The music wafted over the hills, and when the sheep heard it, they loved it so much that they followed the sound into the forest.

When Rafe saw the sheep coming toward him, his heart swelled with joy. As it did, the music changed, and instead of sadness, his music was filled with joy. Soon his cat began to dance to the tune, and this pleased Rafe so much that the songs grew livelier.

Pretty soon the sheep could not resist. They too began to dance to Rafe's violin music, and this pleased him so much that he played louder and faster and more beautifully.

He began to dance through the forest, leading the dancing cat and the dancing sheep. Before long they passed by a tree where the squirrel monkeys were resting. When they saw the festivities below, they began to chatter, spreading word of the beautiful music. Soon the squirrel monkeys and the woolly monkeys and the red-eyed frogs were all dancing.

When the tapir heard the sound, he too began to dance, and so did the jaguar and the marmoset and the armadillo in his heavy armor. When the alligator heard the music, he swam out of the river to dance. Snakes curled themselves around tree trunks to dance with the trees. The toucans danced upon the air, and soon every creature in the rain forest was celebrating Rafe's beautiful music.

Rafe and his followers danced through the forest, until at long last they reached the high wall that surrounded the land of the terrible giants.

Crazy About Christmas

One menacing giant guarded the wall, but when he saw Rafe and his merry band, he began to laugh so hard that he nearly fell from the wall. He couldn't resist taking them inside to see the giant king.

"Look at this," the giant guard said to the giant king, pointing at Rafe and his dancing procession. The king began to laugh so hard that he nearly cried.

Now all the giants were howling with laughter, and because they were so large, the earth began to shake beneath their feet. Outside those walls, the people did not know what was happening. They cowered in fear.

But Rafe was not afraid. He loved the sight of all these animals dancing and these giants laughing, and so his music became lighter and prettier and quicker. Soon the giant's daughter heard the sound, and she came to see what was happening.

The giantess had never in all her life laughed, but when she saw all of those giants and animals dancing to the tune this handsome lad played, she could not help but smile.

The king turned to look at his daughter and was amazed to see her smile. And then he turned back to Rafe and said, "If you can make my daughter laugh, I'll give you half my kingdom!"

"I'll do my best," Rafe said. He turned toward his band of animals and said, "Dance, dance, dance!" and played that magical violin.

All of a sudden the world shook with the sound of the giantess's laughter -- the first laugh she had ever uttered.

"You have earned half my kingdom," the giant said to Rafe.

"Thank you," Rafe said. "We shall live in peace with all the people!"

Rafe served as a prince in the land of giants. The giants no longer threatened the people. And if anyone refused to obey Rafe's call for peace, all he had to do was play his violin. Soon everyone forgot their quarrels and swayed to the sound of his music.

"Let joy and music rule this earth!" Rafe declared, and ever after that, everyone in the land loved music and dance.

November 25

Musical Chairs
group activity

Musical chairs is a fun game to play with a group of friends. This traditional game is easy to play with a few simple supplies. Once you learn the basics of musical chairs, you can try adding some variations to the traditional game for a fun, modern approach. The more chairs and players the longer the game will take.

Choose music to play. Musical chairs is played by walking around chairs to music. When the music is turned off the players find a chair to sit down in. You want music that has a good beat for walking. Using upbeat, party music will create a festive environment encouraging the players to have fun. Make a playlist of songs or pick an entire album of party music to use because the game may last more than one song if you have lots of players.

You need to have one person be in control of the music for each round of musical chairs that you play. This person will be responsible for starting and stopping the music.

Find a space to play. Musical chairs is a game that needs a lot of space in order to play it. Make sure you have a wide open space in a room or outside to easily play the game. You need enough space to have chairs set up in a circle and room for the players to walk around the outside of them.

How to Set Up Musical Chairs:
1. Count the number of players.
2. Collect chairs equivalent to the number of players, minus one.
3. Arrange the chairs in a double line, back to back or in a circle.
4. Instruct the players to walk clockwise in a tight circle around the chairs.

How to Play Musical Chairs:
5. Start the music and have the players walk clockwise in a circle around the chairs.
6. Stop the music suddenly, and all players need to sit quickly in an empty chair.
7. One person will be left standing without a chair, and they will be out of the game.
8. Another chair is then removed.
9. The game continues until there is only one person seated in a chair.
10. That person is the winner of the game.

Crazy About Christmas

Brigadeiro
A Classic Brazilian Candy

INGREDIENTS
1   can (14 ounce) sweet condensed milk
4   tablespoons cocoa powder or Nesquik™
2   tablespoon butter
     A pinch of salt
     Chocolate sprinkle, non-perils, cocoa, toasted coconut, chopped nuts
     Candy cups or small cupcake papers

INSTRUCTIONS
1. Butter a small bowl.
2. In a small sauce pan, stir together sweetened condensed milk, and cocoa powder. Add butter and warm over medium heat.
3. With a wooden spoon or silicon spatula stir constantly until it thickens, about 10 minutes. It should be thick enough to hold the trail of your spoon across the bottom of the pan for a few seconds as you stir.
4. Pour mixture into prepared bowl.
5. Chill until firm, about 40 minutes.
6. While the mixture is chilling place the sprinkles, coconut, chopped nuts... in bowls.
7. Grease your hands, and roll about 1 tablespoon of mixture into a small balls. Roll them in the sprinkles till coated and then place them in paper/foil candy cups.
8. You can leave them out a room temperature for up to three days, refrigerate them for a week, or freeze them for up to three months.

NOTE: In Brazil these tasty morsels often don't even make it into the refrigerator as a spoon goes from bowl to mouth. Some people use it to put over ice cream or dip fruit into. You can also add a teaspoon of orange oil for a different taste. They are easy to make and tasty to eat. Brigaderio's are served

November 26

The Three Skaters
by Lynne Roberts

In the faraway land of Holland, a baker sadly closed up his shop. He carried a worn sack with a few loaves of bread. Not many people came into the bakery that day, because times were hard and people did not have extra money for fresh bread. The baker had to bring home the leftovers so that they would not go to waste.

"Maybe I can make a nice bread pudding with these loaves," said the baker to himself. "It would be a shame not to use such delicious bread." The baker walked off into the cold, gray afternoon.

The baker's mind drifted to visions of his family. He pictured them all warm and snug by the fireplace, waiting for his arrival. He knew his wife would be a little disappointed with the sales at the bakery, but she would take the loaves of bread and cheerfully make the best of them. He smiled beneath the scratchy wool of his scarf. His eyes watered, from the icy wind and from the joy that his family brought to him.

The baker blinked the tears away and kept walking. When he reached the frozen canal, he sat down upon a log and strapped his wooden skates to his feet. As he secured the straps, he looked down the icy canal. The land seemed to stretch out endlessly before him. The air was crisp and the wind was bitter. The baker shivered and pulled his scarf higher on his face.

About a half-mile down the canal, the baker could see the farmer coming toward him. Soon he was joined by the farmer, who was also his neighbor. He, too, carried a sack. The two men greeted each other quietly and began skating together. Their skates soon fell into a rhythm.

"Have you been to the market today?" asked the baker.

The farmer nodded slowly. "Not much luck, though," he said.

"Same here. I still have f few loaves of bread," said the baker. He turned his gaze down the canal and continued to skate.

The farmer also could not wait to be home with his family. He looked forward to warming

Crazy About Christmas

himself by the fire and playing with his children. His youngest child, Lily, had been ill, and the farmer wanted to get her something special at the market. But he did not sell many apples and had to bring a sack of them back home.

"Perhaps a nice apple pie will warm little Lily and make her smile," said the farmer to himself.

Times were tough for everyone. It was clear that both men did not need to say much to each other.

They knew exactly how the other one felt.

As they continued to skate, the clouds grew thicker. The two men wanted to get home as quickly as possible. Soon they came to where another canal met up with theirs. They could see another figure coming toward them from the other canal. With a wave, they saw that it was their friend, the weaver.

"Hello, gentlemen," said the weaver. He skated right up to the farmer and the baker. They greeted the weaver warmly, and they all began to skate together. Now the sound of the three men's skates was all that could be heard on the smooth ice of the canal.

The weaver had also come from the market, where he had been trying to sell the beautiful blankets he had woven. Since no one had any extra money to spend, the weaver left the market with all of his blankets and no money. He tried to keep his spirits up, however, by taking pride in knowing that his blankets were beautifully crafted and woven out of love.

"It will be wonderful when we get home and out of the chill," said the weaver, trying to start some cheerful conversation.

The other two men just nodded their heads in agreement. Their thick scarves and the biting wind made it hard to talk to one another. They continued along the canal in silence.

As they passed an abandoned farm, the weaver suddenly stopped skating. He turned his gaze toward the old rundown barn in the middle of the field. He thought he heard an unusual noise.

"Stop! Listen!" the weaver called to his companions.

The farmer and the baker quickly stopped. They returned to the spot where the weaver was standing.

The three men stood on the icy canal, staring at the old barn. Suddenly a slice of sunlight split through the clouds and shone brightly onto the barn. It was a most unusual sight!

"Listen. Do you hear that?" said the farmer.

The farmer and the baker held their breath and listened. All at once, the three men heard the familiar sound of a baby crying. It seemed to be coming from the old barn, now cast in an eerie glow.

"It sounds like a child," said the farmer.

November 26

"But how could it be? That farm has been abandoned for years," said the weaver. "Perhaps a lamb was left in the barn," said the baker. "It sounds like a lamb."

The three men heard the sound again and knew in an instant that it was not a lamb. It sounded, most definitely, like a child.

Without another word, all three men stepped off the ice and into the snow. They took off their skates and began walking toward the barn. As they reached the doorway, they could hear the baby's cries beginning to soften as the gentle sound of a mother's voice sang a soulful lullaby. The men opened the barn door without knocking. It was as if they knew that it was all right—that whoever was inside wanted them to come in.

Inside the barn, thin beams of sunlight streamed through the holes in the roof and walls. There was not a lamb that had been abandoned by the barn's owner, but the scene inside the barn was most incredible. In the center of the barn sat a young woman holding a newborn infant. She was singing the most beautiful and unusual lullaby. She stopped singing as she looked up at the men. Then she smiled.

The men could not help but smile shyly back at the new mother. They were very surprised that anyone was in the abandoned barn, but even more surprised to see a lovely young mother holding a newborn infant. The three men looked around the barn and saw a man raking hay in a stall. The man looked very tired. After a moment, he stopped his chore and addressed the three strangers.

"It's not much of a home, but we had nowhere else to go," he explained. "We are on our way to visit relatives. My wife had the baby before we could reach our destination."

The farmer, the baker, and the weaver all turned back to look at the mother and her newborn baby. "Are your relatives expecting you arrival?" asked the weaver.

"Yes, but traveling will be difficult now with the infant. We can't stay here long, though. We have no food, and it is very cold and drafty inside this barn," the man said. He then finished raking a soft pile of hay and laid down a thin piece of cloth on top. Then the man walked over to the mother, took the baby, and placed it on its makeshift bed.

The mother father gathered around the child. It was obvious to the men that the young family was happy despite their hardship. The man and woman looked lovingly at each other and their new baby. The family scene touched the three men and, all at once, they took their items from their sacks and laid them on the floor near the child's bed. They smiled at the family, then quietly left the drafty barn

Without a word, the farmer, the baker, and the weaver walked through the snow to the edge of the canal. They bent down to put on their skates, then skated off once again.

Now all three of the men's sacks were empty. They did not seem concerned with coming home empty-handed, however. They felt in their hearts that what they had done was right. Once again, the only sound to be heard was their skates on the ice.

Crazy About Christmas

As he skated, the baker thought of his home. The mother and child reminded him of his wife and children waiting to see him walk through the door. He felt blessed knowing that they were safe and warm in their small, but cozy house.

The farmer's thoughts drifted to his sick daughter. How fragile and tiny she looked when he left her that morning, bundled up in her blanket. He thought of the newborn child and how fragile it looked in its young mother's arms. He said a blessing for the young family left alone in that old barn.

The weaver's prayers also went out to the mother and her child. He hoped that his handmade blankets would provide enough warmth and shelter for the family until they could continue on their journey.

The three men were so deep in thought that they did not notice their sacks getting heavier. Slowing each sack was filling, as if someone was dropping items into each one. But the men did not perceive the growing heaviness. They did notice, however, that they were nearing the village where they all lived. A smile crossed each of their lips, because they knew that they would be home soon. It had been a truly strange, but amazing day.

As they reached the edge of town, the three men stepped off the ice. The crisp snow crunched under their skates. They still did not speak to one another. Each one took off his skates and slung them over his shoulders. Their sacks were quite full by this time, but still not one man made mention of it.

The farmer said good-bye to the baker and the weaver and headed toward his home. The baker and weaver also said good-byes and parted company. It had been an unusual day, but neither the farmer, the baker, nor the weaver felt like talking. It was as if they all knew what the other one was thinking.

By the time the baker reached his front door, his sack was brimming and very heavy. He walked into his home and found his family just as he had pictured, all huddled around the warmth of the fireplace. When they saw him come through the door, all the children shouted at once, "Daddy! Daddy! Daddy's home!"

His wife walked over to the baker and gave him a warm hug. That is when she noticed the sack he was carrying. "Oh, dear! What a day at the shop!" she said, her eyes wide with wonder.

The baker put down the sack. Immediately cookies and cakes, hams and bread, teas and spices, fruits and vegetables came flooding out! There were also wrapped presents for everyone. The whole family began to dry with delight.

"Oh, Daddy! How wonderful!" cried the baker's daughter.

"Dear, we are blessed!" cried the baker's wife.

The baker had no idea how his sack got so full with such wonderful gifts, but he knew it must have something to do with the amazing scene in the barn.

November 26

That night the baker and his family had the best dinner ever. Not only did they have enough for that night, but for forty nights after!

When it was time for bed, the baker gathered the children in front of the fire and told them the amazing story of the family in the old barn on the abandoned field. He described how the sunlight broke through the clouds and shone only on the little barn where they were staying.

"It was a wonderful sight, indeed!" he told the children.

After he put his family to bed with full bellies and wondrous visions in their heads, the baker sat up and looked out the window. He thought of the farmer and the weaver. He knew that their night was as joyous and amazing as his had been. They all gave everything they had out of pure generosity and the goodness of their hearts. And even though the winter winds howled outside, it was the warmest night the farmer, the baker, and the weaver had ever had.

Sock Snowman
Craft

MATERIAL LIST
white sock -any size
colored or patterned sock
Tacky Glue® or hot glue gun
buttons
black permanent marker
rice
rubber bands or twine
orange pipe cleaner

DIRECTIONS

1. Place your white sock on table and cut off at the heel. Save the excess for another snowman. Don't use a thin sock as they stretch too much when filled.

2. To fill your sock with rice, place sock inside of a tall glass and pull top of sock over edge of glass for easy filling. Add rice to sock until it is nearly full then pull the rice filled sock out of glass and use rubber bands or twine to tie off the top of the sock.

3. Use a second rubber band to form a head then tie twine around the neck section to make it secure.

4. Cut the colored sock straight across at the heel. Then cut two strips for the scarf

5. Use the toe of the colored sock to make a hat. Slide over his head and roll up the bottom edge. If you want a poof on the top use another rubber band to make pom-pom like top. Hot glue in a couple of spots under the hat to keep it in place.

6. Place one strip of the colored scarf that you already cut around neck. Cut second strip in half and slide under the first to make the tied length of the scarf.

7. Complete by gluing colored buttons on their belly. Use a marker to make dots for the eyes and smile to represent coal. Add a little blush for cheeks if you want. For nose cut a small length about 2-inches long, put glue on one end and gently push through sock till nose is the length you want. If you are worried about the pointy end just fold it over.

8. If you want to add arms use glue on white pom-poms or sticks. Make an army of them and pretend this is a scene from Calvin and Hobbes® Just have fun decorating and giving them personalities.

November 26

Ontbijtkoek or Peperkoek
Dutch Honey Breakfast Bread

INGREDIENTS

DRY INGREDIENTS
- 2 cups rye flour
- 1 cup all purpose flour
- 2/3 cup brown sugar
- 2 teaspoons baking soda
- 1 teaspoon baking powder
- 2 teaspoons ground cinnamon
- 1 teaspoon ground cardamon
- ½ teaspoon ground ginger
- ¼ teaspoon ground nutmeg
- ¼ teaspoon ground allspice
- ¼ teaspoon ground coriander
- ¼ teaspoon ground cloves
- 1/8 teaspoon ground anise
- 1/8 teaspoon ground black pepper
- ¼ teaspoon salt

WET INGREDIENTS
- ½ cup honey
- 1/3 cup molasses NOT blackstrap!
- ¾ cup milk plus extra for brushing

INSTRUCTIONS

1. Preheat the oven to 350°C. Line a 9x5 inch loaf pan with parchment paper.
2. Place all dry ingredients in a large bowl and mix well.
3. Place wet ingredients in a small saucepan and gently warm (do not boil) over medium heat and gently stir to combine syrup ingredients.
4. Pour the syrup into the dry ingredients and mix using a rubber spatula until a sticky batter forms. Do not overmix.

5. Pour the batter into your prepared loaf pan and flatten the surface. Lightly brush the top with milk.
6. Bake for 60 minutes or until a toothpick inserted comes out clean. Cool in the pan and serve warm or cold with butter.

Note: If you don't have all the individual spices the recipe calls for can substitute 2 teaspoons of ground cinnamon and 1.5 teaspoons of either pumpkin pie or apple pie spice mix.
Unlike American-style quick breads, this one is meant to be sliced into fairly thin slices. And since the bread is baked without any added fat you will most definitely want to serve it slathered with butter.

INTERESTING FACTS:
Ontbijtkoek is not only one of the favorite breakfasts of the Dutch. It turns out that this cake is also at the heart of the country's traditions, and the main element of the koekhappen game.

This traditional and very old Flemish game is particularly popular at children's parties. The Dutch also often play it during festivities and family gatherings of Koningsdag (King's birthday), which is celebrated annually on April 27.

The game of koekhappen involves tying slices of peperkoek to the end of a string or wire and hanging them in the air above the players' heads. The latter are blindfolded and their hands behind their backs. They then try to bite on a piece of cake while the adults have fun pulling the string to put the slices of cake out of their mouths.

November 27

Luda, The Reindeer Maiden
A Tale of Siberia
As told by MyLinda Butterworth

On a wintry day in Siberia, long, long time ago, the Moon gazed down on the snowy fields. He watched the people traveling across the land together, he grew lonely, and so he drifted nearer and nearer to watch them more closely. After a while he decided that he needed to visit this place and get to know the people better, so the Moon transformed into human form so that he could move more freely about the world mingle with the people and studying their ways.

While he was traveling about he came upon a wandering herd of reindeer led by the reindeer herder's daughter, Luda.

Every winter, the reindeer herder gave Luda a magical reindeer and sent her to lead his large herd from their home deep in the snowy land to lush faraway pastures. As the reindeer traveled towards the pastures, Luda played her flute to entertain herself and to fill the long, dark, lonely days.

Many times, as the Moon traveled across the sky he had heard the maiden's melodies. Now that the Moon was traveling on earth, he heard the familiar music, and it beckoned to him. He began to follow the reindeer maiden and her herd. He watched her every movement; he gazed at her face. He listened to her wistful tunes and his heart swelled within in him and before long he felt like he could not live without her and must marry her and take her back to the sky. So much did he believe that would cure his loneliness he resolved to capture her..

But the magical reindeer sensed the Moon growing closer, and she heard the voice of one of her reindeer whispering, "The Moon wishes to capture you. You must take care." Luda also felt the Moon's presence and wondered what she should do. You see, she had no desire to be captured - not by the Moon or anyone. She loved her life just as it was. She loved taking those long treks across the snowy landscape. She loved her music. She loved the friendship of she had with her animal herd. And fear began to swell up in her heart.

The reindeer sensed Luda's fear and slowed down enough that the Moon caught up with the herd. The reindeer maiden whispered to her magical reindeer, "Help," and with his magical powers, he turned the maiden into a snowdrift and so that she disappeared.

When the Moon reached the herd, he looked around, puzzled, he asked, "Where has your maiden gone?"

The creatures ignored him. They simply moved on, trampling icy snow underfoot, taking great care not to step upon Luda. As soon as the magical reindeer saw that the Moon

was lost among the herd, he turned the maiden back into human form, and together they dashed toward the sturdy yaranga, the tent where the maiden slept at night.

Meanwhile, the Moon searched through the herd and found her not. Suddenly he saw a light, he looked up, and he rushed toward the tent, but just before he reached the opening, the magical reindeer turned the maiden into an oil lamp.

The Moon walked inside and cried, "I've found you," but there he saw only a bed and the tent poles, a block and a hammer, and in one corner a shimmering oil lamp. He scratched his head and wondered, "Where are you? Please come out I wish to marry you..." He listened and looked but all he saw was the flickering light of the lamp and heard only the steady breathing of the great herd of reindeer outside.

The Moon called again. "Where are you? Please come to me," he pleaded. But there was no one answer.

He walked outside and once again began to search through the herd, and the moment he was outside, the maiden transformed into her own body. There was a twinkle in her eye and a smile on her face as she opened the tent flap. She cried into the frigid air, "What's wrong with you? Can't you see I'm right here!"

Hearing her voice, the Moon raced back toward the yaranga, but before he reached it, the reindeer maiden again turned into an oil lamp. Now the Moon was growing frantic. "Where are you? I hear your voice but where have you gone?"

Again, nobody answered, and again the Moon walked outside to search, and once more the reindeer maiden turned into herself, and again she walked to the opening of the tent and called, "What's wrong with you? I'm right here..."

Each time the Moon tried to find her, the Luda transformed her shape once more, and in this way, she remained hidden from his sight.

The Moon was desperate. He rushed this way and that, crying, "Please, please...let me find you, let me see you..." And in his frantic search, he grew exhausted.

When the maiden saw that the Moon had grown weak and tired, she grabbed a sack, slipped out of the tent and threw the bag over the Moon's head. Then she bound his legs and arms and pulled him inside her warm tent. She smiled. "Now I have captured you! How do you like it?"

The Moon begged, "Please, set me free."

"And if I do? What will you offer me in return?"

The Moon thought awhile. Trapped inside that tent, unable to move, he longed for the sky, for the sweetness of his nighttime journeys, for the freedom he had so loved. "I promise if you set me free, I shall return to the sky, and I will offer light to your people."

The maiden thought about this for a while. Then she said, "But sometimes we will wish for darkness."

November 27

And so the Moon agreed. "When the people wish for darkness, I shall disappear, and I shall measure out the year, season by season. Each month I will give you a different light. There will be times for hunting and times for frost, times for new leaves and times for newborn calves and brand new days."

The reindeer maiden smiled, but then she thought again. "If I let you go, you will grow stronger and try and capture me again. I too love my freedom."

The Moon realized they both wanted similar things and as much as he loved Luda, the reindeer maiden he had learned his lesson. He now understood why the maiden loved her life just as it was. "You have my word. As much as I love you I love my freedom too so I will care for you and your people from my place in the sky."

And so, the reindeer maiden set the Moon free, and he changed from his human form and drifted back to the sky.

From that day forward the Moon kept his word and spread his light upon the earth, and sometimes he hides his face as his heart sighs when he remembers the reindeer maiden, and his light fades or even goes out. It is in those times that the people know the Moon is dreaming of Luda that courageous and wondrous reindeer woman he loves.

 Crazy About Christmas

Handprint Reindeer Shirt
Craft/Wearable Art

MATERIALS LIST:

T-shirt or sweatshirt (pre-washed no fabric softener)
cardboard
brown, white, black, and red Acrylic Paint
textile medium for acrylic paint
1 inch paint brush
foam or paper plate

DIRECTIONS:

1. Pre-wash t-shirt to remove sizing or recycle an existing shirt for this project.

2. Take a piece of cardboard and fit inside the shirt, it should be the same width as your shirt to hold the fabric flat. Place cardboard form inside of T-shirt with the front of shirt facing you. Secure shirt around cardboard with masking tape if the cardboard is not a tight fit.

3. Mix 1/3 medium to 2/3 paint and mix well on your paper plate. *Hint: You can do this without the medium, but the medium makes it flexible and it washes better. You can also just buy fabric paint.*

4. Using paintbrush, paint the bottom of one foot, cover evenly. Place T-shirt on floor and center foot (toes up please) in middle of T-shirt. Now do what your mother never let you do to your clothes, step down hard and leave your dirty footprint in the middle of your shirt. This becomes the head of the reindeer with your toes becoming his curly hair. Pull the foot straight up so you don't get any smears. NOW WASH YOUR FOOT!

5. Now that your foot is clean, make sure that there is plenty of paint left on the plate and place your hands one at a time in the paint. Check to see that they are evenly covered in paint, if you have too much paint on your hands blot them lightly on newspaper. Spread your fingers wide and carefully place your hands on either side of his head to make the antlers. Apply equal pressure to make a good imprint, but don't move them. Lift them straight up to avoid smearing.

6. Let it dry to the touch before attempting eyes or nose. For the eyes just paint two white circles and then with black paint a smaller circle inside. For the nose you can either give

November 27

him a red nose or a black nose. As an option after it all dries you can use a good fabric glue or sew on wiggly eyes and use a pom-pom for the nose

7. Let dry overnight. Pull out the cardboard. Then enjoy wearing it.

Options: While you can totally make this craft and put it on a shirt you can also put it straight on a piece of card stock and make a picture or a greeting card and if you don't want to deal with the paint then trace their hands and feet and cut them out of paper and glue them on paper

Option 2: Could add a bow and jingle bells at neck. Use your own imagination to decorate your reindeer. Perhaps you want to add lights that twinkle (kits are available at your local craft store).

Harvest-Nut Granola

If you lived in Russia you would probably be eating a sweet and fruity cereal made with grains in the cooler weather. Here is my favorite granola recipe that you can eat with milk, crumble on top of cooked fruit or ice cream or just eat it dry, it is very tasty and easy to make.

INGREDIENTS

5 cups old-fashioned rolled oats
1 cup shredded coconut or chips, preferably unsweetened
½ cup sliced almonds
½ cup coarsely chopped pecans
½ cup light brown sugar
½ cup unsalted pumpkin seeds
½ cup unsalted sunflower seeds
½ cup water
½ cup pure maple syrup
½ cup coconut oil, melted or canola oil
½ cup dried cranberries
½ cup dried dates, diced
½ cup raisins

INSTRUCTIONS

1. Preheat oven to 275°F.
2. Combine oats, coconut, almonds, pecans, brown sugar, pumpkin seeds and sunflower seeds in a large bowl.
3. Combine syrup, water and oil in a medium bowl or large measuring cup and pour over the oat mixture; stir until well combined.
4. Spread the mixture into a large (12-by- 15-inch) roasting pan or large rimmed baking sheet.
5. Bake for 45 minutes. Remove from the oven, stir, and continue baking until golden brown and beginning to crisp, about 30-45 minutes more.
6. Remove from oven and let cool completely. Stir in cranberries, dates, and raisins.
7. Store in an airtight container for up to 2 weeks or in the freezer up to 3 months.

November 28

The Gingerbread Bees
A tale of Poland

There was once a little town called Torun which always smelt of gingerbread. On spring mornings when the breeze blew towards the river, merchants arriving there could smell the ginger wafting through the streets of bakeries. As soon as they had unloaded their wares, they would rush to have breakfast in one of the little waterfront shops where tea and a gingerbread cake were sold.

The most popular baker of all was Bartholomew's, run by a man whose name was not surprising – Mr. Bartholomew. This old baker had a prosperous business and his reputation for baking excellent cakes was the talk of the whole town.

"Your husband must be a happy man, Mrs. Bartholomew. Surely, if anyone has a claim to happiness it would be him," said a customer one day, gingerbread crumbs dropping from her mouth as she spoke.

"Mr. Bartholomew – happy?" replied his wife, brushing cake crumbs from her lap. "He won't be happy until the king tells him his gingerbread is the best in the country." She took another mouthful of tea to wash the cake down, then continued, "And he wishes he'd never hired that rascal of an apprentice Bogumil."

It was known that Bartholomew had designs to marry his lovely daughter, with her honey hair and blue eyes, to a wealthy man. It was equally well known that the girl was not interested in the crusty old men who showered her with amber necklaces, silver ribbons and pearl embroidered gloves in a bid to win her affections, and that her heart was moved more by the bunches of wild flowers and gingerbread hearts given to her by young Bogumil.

"Sack him! That's the only answer, husband. Sack Him!" said Mrs. Bartholomew one day, as she watched her daughter putting a bunch of freshly picked flowers into a vase. "For pity's sake, the lad can't even afford to buy his own flowers! What sort of husband would he make our Katarzyna? Sack him, I say!"

Her husband put a hand to his brow. "I can't sack him, my dear. The king is coming to Torun soon and I need all the help I can get. Besides, Bogumil is a good baker."

Light hearted, Happy go luck Bogumil thought of nothing but Katarzyna by day and by night. Although he loved his work at the baker, there were times when the young man longed only to get away from the hot ovens, and walk dreamily through the forest looking for flowers for his love.

So it was, one morning, that he was walking in a forest outside the town when he spotted a bunch of forget-me-nots growing beside a lake. They were as blue as Katarzya's eyes. Bogumil was on his hands and knees and about to pick the flowers, when he heard a faint droning sound. He looked up and saw a huge, round, black and orange striped bumblebee drowning the lake.

Without thinking, Bogumil snatched up a giant sorrel leaf and, leaning out into the water, helped the bee clamber on to it. He put the leaf down upon the bank and, seeing that the bee's wings were wet, moved it into the sun. Soon the bee began to revive and started rubbing its wings. When it was dry, its buzzing grew louder, and eventually it flew off into the forest, leaving the young man alone.

Bogumil was kneeling down again to pick the forget-me-nots when he heard the chirp of a small bird perched upon a twig at the side of the lake. Imagine his surprise when he looked closer, and saw that it was not a bird at all, but a little woman no bigger than his middle finger sitting, not on a twig, but a throne! She wore a tiny crown upon her head.

Bogumil bowed.

The queen spoke, not in a chirp this time, but in a beautiful voice.

"I am the Queen of the Honey-dwellers, and I have come to reward you for your good deed. My people live on the golden honey made by the bees of this forest. When the queen bee fell into the lake, we thought the end had come, for without her the bees cannot work. If she had died the worker bees would also have died and there would have been no more honey for my people."

Bogumil was speechless.

"Listen to me careful," she continued, "and you will become the most famous baker in Torun, and your town will be known forever as the Gingerbread town. Remember, when you bake your gingerbread, as well as adding spices, to add a spoonful of honey to the recipe." And she gave him a little pot of forest honey.

Then, before Bogumil could thank her, the queen disappeared. The throne had turned back into a twig and there was a bird perched on it.

Bogumil rubbed his eyes, not sure if he had been dreaming, and forgetting about the flowers, ran all the way back to town.

The streets were full of people. Bogumil stopped and asked a man what was happening.

"Good God, my boy, where on earth have you been? The king is coming Torun tomorrow!"

Bogumil went red in the face. The king coming tomorrow! He must get back to the bakery at once.

Old Bartholomew was furious when he saw his apprentice. The ovens in the kitchen were already hot and the baker had rolled out his gingerbread dough.

"Where the devil have you been, you young scoundrel? Don't you know the king is coming tomorrow? he fumed.

His wife shouted, "Every apprentice in town is baking gingerbread, except you. Get to work at once!"

November 28

Young Bogumil said sorry a thousand times and quickly gathered together his cooking utensils. He added cloves, cinnamon, black pepper and ginger to his dough, and when the old baker and his wife were not looking he took out the jar of forest honey and added a spoonful to the mixture. He cut the gingerbread into different shapes: knights, flowers, hearts, elks – even bees –and, he remembrance of the little queen, he cut out some tiny crowns too.

Early the next morning, Bartholomew was up rapping on his apprentices' bedroom door.

"Up, you lazy rascal! There's work to be done!"

His wife already up and about, laying a clean linen cloth over the table outside the baker. Her husband carried out the trays of gingerbread, eying Bogumil's golden creations, which were arranged on a silver tray. The apprentice might have been a rascal, but there was no denying he had a gift for baking. There was such a gleam about his gingerbread biscuits today, they might almost have been made of gold! Bartholomew didn't utter his thoughts out loud. Instead, he shouted, "Bogumil, fetch a ladder my boy, and polish the shop sign until it sparkles."

Bogumil rubbed the old sign until he could see his face in the letters. Then, looking into it, he saw reflected the king's horses approaching the town. There was a great roar from the crowds in the streets, and turning around, he nearly fell off his ladder.

Bartholomew shouted, "Get down off that ladder boy, and put it away."

"Then clean up your hands and get yourself out here!" added Mrs. Bartholomew.

Bogumil meekly did as he was told.

By the time the king arrived at Bartholomew's shop, he and the royal children were already stuffed full of gingerbread. The old baker silently cursed the fact that his shop was in the center of the town so far along the royal route. When the king approached, Bartholomew bowed, his wife curtsied and Bogumil held his breath, as the king stepped forward and chose a ginger bread crown from the silver tray. The king's little son and daughter each picked up a gingerbread bee.

The king ate one crown…then another,,,and then another. His children munched their way through a swarm of gingerbread bees and a bunch of gingerbread flowers.

"Who baked these biscuits?" cried the king.

The old baker bowed again, Mrs. Bartholomew smile smugly, and they both pointed proudly at Bogumil.

"This is the most delicious gingerbread I have ever tasted," the king said. He picked up another ginger bread crown. "Tell me, young man what did you do to make this gingerbread so special?"

Bogumil told the king that he had added forest honey to the recipe, and the king nodded approvingly.

"Ingenious!" he said, Bartholomew smiled. What a clever apprentice!

"Get me a scribe at once," said the king, through a mouthful of Bogumil's biscuits. "I wish to grant this town a royal charter, and bestow upon it the exclusive right to bake honey ginger bread for the King's Market."

Bartholomew patted his young apprentice on the back, forgiving him his errant ways. He promoted Bogumil to senior baker, and gave his her daughter's hand in marriage.

Bogumil was delighted by all this. But he couldn't help wondering if his luck would run out once the little pot of forest honey was finished. He needn't have worried, for one afternoon when he was in the garden of his new cottage, he heard a faint buzzing and discovered that a swarm of bees had moved into one of his cherry trees. The little queen had sent them so that Bogumil would never have to look for honey again!

His gingerbread got better and better, and when old Bartholomew died, Bogumil took over the baker and Torun became known as the Gingerbread Town. Bogumil lived happily with his beautiful wife, but he never told anyone about the little Queen of the Honey-dwellers whom he had met long ago in the Forest of the Bees.

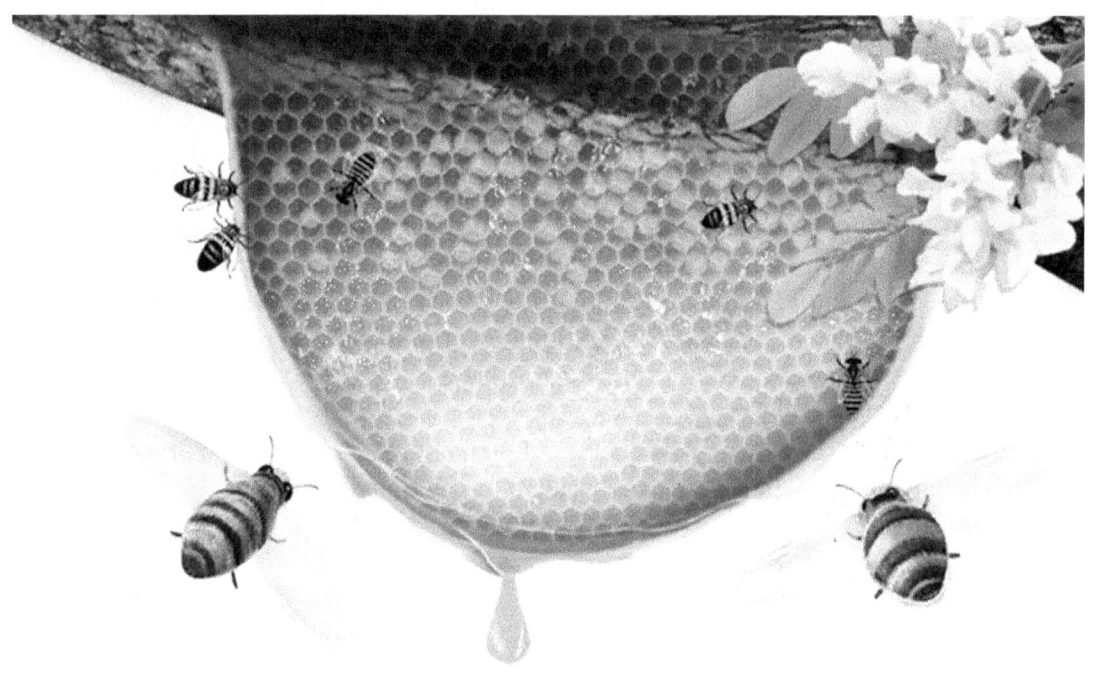

November 28

Chief Cookie Baker Apron
Craft/Wearable Art

MATERIALS:
- Chef style apron - any color
- Fabric pens or dimensional fabric paint
- Brown fabric paint
- brush for paint
- Tracing paper
- Carbon or graphite paper

DIRECTIONS:
1. Begin by pre washing the apron to get out the sizing, and then dry and iron if necessary.
2. Trace you pattern on a sheet of paper from the book (page 16) or print a copy.
3. Place your design on the apron where you like it, then place the carbon paper between your design and the apron with the black side facing down. Tape it in place and trace the lines of the design with a pen or pencil.* Make sure you do this on a hard surface.
4. Use your fabric pens and trace your words on the fabric where your transfer is. Be creative.
5. For the gingerbread man, paint him with brown fabric paint. Let dry completely and then use your markers to decorate him however you want. You can also outline him in a darker color to make him stand out.
6. Once completely dry then put a pressing cloth over your design and iron on cotton setting to set the paint.

Optional technique: If you don't have carbon paper then shade the back of your paper printout with a pencil. Tape your printout to the apron with a piece of tape and trace the design with a pencil or pen so that the shading on the back of the page transfers to your art material. If you are transferring to a dark fabric use chalk in the same way as the pencil technique.

Want to have some fun? Add your name under the word baker or change the word baker to taster (that word pattern is on page 17). Or maybe draw a line of Christmas Lights with your paint markers. Having aprons for different seasons or occasions is simple and fun!

 Crazy About Christmas

CHIEF COOKIE BAKER

November 28

Gingerbread Cookies

Soft in the middle, crisp on the edges, and perfectly spiced.
A smell that reminds you of childhood.
Good for more than just the holidays.

INGREDIENTS
- 2/3 cup unsalted butter, softened
- 3/4 cup packed light or dark brown sugar
- 1/2 cup unsulphured molasses
- 3 tablespoons honey
- 1 large egg, at room temperature
- 1 teaspoon pure vanilla extract
- 3 ½ cups unbleached flour (spoon & leveled)
- 1 teaspoon baking soda
- 1/2 teaspoon salt
- 3 teaspoons ground ginger
- 2 teaspoons ground cinnamon
- 1/4 teaspoon ground allspice
- 1/4 teaspoon ground cloves
- Optional: cookie icing or royal icing

Image by Becca Clark from Pixabay

INSTRUCTIONS
1. In a large bowl using a hand-held mixer or stand mixer fitted with a paddle attachment, beat the butter for 1 minute on medium speed until completely smooth and creamy.
2. Add the brown sugar and molasses and beat on medium high speed until combined and creamy-looking. Scrape down the sides and bottom of the bowl as needed.
3. Beat in egg and vanilla on high speed for 2 full minutes. Scrape down the sides and bottom of the bowl as needed.
4. In a separate bowl, whisk the flour, baking soda, salt, ginger, cinnamon, allspice, and cloves together until combined.
5. On low speed, slowly mix into the wet ingredients until combined. The cookie dough will be quite thick and slightly sticky. Divide the dough in half. Form each piece of dough into a ball, place in center of plastic wrap, then flatten and shape into a thick square and wrap tightly in plastic wrap. It is very important that you chill dough for at

Crazy About Christmas

least 3 hours or up to 3 days. Making these cookies are best when we do it in stages. Mix and chill. Roll and bake. Cool and decorate. Eat. Pretty easy steps don't you think?

6. Preheat oven to 350°F. Line 2-3 large baking sheets with parchment paper or use a silicone baking mats so they will easy to take off the baking sheets after they are baked.
7. Take one ball of dough out of the refrigerator. Generously flour a work surface, as well as your hands and the rolling pin. Roll out dough to about 1/4-inch thick. Note: It is not unusual for the dough to crack or crumble while you are rolling it out. It will help if you pick it up and turn it as you go, this also helps it from sticking to the surface. Worst case scenario use your fingers and squish the cracks back together. Use whatever type of cookie cutter you want and cut into shapes. Place shapes 1 inch apart on prepared baking sheets. Re-roll dough scraps until all the dough is shaped. Repeat with remaining disc of dough. If the dough gets too soft after placing on cookie sheet place the cookie sheet in the refrigerator and re-chill this will help your cookies from spreading and keep them soft after baking.
8. At this point you can use raisins or some small candies to decorate before you put them in the oven. This is an optional step.
9. Bake cookies for about 9-10 minutes. If your cookie cutters are smaller than 4 inches, bake for about 8 minutes. If your cookie cutters are larger than 4 inches, bake for about 11 minutes. Note that the longer the cookies bake, the harder and crunchier they'll be. For soft gingerbread cookies, use the times above.
10. Let cookies cool for 5 minutes on the cookie sheet, then transfer cookies to a cooling rack to cool completely. Once completely cool, decorate however you like.
11. To decorate you can either make your own Royal Icing or pick up a tube of cookie icing at the store. Set out different items to dress your gingerbread cookies, gumdrops, small hard candies, chocolate chips, sprinkles... use your imagination.
12. Cookies stay fresh covered at room temperature for up to 1 week or you can freeze them for up to 3 weeks. They never last that long.

Makes 24   4-inch gingerbread cookies

TASTER

optional word pattern for apron

November 29

The Story of Childe Charity
By Frances Browne

Once upon a time, there lived in the west country a little girl who had neither father nor mother. They both died when she was very young, and left their daughter to the care of her uncle, who was the richest farmer in all that country. He had houses and lands, flocks and herds, many servants to work about his house and fields, a wife who had brought him a great dowry, and two fair daughters.

All their neighbors, being poor, looked up to the family—insomuch that they thought themselves great people. The father and mother were as proud as peacocks. The daughters thought themselves the greatest beauties in the world, and not one of the family would speak civilly to anybody they thought low.

Now it happened that though she was their near relation, they had this opinion of the orphan girl, partly because she had no fortune, and partly because of her humble, kindly nature. It was said that the more needy any creature was, the more ready was she to befriend it. So the people of the west country called her Childe Charity, and if she had any other name, I never heard it.

Childe Charity was thought very mean in that proud house. Her uncle would not own her for his niece. Her cousins would not keep her company. Her aunt sent her to work in the dairy, and to sleep in the back garret, where they kept all sorts of lumber and dry herbs for the winter.

All the servants learned the same lesson, and Childe Charity had more work than rest among them. All the day she scoured pails, scrubbed dishes, and washed crockery ware. But every night she slept in the back garret as sound as a princess could in her palace.

Her uncle's house was large and white, and stood among green meadows by a river's side. In front it had a porch covered with a vine; behind, it had a farmyard and high granaries. Within were two parlors for the rich, and two kitchens for the poor, which the neighbors thought very grand; and one day in the harvest season, when this rich farmer's corn had been all cut down and housed, he invited them to a harvest supper.

The west-country people came in their holiday clothes. Such heaps of cakes and cheese, such baskets of apples and barrels of ale had never been at a feast before. They were making merry in kitchen and parlor, when a poor old woman came to the back door, begging for scraps of food and a night's lodging. Her clothes were coarse and ragged; her hair was scanty and grey; her back was bent; her teeth were gone. She had a squinting eye, a clubbed foot, and crooked fingers. In short, she was the poorest and ugliest old woman that ever came begging.

Crazy About Christmas

The first who saw her was the kitchen maid, and she ordered her to be gone for an ugly witch. The next was the herd-boy, and he threw her a bone. But Childe Charity, hearing the noise, came out from her seat at the foot of the lowest table, and asked the old woman to take her share of the supper, and sleep that night in her bed in the back garret.

The old woman sat down without a word of thanks. All the people laughed at Childe Charity for giving her bed and her supper to a beggar. Her proud cousins said it was just like her mean spirit, but Childe Charity did not mind them. She scraped the pots for her supper that night, and slept on a sack among the lumber, while the old woman rested in her warm bed. And next morning, before the little girl awoke, she was up and gone, without so much as saying thank you, or good morning.

That day all the servants were sick after the feast, and mostly cross too—so you may judge how civil they were; when, at supper time, who should come to the back door but the old woman, again asking for broken scraps of food and a night's lodging. No one would listen to her or give her a morsel, till Childe Charity rose from her seat at the foot of the lowest table, and kindly asked her to take her supper, and sleep in her bed in the back garret.

Again the old woman sat down without a word. Childe Charity scraped the pots for her supper, and slept on the sack. In the morning the old woman was gone; but for six nights after, as sure as the supper was spread, there was she at the back door, and the little girl always asked her in.

Childe Charity's aunt said she would let her get enough of beggars. Her cousins made game of what they called her genteel visitor. Sometimes the old woman said: "Child, why don't you make this bed softer? and why are your blankets so thin?" but she never gave her a word of thanks, nor a civil good morning.

At last, on the ninth night from her first coming, when Childe Charity was getting used to scrape the pots and sleep on the sack, her knock came to the door, and there she stood with an ugly ashy-coloured dog, so stupid-looking and clumsy that no herd-boy would keep him.

"Good evening, my little girl!" she said, when Childe Charity opened the door. "I will not have your supper and bed to-night. I am going on a long journey to see a friend. But here is a dog of mine, whom nobody in all the west country will keep for me. He is a little cross, and not very handsome; but I leave him to your care till the shortest day in all the year. Then you and I will count for his keeping."

When the old woman had said the last word, she set off with such speed that Childe Charity lost sight of her in a minute. The ugly dog began to fawn upon her, but he snarled at everybody else. The servants said he was a disgrace to the house. The cousins wanted him drowned, and it was with great trouble that Childe Charity got leave to keep him in an old ruined cow-house.

November 29

Ugly and cross as the dog was, he fawned on her, and the old woman had left him to her care. So the little girl gave him part of all her meals; and when the hard frost came, took him to her own back garret, because the cow-house was damp and cold in the long nights. The dog lay quietly on some straw in a corner. Childe Charity slept soundly, but every morning the servants would say to her:

"What great light and fine talking was that in your back garret?"

"There was no light but the moon shining in through the shutterless window, and no talk that I heard," said Childe Charity; and she thought they must have been dreaming.

But night after night, when any of them awoke in the dark and silent hour that comes before the morning, they saw a light brighter and clearer than the Christmas fire, and heard voices like those of lords and ladies in the back garret.

Partly from fear, and partly from laziness, none of the servants would rise to see what might be there; till at length, when the winter nights were at the longest, the little parlor maid, who did least work and got most favor, because she gathered news for her mistress, crept out of bed when all the rest were sleeping, and set herself to watch at a small hole in the door.

She saw the dog lying quietly in the corner, Childe Charity sleeping soundly in her bed, and the moon shining through the shutterless window. But an hour before daybreak there came a glare of lights, and a sound of far-off bugles. The window opened, and in marched a troop of little men clothed in crimson and gold, and bearing every man a torch, till the room looked bright as day.

They marched up with great respect to the dog, where he lay on the straw, and the most richly clothed among them said: "Royal Prince, we have prepared the banquet hall. What will your Highness please that we do next?"

"You have done well," said the dog. "Now prepare the feast, and see that all things are in the best order; for the Princess and I mean to bring a stranger who never feasted in our halls before."

"Your Highness's commands shall be obeyed," said the little man, making another bow; and he and his company passed out of the window. By and by there was another glare of lights, and a sound like far-off flutes. The window opened, and there came in a company of little ladies clad in velvet, and carrying each a crystal lamp.

They also walked up to the dog, and the gayest one said: "Royal Prince, we have prepared the carpets and curtains. What will your Highness please that we do next?"

"You have done well," said the dog. "Now prepare the robes, and let all things be of the best; for the Princess and I will bring with us a stranger who never feasted in our halls before."

Crazy About Christmas

"Your Highness's commands shall be obeyed," said the little lady, making a low curtsy; and she and her company passed out through the window, which closed quietly behind them.

The dog stretched himself out upon the straw, the little girl turned in her sleep, and the moon shone in on the back garret. The parlor maid was so much amazed, and so eager to tell this story to her mistress, that she could not close her eyes that night, and was up before cock-crow. But when she told it, her mistress called her a silly wench to have such foolish dreams, and scolded her so that she did not dare to speak about what she had seen to the servants.

Nevertheless, Childe Charity's aunt thought there might be something in it worth knowing. So next night, when all the house was asleep, she crept out of bed, and set herself to watch at the back garret door. There she saw just what the maid told her—the little men with the torches, and the little ladies with the crystal lamps, come in to the dog, and the same words pass, only he said to the one, "Now prepare the presents," and to the other, "Prepare the jewels." When they were gone, the dog stretched himself on the straw, Childe Charity turned in her sleep, and the moon shone in on the back garret.

The mistress could not close her eyes any more than the maid, so eager was she to tell the story. She woke up Childe Charity's rich uncle before cock-crow. But when he heard it, he laughed at her for a foolish woman, and advised her not to repeat the like before her neighbors, lest they should think she had lost her senses.

The mistress could say no more, and the day passed. But that night the master thought he would like to see what went on in the garret. So when all the house were asleep he slipped out of bed, and set himself to watch at the hole in the door. The same thing happened again that the maid and the mistress saw. The little men in crimson with their torches, and the little ladies in rose-colored velvet with their lamps, came in at the window and bowed low to the dog, the one saying, "Royal Prince, we have prepared the presents," and the other, "Royal Prince, we have prepared the jewels."

The dog said to them all: "You have done well. Tomorrow, come and meet me and the Princess with horses and chariots, and let all things be done in the best way. For we will bring a stranger from this house who has never traveled with us, nor feasted in our halls before."

The little men and the little ladies said: "Your Highness's commands shall be obeyed."

When they had gone out through the window, the ugly dog stretched himself out on the straw, Childe Charity turned in her sleep, and the moon shone in on the back garret.

The master could not close his eyes any more than the maid or the mistress. He remembered to have heard his grandfather say, that somewhere near his meadows there lay a path leading to the fairies' country, and the haymakers used to see it shining through the grey summer morning, as the fairy bands went home.

Nobody had heard or seen the like for many years; but the master thought that the doings in his back garret must be a fairy business, and the ugly dog a person of great account. His chief wonder was, however, what visitor the fairies intended to take from his house; and after thinking the matter over, he was sure it must be one of his daughters—they were so handsome, and had such fine clothes.

So Childe Charity's rich uncle made it his first business that morning to get ready a breakfast of roast mutton for the ugly dog, and carry it to him in the cow-house. But not a morsel would the dog taste.

"The fairies have strange ways," said the master to himself. But he called his daughters and bade them dress themselves in their best, for he could not say which of them might be called into great company before nightfall. Childe Charity's cousins, hearing this, put on the richest of their silks and laces, and strutted like peacocks from kitchen to parlor all day.

They were in very bad humor when night fell, and nobody had come. But just as the family were sitting down to supper the ugly dog began to bark, and the old woman's knock was heard at the back door.

Childe Charity opened it, and was going to offer her bed and supper as usual, when the old woman said: "This is the shortest day in all the year, and I am going home to hold a feast after my travels. I see you have taken good care of my dog, and now if you will come with me to my house, he and I will do our best to entertain you. Here is our company."

As the old woman spoke there was a sound of far-off flutes and bugles, then a glare of lights. And a great company, clad so grandly that they shone with gold and jewels, came in open chariots, covered with gilding and drawn by snow-white horses. The first and finest of the chariots was empty. The old woman led Childe Charity to it by the hand, and the ugly dog jumped in before her.

The proud cousins, in all their finery, had by this time come to the door, but nobody wanted them. No sooner was the old woman and her dog within the chariot than a wonderful change passed over them, for the ugly old woman turned at once to a beautiful young princess, with long yellow curls and a robe of green and gold; while the ugly dog at her side started up a fair young prince, with nut-brown hair and a robe of purple and silver.

"We are," said they, as the chariots drove on, "a prince and princess of Fairyland, and there was a wager between us whether or not there were good people still to be found in these false and greedy times. One said 'Yes', and the other said 'No'."

"And I have lost," said the Prince, "and must pay the feast and presents."

Childe Charity never heard any more of that story. Some of the farmer's household, who were looking after them, said the chariots had gone one way across the meadows, some said they had gone another, and till this day they cannot agree upon the way they went.

Crazy About Christmas

But Childe Charity went with that noble company into a country such as she had never seen—for primroses covered all the ground, and the light was always like that of a summer evening. They took her to a royal palace, where there was nothing but feasting and dancing for seven days. She had robes of pale green and velvet to wear, and slept in a room inlaid with ivory.

When the feast was done, the Prince and Princess gave her such heaps of gold and jewels that she could not carry them; but they gave her a chariot to go home in, drawn by six white horses. On the seventh night, which happened to be Christmas time, when the farmer's family had settled in their own minds that she would never come back, and were sitting down to supper, they heard the sound of her coachman's bugle, and saw her alight with all the jewels and gold at the very back door where she had brought in the ugly old woman.

The fairy chariot drove away, and never again came back to that farmhouse after. But Childe Charity scoured and scrubbed no more, for she grew a great lady, even in the eyes of her proud cousins.

From "Granny's Wonderful Chair" by Frances Browne , By Blackie & Son, Limited, Glasgow, 1856. Illustrator: A.A. Dixon

November 29

Tug Dog Toy
Craft/Recycle Project

A simple and fun way to make something special for your canine friend!

MATERIALS:
scissors
old T-shirt

DIRECTIONS
1. Take a used t-shirt (because they smell like you) and begin by cutting off the seams, sleeves and collar of your t-shirt.
2. Cut a wide slit at the bottom of your t-shirt 2-3 inches wide. Note that if you have more than two colored t-shirts you can make a multi-colored version.
3. Now that you have cut your slits either rip along the slit or cut into strips.
4. Take two strips and set aside. Now gather all your strips together and take one strip and tie off one end or you can tie a knot.
5. Divide your strips into thirds and braid them together snuggly if you want your toy to last.
6. Take that last strip of fabric and tie off the other end or tie a knot. Cut off any stragglers.
7. You are now ready to give it a toss or begin an epic tug of war game with your dog.

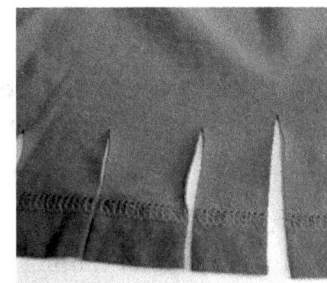

Crazy About Christmas

Tasty Dog Treats

Your dog will love the way you love them if you make them these tasty treats!

INGREDIENTS
- 1 cup pumpkin
- 1/2 cup peanut butter*
- 2 eggs
- 2 1/2 cup whole wheat flour
- 1/2 teaspoon cinnamon

INSTRUCTIONS
1. Preheat oven to 350° degrees F. Line a baking sheet with parchment paper of use a silicone baking mat. Set aside.
2. In a large sized bowl combine pumpkin, peanut butter and eggs. Whisk together
3. Add whole wheat flour and cinnamon. Stir until the mixture until flour is incorporated, like you do for muffins.
4. Lightly flour surface and roll out the dough with a rolling pin to 1/2-inch thick.
5. Use a cookie cutter in the shape of a bone or any other shape you want. You can also just roll them into balls and give them a slice press to make a c
6. Bake for 20 to 40 minutes - depending on how crunchy your d
7. Remove treats from oven and put on a cooling rack.
8. Store in an airtight container for up to a month or 6 months in the freezer.

Note: When it comes to peanut butter, natural is best, make sure it does not contain Xylitol as it is toxic to dogs. All ingredients are considered safe for dogs and humans, but as a cautionary note please be aware of your pets allergies or sensitivities before feeding them any treat. This is a note from my daughter the vet tech.

Have friends with dogs? Stack up a few and tie with a ribbon or find a jar to fill with dog treats and give as a gift.

The Young King and the Stones
By Frederick N. Bosworth

Long ago in a faraway country an old king died. His son was changed from a young to a king in a single day. Now the kingdom was his own, and he went about reordering things to suit himself. He ordered the cooks not to prepare food he did not wish to eat, like Yorkshire pudding, no matter how much the old king, his father, had like it. And he changed the draperies in the royal bedchamber from red and gold to sky blue, even though his mother pouted about it. And there were some things he wanted to change about his people at court. Or maybe just change the people, like the drapes or his food; he hadn't made up his mind quite yet what would please him most. But he knew where he wanted to start.

He took a troop of big guardsmen and went to the house of the old man who had been his father's chief advisor. On the way he talked under his breath, trying out different speeches he might make, thinking how the proud old man would tremble before him now that he was the king. He decided on, "Now old beak-nose, I have the power! You always sided with my father and looked down on me as a child. See if you can ignore my words now!"

He entered the house boldly without knocking on the door, his big guardsmen right behind him in a towering crowd. He found the old counselor playing with his grandchildren. The littles one, squealing and laughing, climbed about his knees and arms as he sat in his chair. It made the young king remember a little hill topped by an oak tree in the palace garden, where he used to play as a small boy, not so many summers ago. Whatever else made him unhappy, the old tree was always there waiting for him there with its arms out in welcome.

When the children saw the new king standing there in the hallway with his crowd of guardsmen towering behind him, they took fright and hid behind their grandfather as he came to his feet and offered a bow to his new master. The remnants of his happy laughter were not altogether gone from his voice as he cleared his throat and welcomed the rude intruders:

"Welcome to my home, Your Majesty! As I served my king, your father, and sought to please none else at his expense, or cross his purpose, may I continue to serve my king if my offer is acceptable."

This was not at all how the young king had imagined things would go. The memories of the many times the old counselor had smiled or chuckled at things he said and did were no longer so irritating; now that the young king saw how freely laughter was given with kindness here among the old man's loved ones. He saw now that the old counselor did not want to laugh at anyone because that person said something childish; he loved laughing with children and delighted in their ways. And more than this, it occurred to the young king that the old man had not played the "flatterer's game" of neglecting his duty toward an aging king to gain the favor of the man soon to replace him. He just stood there not sure what to do, while the guards went from glaring down at all around them to glancing sideways at each other and shrugging their shoulders. Finally, the young king spoke:

"Rest a day or two in memory of the loss of your old friend, my father, and then come to the palace to resume your duties. Until then, peace be with you and all in your house."

The young king led his guardsmen to the servants' quarters to find a gardener who had often irritated him with slow answers and clumsiness. This time the guardsmen stayed outside while the young king walked in alone. As he entered, he saw the gardener on a little stool next to the small fireplace. The long-limbed, gawky man was handing a toy horse, one of the wooden legs of which had obviously been broken off and just as obviously not mended very skillfully, to a little girl. The gardener tried to swallow his huge, ridiculous Adam's apple and in his irksome, hit-pitched voice said, "I'm sorry Sunshine. It's the best I can do." The young king had no idea the gardener was a father, but the child's father he surely was, for by some miracle the gardener's features, which before had always seemed something to inspire a clown's mask, had been softened and molded into a surprisingly pleasing face on the little girl. The gardener seemed in awe of the miracle, and looked at the child as if she were an angel that had chosen to spend a vacation in his house on a whim. The little girl looked up at him all unaware that the man's face was anything other than lovable and took the wooden horse from his hands. She tried to stand it up the horse fell over on the broken leg, which bent back. The gardener bit his lip, but the little angel picked the horse up again and shook it slightly as she walked it along, the mended leg swinging with her rhythm.

"Hey," she said, "now he can dance and paw the ground like a real horse."

Her father relaxed in relief, but then he saw the new king in the doorway. The gardener blushed and stuttered, started to stand up, then went down on his knee without getting out a coherent greeting at all. The little girl looked up at her father, then at the king, and froze as stiff as he wooden horse. The young king looked down at the gardener, then at his little daughter who watched him as steadily as the gardener stared at the floor under his knee. This wasn't turning out like he had expected either. The young king started t speak, but the intent gaze of the little angel's face made him stumble to clear his throat. Immediately he realized that this is just what the gardener did every time he met him at work in the gardens: the man just stood there making noises in his throat and shifting his weight back and forth from one foot to the other — maddening! At least, it had always disgusted the young king before.

"Do you servants live well here?" the young king finally got out.

"Yes, Your Royal Highness — I mean, Your Majesty!" answered the servant.

There was silence for a moment, and the young king finally said, "That is good." Then the young king turned and went back outside. He went up to his guardsmen and started to give them an order when the little girl called from the doorway.

"See my horse! My dad made it for me all by himself just for me! I broke it, but he fixed it for me."

The gardener pulled her back into the house and gave a hurried bow. The young king blinked and opened his mouth to tell the guardsmen what he wanted them to do, but the child's interruption made his mind go blank. He stood there motionless while they waited for him to say something. To his amazement, the young king realized he was shifting his weight back and forth from one foot to the other. He looked at his guardsmen, turned as red in the face as the gardener who had been bowing in the doorway just now, and he had to laugh. He just started walking back away from the house and waved the guards on after him. But he sent one of them to go take some meat and fruit to the gardener to go along with the simple bread he had seen on the table.

He walked much more slowly on the way back to the palace. He was thinking how glad he was that he had not sent someone else to arrest the old counselor or dismiss the gardener from his service. What would the little grandchildren be doing now if their grandfather were in the dungeon? What would the little girl's face look like if she and her father had been thrown out into the street?

Near the palace gate the young king saw the beggar. The sight and smell of the beggar so close to his palace were very offensive to the young king. But when he got closer, the light of the setting sun fell upon the bronze work in such a way that for a moment it didn't look like his gate at all, but the very gates of Paradise made of living gold, and the beggar looked like the one who watched there and tested each man who would pass through the gates, be that man prince, townsman, or peasant.

The young king sent a guardsman for a blanket and some food for the beggar and had another guardsman take the beggar to a stable where he could sleep on some clean straw. He sent a third guardsman to find out whether the beggar had any relatives who should be helping him, and to see what work he might be fit to do in the king's service. Then the young king went to the place where his father's body lay entombed and asked to be left alone.

The king spent the second day of his reign riding in his woods and fields, speaking but little. On the morning of the third day he declared a new law. Henceforth, if any man were offended by another, satisfaction and justice were to be had at the king's court. But there had to be a period of waiting: for not less than a year the accuser had to carry on his person a stone no smaller than his own fist, on which would be written the name of the accused and the name of the offense. Having done this, the young king grinned at the old counselor and took him on a walk in the garden to show him the tree he used to play on. Some say he even climbed up into its arms again for a while.

When a year had passed, the young king called for the accusers to be let into his courtroom. No one entered. No one waited outside the court. No one waited at the gates of his palace. No one waited in the marketplaces. The king called for the elders of his villages and towns to come and report. They did come, and were happy to see him. They told how they had begun by gathering stones themselves, fitting pockets into their robes and sashes. But soon they became too heavy to keep carrying around in spite of the oaths they had sworn in their anger. They began to be more careful before adding another stone to their collection and finally began to throw some away. When they threw some away, they found that their hearts were lighter as well as their pockets. They decided to let the law carry their burdens. If none was broken, they took no offense. Some realized that they had replaced their friends and neighbors with their stones, that they had forgotten their friends as real people and remembered only the one moment that angered them, keeping the stones as a monument to their anger and a memorial to a friendship that was now dead. They cast away their stones and made room in their hearts again for their friends, relatives, and neighbors as whole people.

It was said that some still kept their stones, and were content to reduce their friends and neighbors down to one most unhappy moment, but such as like to feel the heat of their own anger that much now had so many stones that they were too weighted down to travel to the king's palace, or even out of their houses.

In some towns they gathered the discarded stones and used them to repair wells, walls, bridges, and public monuments in order to put them to some good use, and to keep people from forgetting and repeating their foolishness. And the king was happy with his people.

@1982 Frederick N. Bosworth - printed with permission.

November 30

Word Rocks
Craft/Gift

MATERIALS

Assorted small flat rocks
acrylic paint
Paint brush
Permanent markers
Spray lacquer- clear

DIRECTIONS

1. Wash rocks so that they are free of dirt and debris. Allow to dry.
2. Apply a layer of paint to one side of your rock. allow paint to dry.
3. Decorate rock using more paint, sharpies and decorative pens. Write positive words and phrases on the rocks.
4. If you want your art to be more permanent then after the paint is dry spray with a clear spray lacquer.

   When I was growing up Pet Rocks were popular and they were decorated with faces or like animals. They were fun. Later when my daughter was young I was introduced to Prayer Rocks. Recently I was reintroduced to decorated rocks through something called the Word Rocks Project where you write inspirational words or paint pictures on the rocks and then leave them on trails or in gardens or give them to people, leaving positive vibes for others to find. Find them, keep them, pass them along - filling the world with goodness.

Savory Cheese Coins

These tasty crackers will melts in your mouth and surprise you with its spicy kick.

INGREDIENTS:

- 2 cups shredded extra-sharp Cheddar cheese
- 1/2 cup butter, chilled, cut into 8 pieces
- 1 ½ cup all-purpose unbleached flour
- 1 tablespoon cornstarch
- 1/4 teaspoon salt
- 1/4 teaspoon cayenne pepper*
- 1/4 teaspoon paprika (optional)
- pinch of garlic powder
- sesame seeds- optional

INSTRUCTIONS:

1. In a food processor place cheese, flour, cornstarch, salt, cayenne, paprika and garlic powder until mixed well. Add cheese and process until dough resembles coarse meal.
2. Add butter and process until it makes a dough ball. (option you can mix this with a heavy-duty stand mixer or by hand if you don't mind messy hands). If the dough is too dry you can add water one tablespoon at a time.
3. Divide the dough in half; shape each half into a log about 1¼ -inch in diameter and 10 inches long. If desired you can roll this log in sesame seeds to coat the outside.
4. Wrap the logs in plastic wrap and chill for an 3 to 4 hours or until firm. This can be frozen for up to a month; make sure to thaw it completely before slicing and baking.
5. While the dough is chilling line two baking sheets with a silicone mat or parchment paper.
6. Preheat oven to 350°. When logs are completely chilled, cut each log into ¼-inch slices.
7. Place on prepared baking sheet about 1/2-inch apart.
8. Bake until golden brown, 20-25 minutes. Let cool on baking sheets for about 5 minutes before placing on wire racks to cool completely if you can resist them. Store in a airtight container. Makes about 6 dozen.

Note if you don't like things real spicy cut the amount of the cayenne and paprika in half. Other options are too use different kinds of cheese and spices like Parmesan with black pepper instead of cayenne, and 1 teaspoon of rosemary instead of paprika. Option 2 is replace one cup of sharp cheddar for one cup of Parmigiano-Reggiano.

The ABC's of Christmas
Author unknown

A is for Angels
With halos so bright
Whose carols were heard
On that first Christmas Night.

B is for Bells
So merrily ringing
Joy to the world
Is the message they're bringing.

C is for Candles
That so brightly shine
To give a warm welcome
To your friends and mine.

D is for Doorway
With garlands of green
To make Christmas merry
As far as they're seen.

E is for Evergreens
With fragrance so rare
So plentiful at Christmas
Their scent fills the air.

F is for Fun
The whole season long
From trimming the tree
To singing a song.

G is for Greetings
A merry "hello"
With a heart full of love
For people we know.

H is for Holly
With berries so red
To make into wreaths
To hang overhead.

I is for Ice
On snow covered hills
Where sledding is fun
Along with the spills.

J is for Jesus
The Christ child so dear
We honor his birth
On Christmas each year.

K is for Kris Kringle
So merrily he stands
He is who they call Santa
In so many lands.

L is for Lanterns
I am sure that their light
Helped Mary and Joseph
That first Christmas Night.

M is for Mary
Her heart full of love
For her little son Jesus
Who came from above.

N is for Noel
The angels did sing
To herald the birth
of Jesus, our King.

Crazy About Christmas

O is for Ornaments
So shining and bright
With lights on the tree
To sparkle at night.

P is for Packages
With ribbons so gay
All 'round the tree
For our Christmas Day.

Q is for Quiet
Christmas Eve Night
With snow covered hills
Glistening so bright.

R is for Reindeer
Who pull Santa's sleigh
To your house, to my house
They know the way.

S is for Shepherds
Who first saw the star
Over Bethlehem's manger
And followed it far.

T is for Trees
We decorate so gay
Then wait for ole Santa
To hurry our way.

U is for Universe
Where Christmas brings joy
To all in the world
To each girl and each boy.

V is for Visiting
Friends near and far
We travel by plane
Or by bus, or by car.

W is for Wise Men
Who brought gifts so rare
And knelt down and worshiped
The child they found there.

X is for X-mas
Or Christmas by full name
No matter the language
It all means the same.

Y is for Yule Logs
Whose bright sparks fly high
To give a warm welcome
To friends passing by.

Z is for Zeal
We show at this time
In giving to others
And loving mankind.

December 1

Scrabble Ornaments
Craft/Ornament

MATERIALS LIST:

Scrabble tiles*
Snow Tex - snow texture paint (optional)
Ribbon
Paper plate or cardboard
Felt
White craft glue or hot glue

DIRECTIONS:

1. Place scrabble tiles on paper plate and arrange the tiles to say what you want.
2. Trace around the shape of the tiles with a pencil to get a rough outline of the shape of your letters.
3. Cut shape out a little smaller than the actual outline so that you don't see it once the tiles are in place. Use you paper pattern to cut out the outline with felt for later.
4. Glue each letter in place either with craft glue or hot glue. Place something heavy on top of the letters and let them dry for 2-3 hours if using craft glue.
5. If you want to at this point you can apply snow texture paint to the top edges of the letters to make it look like they have freshly fallen snow on them. Use a paint brush or your finger to apply. Let the snow texture dry for at least an hour.
6. Once the snow texture paint has dried, cut a piece of ribbon and fold into a loop. Glue the ribbon hanger to the back of the ornament.
7. Finish by gluing the felt on the back to cover ribbon and give a finished look.

* Scrabble tiles can also be found at garage sales, thrift stores, Amazon and even at craft stores, they even come in sizes up to 9 inches. You can also just use square blank tiles and use vinyl letters.

Get creative, place the letters on plastic snowflakes, ribbon, old Christmas cards, rulers, mini wreaths—the skies the limit. Make them vertical or horizontal. Hang them on the wall, the tree, door knobs or cabinets... Just go crazy.

Taco Stack-Ups

INGREDIENTS

Spanish Rice
2 ½ cup cooked rice (I like brown rice)
1   pound lean ground beef
1   28 to 29-ounce can of crushed tomatoes
1   8 oz can of diced chili peppers
1   medium yellow onion, diced
2   large cloves garlic, minced
1   teaspoon Paprika
1   tsp salt
1   tsp chili powder

Toppers:
Corn chips or tortilla chips
Chopped green onions
Sliced ripe olives
Shredded lettuce
Grated cheese
Diced tomato
Avocado slices or guacamole
Sour Cream
Salsa or hot sauce

INSTRUCTIONS

1. Brown meat with onion and garlic. Add paprika, salt, chili powder and tomatoes, mix together. Simmer sauce until thickened.
2. Add cooked rice and mix well (you just made Spanish Rice).
3. To create your Taco Stack-Ups start by placing a layer of corn chips in the bottom of a bowl or on a plate, next place a spoonful or two of Spanish Rice, and then keep adding whatever extra ingredients you like. Think of this as a flat taco. Finish with a dollop of sour cream and salsa.

In the Great Walled Country
by Raymond Macdonald Alden

Away at the northern end of the world, farther than men have ever gone with their ships or their sleds, and where most people suppose that there is nothing but ice and snow, is a land full of children, called The Great Walled Country. This name is given because all around the country is a great wall, hundreds of feet thick and hundreds of feet high. It is made of ice, and never melts, winter or summer; and of course it is for this reason that more people have not discovered the place.

The land, as I said, is filled with children, for nobody who lives there ever grows up. The king and the queen, the princes and the courtiers, may be as old as you please, but they are children for all that. They play a great deal of the time with dolls and tin soldiers, and every night at seven o'clock have a bowl of bread and milk and go to bed. But they make excellent rulers, and the other children are well pleased with the government.

There are all sorts of curious things about the way they live in The Great Walled Country, but this story is only of their Christmas season. One can imagine what a fine thing their Christmas must be, so near the North Pole, with ice and snow everywhere; but this is not all. Grandfather Christmas lives just on the north side of the country, so that his house leans against the great wall and would tip over if it were not for its support. Grandfather Christmas is his name in The Great Walled Country; no doubt we should call him Santa Claus here. At any rate, he is the same person, and, best of all the children in the world, he loves the children behind the great wall of ice.

One very pleasant thing about having Grandfather Christmas for a neighbor is that in The Great Walled Country they never have to buy their Christmas presents. Every year, on the day before Christmas, before he makes up his bundles for the rest of the world, Grandfather Christmas goes into a great forest of Christmas trees, that grows just back of the palace of the king of The Great Walled Country, and fills the trees with candy and books and toys and all sorts of good things. So when night comes, all the children wrap up snugly, while the children in all other lands are waiting in their beds, and go to the forest to gather gifts for their friends. Each one goes by himself, so that none of his friends can see what he has gathered; and no one ever thinks of such a thing as taking a present for himself. The forest is so big that there is room for every one to wander about without meeting the people from whom he has secrets, and there are always enough nice things to go around.

So Christmas time is a great holiday in that land, as it is in all the best places in the world. They have been celebrating it in this way for hundreds of years, and since Grandfather

Crazy About Christmas

Christmas does not seem to grow old any faster than the children, they will probably do so for hundreds of years to come.

But there was once a time, so many years ago that they would have forgotten all about it if the story were not written in their Big Book and read to them every year, when the children in The Great Walled Country had a very strange Christmas. There came a visitor to the land. He was an old man, and was the first stranger for very many years that had succeeded in getting over the wall. He looked so wise, and was so much interested in what he saw and heard, that the king invited him to the palace, and he was treated with every possible honor.

When this old man had inquired about their Christmas celebration, and was told how they carried it on every year, he listened gravely, and then, looking wiser than ever, he said to the king:

"That is all very well, but I should think that children who have Grandfather Christmas for a neighbor could find a better and easier way. You tell me that you all go out on Christmas Eve to gather presents to give to one another the next morning. Why take so much trouble, and act in such a round-about way? Why not go out together, and everyone get his own presents? That would save the trouble of dividing them again, and everyone would be better satisfied, for he could pick out just what he wanted for himself. No one can tell what you want as well as you can.

This seemed to the king a very wise saying, and he called all his courtiers and counselors about him to hear it. The wise stranger talked further about his plan, and when he had finished they all agreed that they had been very foolish never to have thought of this simple way of getting their Christmas gifts.

"If we do this," they said, "no one can ever complain of what he has, or wish that some one had taken more pains to find what he wanted. We will make a proclamation, and always after this follow the new plan."

So the proclamation was made, and the plan seemed as wise to the children of the country as it had to the king and the counselors. Everyone had at some time been a little disappointed with his Christmas gifts; now there would be no danger of that.

On Christmas Eve they always had a meeting at the palace, and sang carols until the time for going to the forest. When the clock struck ten every one said, "I wish you a Merry Christmas!" to the person nearest him, and then they separated to go their ways to the forest. On this particular night it seemed to the king that the music was not quite so merry as usual, and that when the children spoke to one another their eyes did not shine as gladly as he had noticed them in other years; but there could be no good reason for this, since everyone was expecting a better time than usual. So he thought no more of it.

December 2

There was only one person at the palace that night who was not pleased with the new proclamation about the Christmas gifts. This was a little boy named Inge, who lived not far from the palace with his sister. Now his sister was a cripple, and had to sit all day looking out of the window from her chair; and Inge took care of her, and tried to make her life happy from morning till night. He had always gone to the forest on Christmas Eve and returned with his arms and pockets loaded with pretty things for his sister, which would keep her amused all the coming year. And although she was not able to go after presents for her brother, he did not mind that at all, especially as he had other friends who never forgot to divide their good things with him.

But now, said Inge to himself, what would his sister do? For the king had ordered that no one should gather any presents except for himself, or any more than he could carry away at once. All of Inge's friends were busy planning what they would pick for themselves, but the poor crippled child could not go a step toward the forest. After thinking about it a long time, Inge decided that it would not be wrong if, instead of taking gifts for himself, he took them altogether for his sister. This he would be very glad to do; for what did a boy who could run about and play in the snow care for presents, compared with a little girl who could only sit still and watch others having a good time? Inge did not ask the advice of any one, for he was a little afraid others would tell him he must not do it; but he silently made up his mind not to obey the proclamation.

And now the chimes had struck ten, and the children were making their way toward the forest, in starlight that was so bright that it almost showed their shadows on the sparkling snow. As soon as they came to the edge of the forest, they separated, each one going by himself in the old way, though now there was really no reason why they should have secrets from one another.

Ten minutes later, if you had been in the forest, you might have seen the children standing in dismay with tears on their faces, and exclaiming that there had never been such a Christmas Eve before. For as they looked eagerly about them to the low-bending branches of the evergreen trees, they saw nothing hanging from them that could not be seen every day in the year. High and low they searched, wandering farther into the forest than ever before, lest Grandfather Christmas might have chosen a new place this year for hanging his presents; but still no presents appeared. The king called his counselors about him, and asked them if they knew whether anything of this kind had happened before, but they could tell him nothing. So no one could guess whether Grandfather Christmas had forgotten them, or whether some dreadful accident had kept him away.

As the children were trooping out of the forest, after hours of weary searching, some of them came upon little Inge, who carried over his shoulder a bag that seemed to be full to overflowing. When he saw them looking at him, he cried:

Crazy About Christmas

"Are they not beautiful things? I think Grandfather Christmas was never so good to us before."

"Why, what do you mean?" cried the children. "There are no presents in the forest."

"No presents!" said Inge. "I have my bag full of them." But he did not offer to show them, because he did not want the children to see that they were all for his little sister instead of for himself.

Then the children begged him to tell them in what part of the forest he had found his presents, and he turned back and pointed them to the place where he had been. "I left many more behind than I brought away," he said. "There they are! I can see some of the things shining on the trees even from here."

But when the children followed his footprints in the snow to the place where he had been, they still saw nothing on the trees, and thought that Inge must be walking in his sleep, and dreaming that he had found presents. Perhaps he had filled his bag with the cones from the evergreen trees.

On Christmas Day there was sadness all through The Great Walled Country. But those who came to the house of Inge and his sister saw plenty of books and dolls and beautiful toys piled up about the little cripple's chair; and when they asked where these things came from, they were told, "Why, from the Christmas-tree forest." And they shook their heads, not knowing what it could mean.

The king held a council in the palace, and appointed a committee of his most faithful courtiers to visit Grandfather Christmas, and see if they could find what was the matter. In a day or two more the committee set out on their journey. They had very hard work to climb the great wall of ice that lay between their country and the place where Grandfather Christmas lived, but at last they reached the top. And when they came to the other side of the wall, they were looking down into the top of his chimney. It was not hard to go down this chimney into the house, and when they reached the bottom of it they found themselves in the very room where Grandfather Christmas lay sound asleep.

It was hard enough to waken him, for he always slept one hundred days after his Christmas work was over, and it was only by turning the hands of the clock around two hundred times that the committee could do anything. When the clock had struck twelve times two hundred hours, Grandfather Christmas thought it was time for his nap to be over, and he sat up in bed, rubbing his eyes.

"Oh, sir!" cried the prince who was in charge of the committee, "we have come from the king of The Great Walled Country, who has sent us to ask why you forgot us this Christmas, and left no presents in the forest."

"No presents!" said Grandfather Christmas. "I never forget anything. The presents were there. You did not see them, that's all."

December 2

But the children told him that they had searched long and carefully, and in the whole forest there had not been found a thing that could be called a Christmas gift.

"Indeed!" said Grandfather Christmas. "And did little Inge, the boy with the crippled sister, find none?"

Then the committee was silent, for they had heard of the gifts at Inge's house, and did not know what to say about them.

"You had better go home," said Grandfather Christmas, who now began to realize that he had been awakened too soon, "and let me finish my nap. The presents were there, but they were never intended for children who were looking only for themselves. I am not surprised that you could not see them. Remember that not everything that wise travelers tell you is wise." And he turned over and went to sleep again.

The committee returned silently to The Great Walled Country, and told the king what they had heard. The king did not tell all the children of the land what Grandfather Christmas had said, but, when the next December came, he made another proclamation, bidding everyone to seek gifts for others, in the old way, in the Christmas-tree forest. So that is what they have been doing ever since; and in order that they may not forget what happened, in case any one should ever ask for another change, they have read to them every year from their Big Book the story of the time when they had no Christmas gifts.

@1906

Crazy About Christmas

Gift Tags
Craft/Recycle Project

MATERIALS

Old Christmas Cards
Gift Tag pattern or Cookie Cutters

DIRECTIONS

1. Take old Christmas card and open up. Cut on fold-line. Take the greeting side and set aside.

2. Take the front of the card and place template or cookie cutter over an image you like and trace it with a pencil or fine line marker.

3. Cut along your pencil line.

4. Punch a hole in the top. Cut a small piece of ribbon and thread through hole. Tie in a knot.

5. Either write or rubber stamp, to and from on the backside of the gift tag.

6. Attach as usual to your package.

Hint: If you are going to make lots of gift tags you might want to invest in a paper punch just for doing this.

December 2

Hot Chocolate Sticks
makes 16

INGREDIENTS

1   16 oz package semi-sweet chocolate chips
1   cup sugar (optional)
     Marshmallows - any size (optional)
     Chopped Candy Canes (optional)
     Caramel bits (optional)
     Craft sticks or plastic spoons

INSTRUCTIONS

1. Place chocolate chips in a microwave safe bowl. Heat for 1 minute. Remove and mix until melted. If it needs more time do it in 30 second increments mixing after each heating
2. If you like your hot chocolate a little sweeter add the cup of sugar to the melted chocolate and mix until smooth.
3. Carefully spoon chocolate into a one ounce silicon mold or mini muffin mold, A small cookie scoop is also a great way to get equal amounts into the mold.
4. Place craft stick or stirrer in center of chocolate. If you are going to add candy canes, caramel bits or mini marshmallows to the top do so before chocolate is set.
5. Carefully place in freezer trying to keep craft stick straight..It will take about five minutes to set.
6. Gently grab the stick and pull out of mold. If you are going to attach a large marshmallow to the stick carefully push them onto the stick down to the chocolate.
7. For gift giving wrap in a piece of plastic wrap and tie with a ribbon.
8. To serve place 8 ounces of hot milk in mug and use the chocolate stick to stir. Keep stirring until chocolate is melted. Enjoy.

Suggestion: If you are using mini muffin tins you can put paper liners in like you do for muffins. The paper wrapper makes an easy clean up and is decorative.

Of course there is a Santa Claus.
It's just that no single somebody
could do all he has to do.
So the Lord has spread the task
among us all.
That's why everybody is Santa Claus.
I am...
You are...

—Truman Capote—

December 3

A Kidnapped Santa Claus
by L. Frank Baum

Santa Claus lives in the Laughing Valley, where stands the big, rambling castle in which his toys are manufactured. His workmen, selected from the ryls, knooks, pixies and fairies, live with him, and every one is as busy as can be from one year's end to another.

It is called the Laughing Valley because everything there is happy and gay. The brook chuckles to itself as it leaps rollicking between its green banks; the wind whistles merrily in the trees; the sunbeams dance lightly over the soft grass, and the violets and wild flowers look smilingly up from their green nests. To laugh one needs to be happy; to be happy one needs to be content. And throughout the Laughing Valley of Santa Claus contentment reigns supreme.

On one side is the mighty Forest of Burzee. At the other side stands the huge mountain that contains the Caves of the Daemons. And between them the Valley lies smiling and peaceful.

One would think that our good old Santa Claus, who devotes his days to making children happy, would have no enemies on all the earth; and, as a matter of fact, for a long period of time he encountered nothing but love wherever he might go.

But the Daemons who live in the mountain caves grew to hate Santa Claus very much, and all for the simple reason that he made children happy.

The Caves of the Daemons are five in number. A broad pathway leads up to the first cave, which is a finely arched cavern at the foot of the mountain, the entrance being beautifully carved and decorated. In it resides the Daemon of Selfishness. Back of this is another cavern inhabited by the Daemon of Envy. The cave of the Daemon of Hatred is next in order, and through this one passes to the home of the Daemon of Malice--situated in a dark and fearful cave in the very heart of the mountain. I do not know what lies beyond this. Some say there are terrible pitfalls leading to death and destruction, and this may very well be true. However, from each one of the four caves mentioned there is a small, narrow tunnel leading to the fifth cave--a cozy little room occupied by the Daemon of Repentance. And as the rocky floors of these passages are well worn by the track of passing feet, I judge that many wanderers in the Caves of the Daemons have escaped through the tunnels to the abode of the Daemon of Repentance, who is said to be a pleasant sort of fellow who gladly opens for one a little door admitting you into fresh air and sunshine again.

Well, these Daemons of the Caves, thinking they had great cause to dislike old Santa Claus, held a meeting one day to discuss the matter.

"I'm really getting lonesome," said the Daemon of Selfishness. "For Santa Claus distributes so many pretty Christmas gifts to all the children that they become happy and generous, through his example, and keep away from my cave."

"I'm having the same trouble," rejoined the Daemon of Envy. "The little ones seem quite content with Santa Claus, and there are few, indeed, that I can coax to become envious."

"And that makes it bad for me!" declared the Daemon of Hatred. "For if no children pass through the Caves of Selfishness and Envy, none can get to MY cavern."

"Or to mine," added the Daemon of Malice.

"For my part," said the Daemon of Repentance, "it is easily seen that if children do not visit your caves they have no need to visit mine; so that I am quite as neglected as you are."

"And all because of this person they call Santa Claus!" exclaimed the Daemon of Envy. "He is simply ruining our business, and something must be done at once."

To this they readily agreed; but what to do was another and more difficult matter to settle. They knew that Santa Claus worked all through the year at his castle in the Laughing Valley, preparing the gifts he was to distribute on Christmas Eve; and at first they resolved to try to tempt him into their caves, that they might lead him on to the terrible pitfalls that ended in destruction.

So the very next day, while Santa Claus was busily at work, surrounded by his little band of assistants, the Daemon of Selfishness came to him and said:

"These toys are wonderfully bright and pretty. Why do you not keep them for yourself? It's a pity to give them to those noisy boys and fretful girls, who break and destroy them so quickly."

"Nonsense!" cried the old graybeard, his bright eyes twinkling merrily as he turned toward the tempting Daemon. "The boys and girls are never so noisy and fretful after receiving my presents, and if I can make them happy for one day in the year I am quite content."

So the Daemon went back to the others, who awaited him in their caves, and said:

"I have failed, for Santa Claus is not at all selfish."

The following day the Daemon of Envy visited Santa Claus. Said he: "The toy shops are full of playthings quite as pretty as those you are making. What a shame it is that they should interfere with your business! They make toys by machinery much quicker than you can make them by hand; and they sell them for money, while you get nothing at all for your work."

But Santa Claus refused to be envious of the toy shops.

"I can supply the little ones but once a year--on Christmas Eve," he answered; "for the children are many, and I am but one. And as my work is one of love and kindness I would be ashamed to receive money for my little gifts. But throughout all the year the children

must be amused in some way, and so the toy shops are able to bring much happiness to my little friends. I like the toy shops, and am glad to see them prosper."

In spite of the second rebuff, the Daemon of Hatred thought he would try to influence Santa Claus. So the next day he entered the busy workshop and said:
"Good morning, Santa! I have bad news for you."
"Then run away, like a good fellow," answered Santa Claus. "Bad news is something that should be kept secret and never told."
"You cannot escape this, however," declared the Daemon; "for in the world are a good many who do not believe in Santa Claus, and these you are bound to hate bitterly, since they have so wronged you."
"Stuff and rubbish!" cried Santa.
"And there are others who resent your making children happy and who sneer at you and call you a foolish old rattlepate! You are quite right to hate such base slanderers, and you ought to be revenged upon them for their evil words."
"But I don't hate 'em!" exclaimed Santa Claus positively. "Such people do me no real harm, but merely render themselves and their children unhappy. Poor things! I'd much rather help them any day than injure them."
Indeed, the Daemons could not tempt old Santa Claus in any way. On the contrary, he was shrewd enough to see that their object in visiting him was to make mischief and trouble, and his cheery laughter disconcerted the evil ones and showed to them the folly of such an undertaking. So they abandoned honeyed words and determined to use force.
It was well known that no harm can come to Santa Claus while he is in the Laughing Valley, for the fairies, and ryls, and knooks all protect him. But on Christmas Eve he drives his reindeer out into the big world, carrying a sleighload of toys and pretty gifts to the children; and this was the time and the occasion when his enemies had the best chance to injure him. So the Daemons laid their plans and awaited the arrival of Christmas Eve.
The moon shone big and white in the sky, and the snow lay crisp and sparkling on the ground as Santa Claus cracked his whip and sped away out of the Valley into the great world beyond. The roomy sleigh was packed full with huge sacks of toys, and as the reindeer dashed onward our jolly old Santa laughed and whistled and sang for very joy. For in all his merry life this was the one day in the year when he was happiest--the day he lovingly bestowed the treasures of his workshop upon the little children.
It would be a busy night for him, he well knew. As he whistled and shouted and cracked his whip again, he reviewed in mind all the towns and cities and farmhouses where he was expected, and figured that he had just enough presents to go around and make every child

happy. The reindeer knew exactly what was expected of them, and dashed along so swiftly that their feet scarcely seemed to touch the snow-covered ground.

Suddenly a strange thing happened: a rope shot through the moonlight and a big noose that was in the end of it settled over the arms and body of Santa Claus and drew tight. Before he could resist or even cry out he was jerked from the seat of the sleigh and tumbled head foremost into a snowbank, while the reindeer rushed onward with the load of toys and carried it quickly out of sight and sound.

Such a surprising experience confused old Santa for a moment, and when he had collected his senses he found that the wicked Daemons had pulled him from the snowdrift and bound him tightly with many coils of the stout rope. And then they carried the kidnapped Santa Claus away to their mountain, where they thrust the prisoner into a secret cave and chained him to the rocky wall so that he could not escape.

"Ha, ha!" laughed the Daemons, rubbing their hands together with cruel glee. "What will the children do now? How they will cry and scold and storm when they find there are no toys in their stockings and no gifts on their Christmas trees! And what a lot of punishment they will receive from their parents, and how they will flock to our Caves of Selfishness, and Envy, and Hatred, and Malice! We have done a mighty clever thing, we Daemons of the Caves!"

Now it so chanced that on this Christmas Eve the good Santa Claus had taken with him in his sleigh Nuter the Ryl, Peter the Knook, Kilter the Pixie, and a small fairy named Wisk--his four favorite assistants. These little people he had often found very useful in helping him to distribute his gifts to the children, and when their master was so suddenly dragged from the sleigh they were all snugly tucked underneath the seat, where the sharp wind could not reach them.

The tiny immortals knew nothing of the capture of Santa Claus until some time after he had disappeared. But finally they missed his cheery voice, and as their master always sang or whistled on his journeys, the silence warned them that something was wrong.

Little Wisk stuck out his head from underneath the seat and found Santa Claus gone and no one to direct the flight of the reindeer.

"Whoa!" he called out, and the deer obediently slackened speed and came to a halt.

Peter and Nuter and Kilter all jumped upon the seat and looked back over the track made by the sleigh. But Santa Claus had been left miles and miles behind.

"What shall we do?" asked Wisk anxiously, all the mirth and mischief banished from his wee face by this great calamity.

"We must go back at once and find our master," said Nuter the Ryl, who thought and spoke with much deliberation.

December 3

"No, no!" exclaimed Peter the Knook, who, cross and crabbed though he was, might always be depended upon in an emergency. "If we delay, or go back, there will not be time to get the toys to the children before morning; and that would grieve Santa Claus more than anything else."

"It is certain that some wicked creatures have captured him," added Kilter thoughtfully, "and their object must be to make the children unhappy. So our first duty is to get the toys distributed as carefully as if Santa Claus were himself present. Afterward we can search for our master and easily secure his freedom."

This seemed such good and sensible advice that the others at once resolved to adopt it. So Peter the Knook called to the reindeer, and the faithful animals again sprang forward and dashed over hill and valley, through forest and plain, until they came to the houses wherein children lay sleeping and dreaming of the pretty gifts they would find on Christmas morning.

The little immortals had set themselves a difficult task; for although they had assisted Santa Claus on many of his journeys, their master had always directed and guided them and told them exactly what he wished them to do. But now they had to distribute the toys according to their own judgment, and they did not understand children as well as did old Santa. So it is no wonder they made some laughable errors.

Mamie Brown, who wanted a doll, got a drum instead; and a drum is of no use to a girl who loves dolls. And Charlie Smith, who delights to romp and play out of doors, and who wanted some new rubber boots to keep his feet dry, received a sewing box filled with colored worsteds and threads and needles, which made him so provoked that he thoughtlessly called our dear Santa Claus a fraud.

Had there been many such mistakes the Daemons would have accomplished their evil purpose and made the children unhappy. But the little friends of the absent Santa Claus labored faithfully and intelligently to carry out their master's ideas, and they made fewer errors than might be expected under such unusual circumstances.

And, although they worked as swiftly as possible, day had begun to break before the toys and other presents were all distributed; so for the first time in many years the reindeer trotted into the Laughing Valley, on their return, in broad daylight, with the brilliant sun peeping over the edge of the forest to prove they were far behind their accustomed hours.

Having put the deer in the stable, the little folk began to wonder how they might rescue their master; and they realized they must discover, first of all, what had happened to him and where he was.

So Wisk the Fairy transported himself to the bower of the Fairy Queen, which was located deep in the heart of the Forest of Burzee; and once there, it did not take him long to find out all about the naughty Daemons and how they had kidnapped the good Santa Claus to prevent his making children happy. The Fairy Queen also promised her assistance, and then, fortified by this powerful support, Wisk flew back to where Nuter and Peter and Kilter awaited him, and the four counseled together and laid plans to rescue their master from his enemies.

It is possible that Santa Claus was not as merry as usual during the night that succeeded his capture. For although he had faith in the judgment of his little friends he could not avoid a certain amount of worry, and an anxious look would creep at times into his kind old eyes as he thought of the disappointment that might await his dear little children. And the Daemons, who guarded him by turns, one after another, did not neglect to taunt him with contemptuous words in his helpless condition.

When Christmas Day dawned the Daemon of Malice was guarding the prisoner, and his tongue was sharper than that of any of the others.

"The children are waking up, Santa!" he cried. "They are waking up to find their stockings empty! Ho, ho! How they will quarrel, and wail, and stamp their feet in anger! Our caves will be full today, old Santa! Our caves are sure to be full!"

But to this, as to other like taunts, Santa Claus answered nothing. He was much grieved by his capture, it is true; but his courage did not forsake him. And, finding that the prisoner would not reply to his jeers, the Daemon of Malice presently went away, and sent the Daemon of Repentance to take his place.

This last personage was not so disagreeable as the others. He had gentle and refined features, and his voice was soft and pleasant in tone.

"My brother Daemons do not trust me overmuch," said he, as he entered the cavern; "but it is morning, now, and the mischief is done. You cannot visit the children again for another year."

"That is true," answered Santa Claus, almost cheerfully; "Christmas Eve is past, and for the first time in centuries I have not visited my children."

"The little ones will be greatly disappointed," murmured the Daemon of Repentance, almost regretfully; "but that cannot be helped now. Their grief is likely to make the children selfish and envious and hateful, and if they come to the Caves of the Daemons today I shall get a chance to lead some of them to my Cave of Repentance."

"Do you never repent, yourself?" asked Santa Claus, curiously.

"Oh, yes, indeed," answered the Daemon. "I am even now repenting that I assisted in your capture. Of course it is too late to remedy the evil that has been done; but repentance, you know, can come only after an evil thought or deed, for in the beginning there is nothing to repent of."

"So I understand," said Santa Claus. "Those who avoid evil need never visit your cave."

"As a rule, that is true," replied the Daemon; "yet you, who have done no evil, are about

December 3

to visit my cave at once; for to prove that I sincerely regret my share in your capture I am going to permit you to escape."

This speech greatly surprised the prisoner, until he reflected that it was just what might be expected of the Daemon of Repentance. The fellow at once busied himself untying the knots that bound Santa Claus and unlocking the chains that fastened him to the wall. Then he led the way through a long tunnel until they both emerged in the Cave of Repentance.

"I hope you will forgive me," said the Daemon pleadingly. "I am not really a bad person, you know; and I believe I accomplish a great deal of good in the world."

With this he opened a back door that let in a flood of sunshine, and Santa Claus sniffed the fresh air gratefully.

"I bear no malice," said he to the Daemon, in a gentle voice; "and I am sure the world would be a dreary place without you. So, good morning, and a Merry Christmas to you!"

With these words he stepped out to greet the bright morning, and a moment later he was trudging along, whistling softly to himself, on his way to his home in the Laughing Valley.

Marching over the snow toward the mountain was a vast army, made up of the most curious creatures imaginable. There were numberless knooks from the forest, as rough and crooked in appearance as the gnarled branches of the trees they ministered to. And there were dainty ryls from the fields, each one bearing the emblem of the flower or plant it guarded. Behind these were many ranks of pixies, gnomes and nymphs, and in the rear a thousand beautiful fairies floated along in gorgeous array.

This wonderful army was led by Wisk, Peter, Nuter, and Kilter, who had assembled it to rescue Santa Claus from captivity and to punish the Daemons who had dared to take him away from his beloved children.

And, although they looked so bright and peaceful, the little immortals were armed with powers that would be very terrible to those who had incurred their anger. Woe to the Daemons of the Caves if this mighty army of vengeance ever met them!

But lo! coming to meet his loyal friends appeared the imposing form of Santa Claus, his white beard floating in the breeze and his bright eyes sparkling with pleasure at this proof of the love and veneration he had inspired in the hearts of the most powerful creatures in existence.

And while they clustered around him and danced with glee at his safe return, he gave them earnest thanks for their support. But Wisk, and Nuter, and Peter, and Kilter, he embraced affectionately.

"It is useless to pursue the Daemons," said Santa Claus to the army. "They have their place in the world, and can never be destroyed. But that is a great pity, nevertheless," he continued musingly.

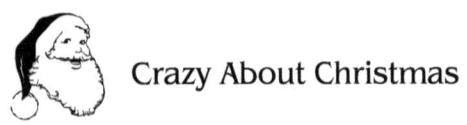 Crazy About Christmas

So the fairies, and knooks, and pixies, and ryls all escorted the good man to his castle, and there left him to talk over the events of the night with his little assistants.

Wisk had already rendered himself invisible and flown through the big world to see how the children were getting along on this bright Christmas morning; and by the time he returned, Peter had finished telling Santa Claus of how they had distributed the toys.

"We really did very well," cried the fairy, in a pleased voice; "for I found little unhappiness among the children this morning. Still, you must not get captured again, my dear master; for we might not be so fortunate another time in carrying out your ideas."

He then related the mistakes that had been made, and which he had not discovered until his tour of inspection. And Santa Claus at once sent him with rubber boots for Charlie Smith, and a doll for Mamie Brown; so that even those two disappointed ones became happy.

As for the wicked Daemons of the Caves, they were filled with anger and chagrin when they found that their clever capture of Santa Claus had come to naught. Indeed, no one on that Christmas Day appeared to be at all selfish, or envious, or hateful. And, realizing that while the children's saint had so many powerful friends it was folly to oppose him, the Daemons never again attempted to interfere with his journeys on Christmas Eve.

The Delineator, December 1904

December 3

Crystal Coal Garden
Craft/Science Project

MATERIALS LIST:

Five charcoal briquets or coal
Hammer
2-quart glass bowl or disposable aluminum pan
Clean, empty glass jar
1 tablespoon ammonia
6 tablespoons non-iodized salt
6 tablespoons of Liquid Bluing (see note)
6 tablespoons water
Food coloring

DIRECTIONS:

1. Break up the charcoal briquets into 1-inch chunks with the hammer, and place the pieces in the bottom of the bowl. You can leave some whole if you want.
2. In a glass measuring cup mix the ammonia, salt, bluing and water.
3. Pour the mixture carefully over the coal.
4. Put a few drops of food coloring over the charcoal. It will be come the color of the flowers.
5. Let the bowl sit undisturbed in a safe place. Your crystals will begin to grow within a few hours. Crystals will continue to grow if you keep watering it.

Historical Note: This project has been around since pioneer times and during the depression was called depression flowers.

Note: Liquid bluing can be found in most markets in with the laundry soaps and products. The most popular brand is Mrs. Stewart's Liquid Bluing and is used as a laundry whitener. If you can't find it the store try their website http://www.mrsstewart.com

Strawberry Santa

A easy tasty snack or a great party pleaser

INGREDIENTS

- 1 pint fresh strawberries
- 1 cup heavy whipping cream
- 2 tablespoons confectioners sugar
- mini chocolate chips or chocolate sprinkles

INSTRUCTIONS

1. Cut the hulls off the strawberries so they can stand up on a plate.
2. Slice off top of strawberry about 1/3 of the way down to make hat and set aside.
3. Place whipping cream into bowl with confectioner's sugar and whip till it makes soft mounds.
4. Spoon whipped cream into a pastry bag with a star tip or a zip-lock bag that you snip the corner off of and pipe whipped cream on top of strawberry base to form a head. Set the hat on top of his head.
5. Note: If you want more of the whipped creme to stay on the Santa use a small melon scoop and take a little of the strawberry out of the top.
6. Carefully add a dot of whipped cream on top of his hat for the pom-pom and two dots on the front of his belly for buttons.
7. Place either 2 mini chocolate chips or two sprinkles for his eyes.

December 4

A Letter from Santa Claus
by Mark Twain

Palace of Saint Nicholas
In the Moon
Christmas Morning

My Dear Susy Clemens,

I have received and read all the letters which you and your little sister have written me . . . . I can read your and your baby sister's jagged and fantastic marks without any trouble at all. But I had trouble with those letters which you dictated through your mother and the nurses, for I am a foreigner and cannot read English writing well. You will find that I made no mistakes about the things which you and the baby ordered in your own letters--I went down your chimney at midnight when you were asleep and delivered them all myself--and kissed both of you, too . . . . But . . . there were . . . one or two small orders which I could not fill because we ran out of stock . . . .

There was a word or two in your mama's letter which . . . I took to be "a trunk full of doll's clothes." Is that it? I will call at your kitchen door about nine o'clock this morning to inquire. But I must not see anybody and I must not speak to anybody but you. When the kitchen doorbell rings, George must be blindfolded and sent to the door. You must tell George he must walk on tiptoe and not speak-- otherwise he will die someday. Then you must go up to the nursery and stand on a chair or the nurse's bed and put your ear to the speaking tube that leads down to the kitchen and when I whistle through it you must speak in the tube and say, "Welcome, Santa Claus!" Then I will ask whether it was a trunk you ordered or not. If you say it was, I shall ask you what color you want the trunk to be . . . and then you must tell me every single thing in detail which you want the trunk to contain. Then when I say "Good-by and a Merry Christmas to my little Susy Clemens," you must say "Good-by, good old Santa Claus, I thank you very much." Then you must go down into the library and make George close all the doors that open into the main hall, and everybody must keep still for a little while. I will go to the moon and get those things and in a few minutes I will come down the chimney that belongs to the fireplace that is in the hall--if it is a trunk you want--because I couldn't get such a thing as a trunk down the nursery chimney, you know . . . .If I should leave any snow in the hall, you must tell George to sweep it into the fireplace, for I haven't time to do such things. George must not use

Crazy About Christmas

a broom, but a rag--else he will die someday . . . . If my boot should leave a stain on the marble, George must not holystone it away. Leave it there always in memory of my visit; and whenever you look at it or show it to anybody you must let it remind you to be a good little girl. Whenever you are naughty and someone points to that mark which your good old Santa Claus's boot made on the marble, what will you say, little sweetheart?

Good-by for a few minutes, till I come down to the world and ring the kitchen doorbell.

Your loving Santa Claus
Whom people sometimes call
"The Man in the Moon"

Suzy Clemens, was born in Elmira, New York, and lived a short life, dying at the age of 23 from meningitis. In childhood, Suzy often had poor health, similar to her mother. At 13, she wrote a biography of her father, which was included as part of Twain's Chapters From My Autobiography. Mark Twain wrote a letter to his daughter, which he sent from Santa Claus, during one of her childhood illnesses. Written in 1875. and published in Clara Clemen's 1931 book "My Father, Mark Twain".

December 4

Handsy Santa
Craft/Ornament/Decoration

MATERIALS LIST:

Red, pink, white, green construction paper *or* fun foam
white cotton ball *or* pompom
pair of wiggly eyes
Ribbon for hanging

DIRECTIONS:

1. Trace hand on white construction paper and then cut out. The hand becomes Santa's beard.
2. Trace mustache, hat brim and eyebrows on white paper, cheeks on pink, hat and berries on red, face and nose on peach, and holly on green.
3. Cut all the pieces out and glue into place in this order: Face, hat, hat brim, cheeks, mustache, nose, wiggly eyes, eyebrows, holly and holly berries. Refer to the picture if you get lost.
4. Glue cotton ball on edge of hat.
5. You can now either glue a ribbon to the back and hang on the tree or mount on another piece of paper as a piece of holiday art or hang it over your door knob.
6. As an option you can stuff a white cloth glove, felt for his features, and a small sock for his hat. Above all have fun.

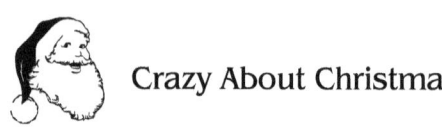

Crazy About Christmas

Furry Hat Brim cut 1 in white

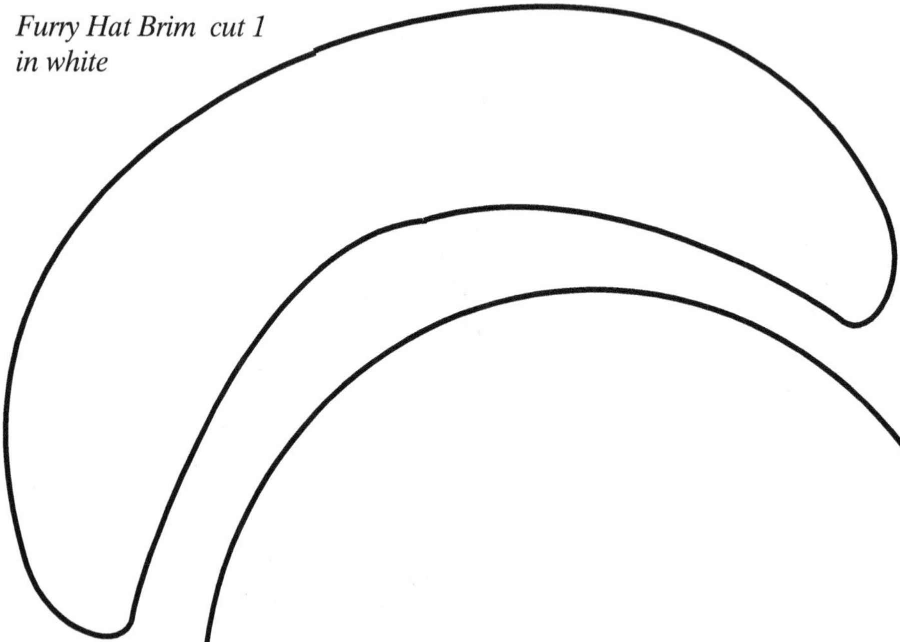

Face cut 1 in peach

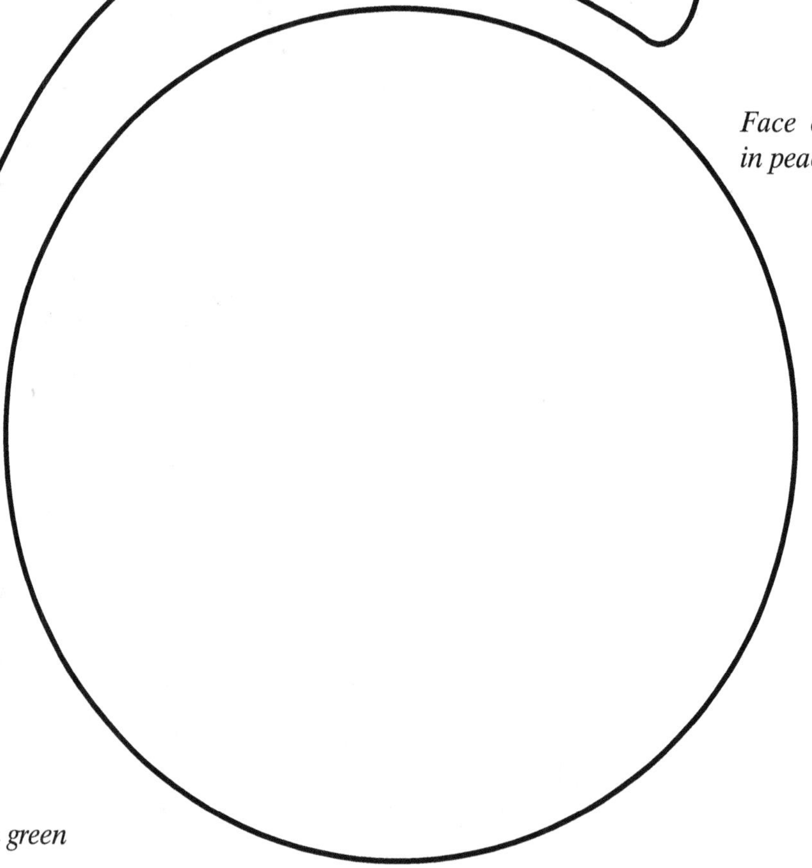

Holly Berries cut 3 in red

Holly cut 1 in green

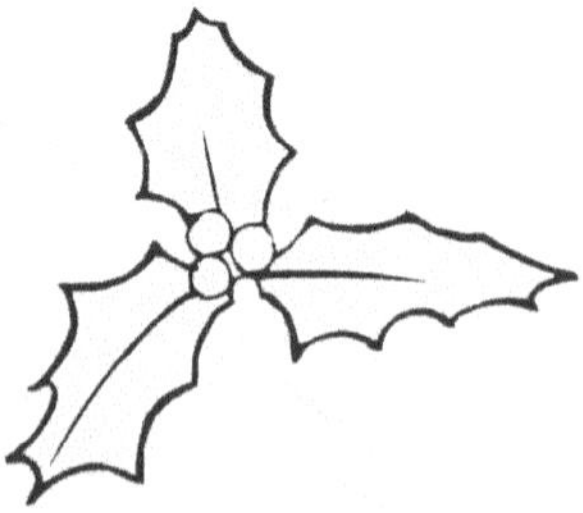

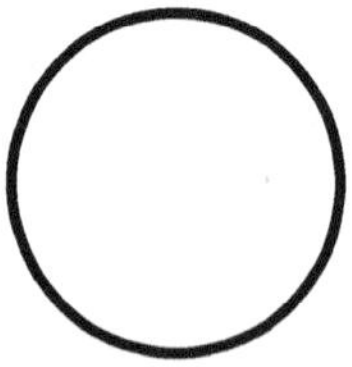

Nose cut 1 in peach

Eyebrows cut 2 in white

December 4

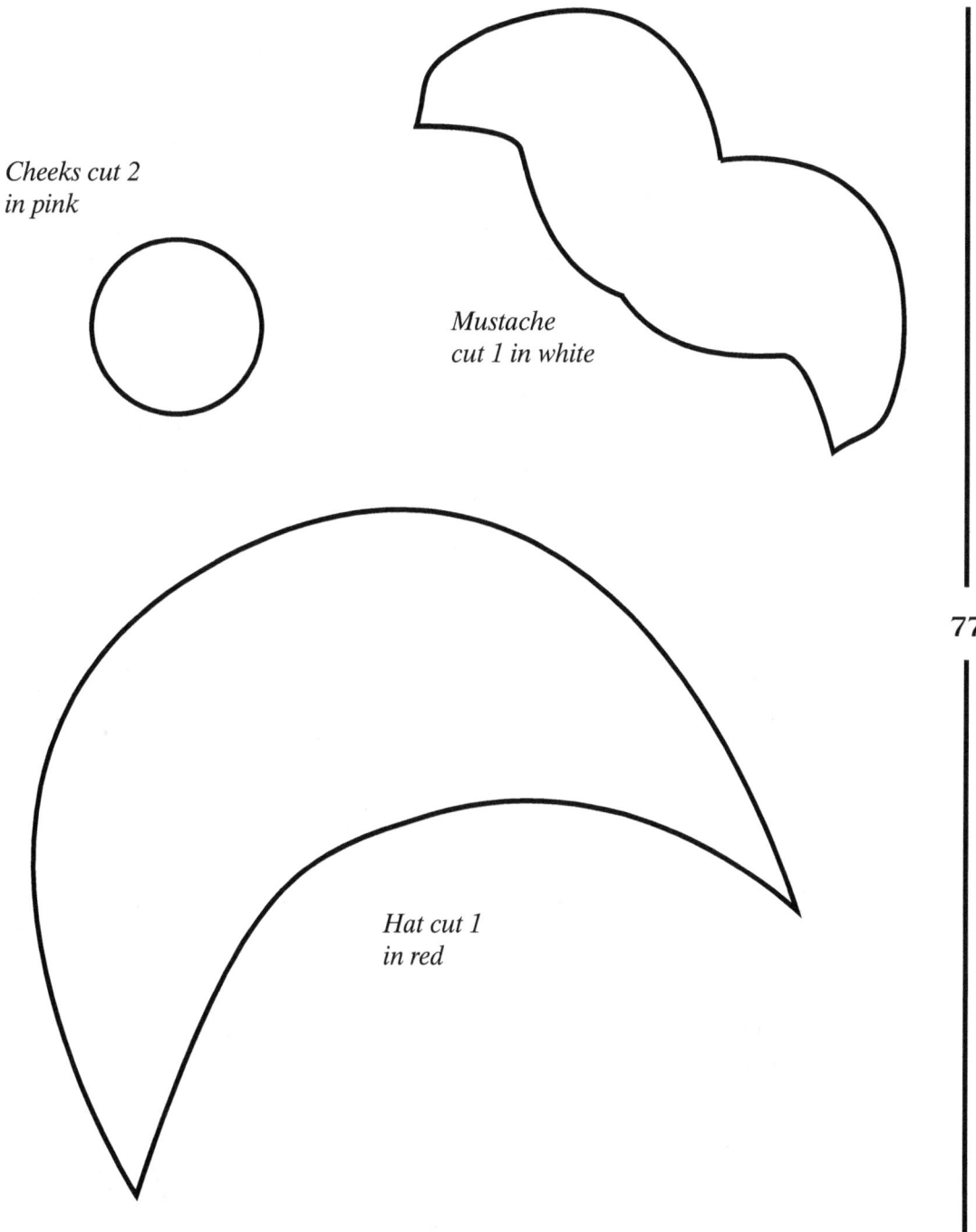

Cheeks cut 2 in pink

Mustache cut 1 in white

Hat cut 1 in red

Carrot-Apple Cake

INGREDIENTS

1 ½ cups sugar
1 ½ cups vegetable oil*
3 eggs
2 teaspoons vanilla

2 cups sifted all-purpose flour
2 teaspoons cinnamon
1 teaspoon baking soda
1 teaspoon baking powder

1 teaspoon salt
2 cups shredded carrots
1 cup chopped apples
1 cup golden raisins
1 cup chopped pecans

INSTRUCTIONS

1. Preheat oven to 350°.
2. Combine sugar, oil, eggs and vanilla in a large bowl; blend well.
3. Sift together the dry ingredients; add to the first mixture and mix well.
4. Stir in carrots, apples, raisins and pecans ingredients until well blended.
5. Pour into 2 greased and wax paper lined 9-inch cake pans.
6. Bake for 35 to 45 minutes until center of cake is firm to touch.
7. Cool in pans 10 minutes. Remove from pans and finish cooling on cake racks.
8. Frost with Pecan Cream Cheese Frosting.

Note: if you want to reduce the fat and still be moist and wonderful use 3/4 cup applesauce and 3/4 cup oil

Pecan Cream Cheese Frosting:

INGREDIENTS

2 (3oz) pkgs cream cheese, softened
1 tablespoon milk
2 teaspoons vanilla
   dash salt
1 box (1lb) confectioners' sugar -- sifted
½ cup chopped pecans

INSTRUCTIONS

1. In a medium bowl blend cream cheese, milk, vanilla, and salt thoroughly.
2. Gradually beat in sifted sugar until frosting is smooth and of spreading consistency.
3. Fold in pecans.

December 5

Teach the Children
Author Unknown

Late one Christmas Eve, I sank back, tired but content, into my easy chair. The kids were in bed, the gifts were wrapped, the milk and cookies waited by the fireplace for Santa. As I sat back admiring the tree with its decorations, I couldn't help feeling that something important was missing. It wasn't long before the tiny twinkling tree lights lulled me to sleep.

I don't know how long I slept, but all of a sudden I knew that I wasn't alone. I opened my eyes, and you can imagine my surprise when I saw Santa Claus himself standing next to my Christmas tree. He was dressed all in fur from his head to his foot just as the poem described him, but he was not the "jolly old elf" of Christmas legend. The man who stood before me looked sad and disappointed, and there were tears in his eyes.

"Santa, what's wrong?" I asked, "Why are you crying?"

"It's the children," Santa replied sadly.

"But Santa, the children love you," I said.

"Oh, I know they love me, and they love the gifts I bring them," Santa said, "but the children of today seem to have somehow missed out on the true spirit of Christmas. It's not their fault. It's just that the adults, many of them not having been taught themselves, have forgotten to teach the children."

"Teach them what?" I asked.

Santa's kind old face became soft, more gentle. His eyes began to shine with something more than tears. He spoke softly. "Teach the children the true meaning of Christmas. Teach them that the part of Christmas we can see, hear, and touch is much more than meets the eye. Teach them the symbolism behind the customs and traditions of Christmas which we now observe. Teach them what it is they truly represent."

Santa reached into his bag and pulled out a tiny Christmas tree and set it on my mantle. "Teach them about the Christmas tree. Green is the second color of Christmas. The stately evergreen, with its unchanging color, represents the hope of eternal life in Jesus. Its needles point heavenward as a reminder that mankind's thoughts should turn heavenward as well."

Santa reached into his bag again and pulled out a shiny star and placed it at the top of the small tree. "The star was the heavenly sign of promise. God promised a Savior for the world and the star was the sign of the fulfillment of that promise on the night that Jesus Christ was born. Teach the children that God always fulfills His promises, and that wise men still seek Him."

"Red," said Santa, "is the first color of Christmas." "He pulled forth a red ornament for the tiny tree. Red is deep, intense, vivid. It is the color of the life-giving blood that flows through our veins. It is the symbol of God's greatest gift. Teach the children that Christ gave his life and shed his blood for them that they might have eternal life. When they see the color red, it should remind them of that most wonderful gift."

Santa found a silver bell in his pack and placed it on the tree. "Just as lost sheep are guided to safety by the sound of the bell, it continues to ring today for all to be guided to the fold. Teach the children to follow the true Shepherd, who gave His life for the sheep."

Santa placed a candle on the mantle and lit it. The soft glow from its one tiny flame brightened the room. "The glow of the candle represents how people can show their thanks for the gift of God's son that Christmas Eve long ago. Teach the children to follow in Christ's foot steps...to go about doing good. Teach them to let their light so shine before people that all may see it and glorify God. This is what is symbolized when the twinkle lights shine on the tree like hundreds of bright, shining candles, each of them representing one of God's precious children, their light shining for all to see."

Again Santa reached into his bag and this time he brought forth a tiny red and white striped cane. As he hung it on the tree he spoke softly. "The candy cane is a stick of hard white candy. White to symbolize the virgin birth and sinless nature of Jesus, and hard to symbolize the Solid Rock the foundation of the church, and the firmness of God's promises. The candy cane is in the form of a "J" to represent the precious name of Jesus, who came to earth. It also represents the Good Shepherd's crook, which He uses to reach down into the ditches of the world to lift out the fallen lambs who, like all sheep, have gone astray. The original candy cane had three small red stripes, which are the stripes of the scourging Jesus received by which we are healed, and a large red stripe that represents the shed blood of Jesus, so that we can have the promise of eternal life.

"Teach these things to the children."

Santa brought out a beautiful wreath made of fresh, fragrant greenery tied with a bright red bow. "The bow reminds us of the bond of perfection, which is love. The wreath embodies all the good things about Christmas for those with eyes to see and hearts to understand. It contains the colors of red and green and the heaven-turned needles of the evergreen. The bow tells the story of good will towards all and its color reminds us of Christ's sacrifice. Even its very shape is symbolic, representing eternity and the eternal nature of Christ's love. It is a circle, without beginning and without end. These are the things you must teach the children."

I asked, "But where does that leave you, Santa?"

The tears gone now from his eyes, a smile broke over Santa's face. "Why bless you, my dear," he laughed, "I'm only a symbol myself. I represent the spirit of family fun and the

December 5

joy of giving and receiving. If the children are taught these other things, there is no danger that I'll ever be forgotten."

"I think I'm beginning to understand."

"That's why I came," said Santa. "You're an adult. If you don't teach the children these things, then who will?"

Clay Pot Santa
Craft/Decoration

MATERIAL LIST

2 clay pots - 1 a bit larger than the other
Wooden Head Bead that the smaller pot will fit on
2 small wooden beads for hands
Red and black, acrylic paint or permanent markers
White, Curly Chenille Stem
Red Chenille Stem
White pompom
Low-temp Glue Gun
Tacky glue
Green button
White texture snow paste (see recipe below)
candy cane

DIRECTIONS:

1. Wipe down your clay pot with a damp cloth and let dry completely.
2. Paint both pots with red paint and let dry. If necessary give them a second coat of paint to have a rich red color.
3. Paint the smaller beads black for hands.
4. Use snow paste to paint a beard on Santa's face. Also paint the snow paste on the bottom of both pots and let dry completely.
5. Hot glue the large wooden bead onto the large clay pot.
6. Use paint or markers to draw a face onto the wooden ball.
7. Glue a piece of white chenille around the bottom of small pot to make Santa's hat.
8. Hot Glue the small clay pot you painted on top of the wooden head to be Santa's hat. Run the bead of glue about 1/4 inch from the bottom so you don't see the glue when you press down the pot.
9. Glue the white pompom on top of the hat.
10. To make Santa's arms, Cut a piece of red chenille to be the arms. Dab a bit of tacky glue on the ends and insert the small wooden balls on the ends for hands. Glue the

December 5

piece of red chenille towards the top edge of the clay pot body. Once dry bend the arms however you like. You might even give him a sack to hold or even a candy cane staff.

11. For Santa's belt cut a 1 inch wide piece of felt to fit around the middle of Santa's belly and secure with a dab of tacky glue. Then place a green button over the seam for a belt buckle.

12. *Recipe for Snow Paste*. If you can't find it at your craft store make your own by mixing sand ,white paint and a little bit of spackling paste. Mix until the mixture is thick. Apply it with a small craft spatula and let it dry overnight.

Idaho Style Cinnamon Rolls

Mashed potatoes are the secret ingredient to getting super light and fluffy cinnamon rolls.

INGREDIENTS
- 2 cups hot milk
- ½ cup butter
- 1 cup granulated sugar
- 1 cup finely mashed potatoes (see note)
- 2 teaspoons salt
- 4 ½ teaspoons active dry yeast (2 packets)
- ½ cup warm water
- 2 eggs, lightly beaten
- 7 - 8 ½ cups unbleached bread flour

FILLING
- 4 tablespoons butter, softened
- 1 cup brown sugar or coconut sugar
- 3 teaspoons ground cinnamon
- ½ cup chopped pecans (optional)
- ½ cup raisins (optional)

FROSTING
- 2 ounces cream cheese, softened
- 2 tablespoons butter, softened
- 5 tablespoons milk
- 4 cups powdered sugar
- 1 teaspoon vanilla extract

INSTRUCTIONS
1. In a large stand mixer or a bowl put 1/2 cup butter, then pour the hot milk over the butter. Add sugar, mashed potatoes, and salt. Set aside.
2. Dissolve yeast in the 1/2 cup warm water.
3. Add eggs and 4 cups of the flour to the potato mix and mix until well blended.
4. Add remaining flour a 1/2 cup at a time until a soft dough forms. Then transfer to a clean, well-floured surface and knead for 1-2 minutes by hand. Place in a lightly greased

December 5

large bowl and cover with plastic wrap or a light dish towel. Allow to rise for 45 minutes.
5. Preheat oven to 350° F and lightly grease a baking sheet or large casserole dish.
6. Roll dough into a large rectangle about 1/2 inch thick.
7. For the filling, spread the softened butter onto the dough, I tend to use my fingers to smear it all over the dough. Mix the brown sugar and cinnamon together and sprinkle over buttered dough. If you are like me you are then going to sprinkle the dough with nuts and raisins on top of the cinnamon sugar.
8. Tightly roll one long side to the other long side and pinch the seam to seal. Use a pizza cutter or sharp knife to cut into about 16 pieces.
9. Place sections swirl-side-down onto your greased casserole dish or baking sheet. (see note) Bake for 20-30 minutes until golden brown.
10. To make the frosting. Cream together cream cheese and butter until smooth. Add milk, powdered sugar, and vanilla and mix again for 2-3 minutes until smooth. Drizzle or spread over warm cinnamon rolls and serve.

NOTE: Let's talk about mashed potatoes. You can use homemade mashed potatoes only if you don't heavily season them, in other words just set aside some freshly mashed potatoes before you add the seasonings. In a hurry place a medium sized potatoe in a sandwich bag and place in microwave and bake for 3.5 minutes. Peel under cool water the skin practiallay slides off, then mash it well with a touch of milk. In a pinch, you can use instant potatoes.

If you use a casserole dish they will require a little bit longer baking time than a on a baking sheet because they are touching.

Today is St. Nicholas Day, or the Feast of St. Nicholas

St. Nicholas Day, or Feast of St. Nicholas, is December 6 and marks the anniversary of the death of the third-century Catholic saint who inspired the modern versions of Santa Claus. St. Nicholas Day is rooted in a tradition of giving, stemming from the saint's legendary generosity. It is said he sold all that he owned, giving the money to the poor. He dedicated his entire life serving and caring for the sick and suffering. He is the patron said of children and sailors.

St. Nicholas Day is a time when children are given special cookies, candies, and gifts. In many places, children leave letters for St. Nicholas and carrots or grass for his donkey or horse. In the morning, they find small presents under their pillows or in the shoes, stockings, or plates they have set out for him. Oranges and chocolate coins are common treats that represent St. Nicholas's legendary rescue of three impoverished girls by paying their marriage dowries with gold. Candy canes, which have the shape of a bishop's crosier, are also given.

Isn't nice that St. Nicholas and Jesus don't have to share a day. They each have their own day St. Nicholas Day and Christmas or at least that is how we celebrate it.

St. Nicholas Day — December 6

Little Piccola

Phebe A. Curtiss
Based on a poem by Celia Thaxter

Piccola lived in Italy, where the oranges grow, and where all the year the sun shines warm and bright. I suppose you think Piccola a very strange name for a little girl; but in her country it was not strange at all, and her mother thought it the sweetest name a little girl ever had.

Piccola had no kind father, no big brother or sister, and no sweet baby to play with and love. She and her mother lived all alone in an old stone house that looked on a dark, narrow street. They were very poor, and the mother was away from home almost every day, washing clothes and scrubbing floors, and working hard to earn money for her little girl and herself. So you see Piccola was alone a great deal of the time; and if she had not been a very happy, contented little child, I hardly know what she would have done. She had no playthings except a heap of stones in the back yard that she used for building houses and a very old, very ragged doll that her mother had found in the street one day.

But there was a small round hole in the stone wall at the back of her yard, and her greatest pleasure was to look through that into her neighbor's garden. When she stood on a stone, and put her eyes close to the hole, she could see the green grass in the garden, and smell the sweet flowers, and even hear the water splashing into the fountain. She had never seen anyone walking in the garden, for it belonged to an old gentleman who did not care about grass and flowers.

One day in the autumn her mother told her that the old gentleman had gone away, and had rented his house to a family of little American children, who had come with their sick mother to spend the winter in Italy. After this, Piccola was never lonely, for all day long the children ran and played and danced and sang in the garden. It was several weeks before they saw her at all, and I am not sure they ever would have done so but one day the kitten ran away, and in chasing her they came close to the wall and saw Piccola's black eyes looking through the hole in the stones. They were a little frightened at first, and did not speak to her; but the next day she was there again, and Rose, the oldest girl, went up to the wall and talked to her a little while. When the children found that she had no one to play with and was very lonely, they talked to her every day, and often brought her fruits and candies, and passed them through the hole in the wall.

One day they even pushed the kitten through; but the hole was hardly large enough for her, and she mewed and scratched and was very much frightened. After that the little boy said he would ask his father if the hole might not be made larger, and then Piccola could come in and play with them. The father had found out that Piccola's mother was a good

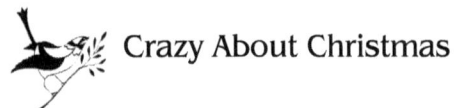
Crazy About Christmas

woman, and that the little girl herself was sweet and kind, so that he was very glad to have some of the stones broken away and an opening made for Piccola to come in.

How excited she was, and how glad the children were when she first stepped into the garden! She wore her best dress, a long, bright-colored woolen skirt and a white waist. Round her neck was a string of beads, and on her feet were little wooden shoes. It would seem very strange to us—would it not?—to wear wooden shoes; but Piccola and her mother had never worn anything else, and never had any money to buy stockings. Piccola almost always ran about barefooted, like the kittens and the chickens and the little ducks. What a good time they had that day, and how glad Piccola's mother was that her little girl could have such a pleasant, safe place to play in, while she was away at work!

By and by December came, and the little Americans began to talk about Christmas. One day, when Piccola's curly head and bright eyes came peeping through the hole in the wall, and they ran to her and helped her in; and as they did so, they all asked her at once what she thought she would have for a Christmas present. "A Christmas present!" said Piccola. "Why, what is that?"

All the children looked surprised at this, and Rose said, rather gravely, "Dear Piccola, don't you know what Christmas is?"

Oh, yes, Piccola knew it was the happy day when the baby Christ was born, and she had been to church on that day and heard the beautiful singing, and had seen the picture of the Babe lying in the manger, with cattle and sheep sleeping round about. Oh, yes, she knew all that very well, but what was a Christmas present?

Then the children began to laugh and to answer her all together. There was such a clatter of tongues that she could hear only a few of the words now and then, such as "chimney," "Santa Claus," "stockings," "reindeer," "Christmas Eve," "candies and toys." Piccola put her hands over her ears and said, "Oh, I can't understand one word. You tell me, Rose." Then Rose told her all about jolly Santa Claus, with his red cheeks and white beard and fur coat, and about his reindeer and sleigh full of toys. "Every Christmas Eve," said Rose, "he comes down the chimney, and fills the stockings of all the good children; so, Piccola, you hang up your stocking, and who knows what a beautiful Christmas present you will find when morning comes!" Of course Piccola thought this was a delightful plan, and was very pleased to hear about it. Then all the children told her of every Christmas Eve they could remember, and of the presents they had had; so that she went home thinking of nothing but dolls and hoops and balls and ribbons and marbles and wagons and kites.

She told her mother about Santa Claus, and her mother seemed to think that perhaps he did not know there was any little girl in that house, and very likely he would not come at all. But Piccola felt very sure Santa Claus would remember her, for her little friends had promised to send a letter up the chimney to remind him.

St. Nicholas Day — December 6

Christmas Eve came at last. Piccola's mother hurried home from her work; they had their little supper of soup and bread, and soon it was bedtime,—time to get ready for Santa Claus. But oh! Piccola remembered then for the first time that the children had told her she must hang up her stocking, and she hadn't any, and neither had her mother.

How sad, how sad it was! Now Santa Claus would come, and perhaps be angry because he couldn't find any place to put the present.

The poor little girl stood by the fireplace, and the big tears began to run down her cheeks. Just then her mother called to her, "Hurry, Piccola; come to bed." What should she do? But she stopped crying, and tried to think; and in a moment she remembered her wooden shoes, and ran off to get one of them. She put it close to the chimney, and said to herself, "Surely Santa Claus will know what it's there for. He will know I haven't any stockings, so I gave him the shoe instead."

Then she went off happily to her bed, and was asleep almost as soon as she had nestled close to her mother's side.

The sun had only just begun to shine, next morning, when Piccola awoke. With one jump she was out on the floor and running toward the chimney. The wooden shoe was lying where she had left it, but you could never, never guess what was in it.

Piccola had not meant to wake her mother, but this surprise was more than any little girl could bear and yet be quiet; so she danced to the bed with the shoe in her hand, calling, "Mother, mother! look, look! see the present Santa Claus brought me!"

Her mother raised her head and looked into the shoe. "Why, Piccola," she said, "a little chimney swallow nestling in your shoe? What a good Santa Claus to bring you a bird!"

"Good Santa Claus, dear Santa Claus!" cried Piccola; and she kissed her mother and kissed the bird and kissed the shoe, and even threw kisses up the chimney, she was so happy.

When the birdling was taken out of the shoe, they found that he did not try to fly, only to hop about the room; and as they looked closer, they could see that one of his wings was hurt a little. But the mother bound it up carefully, so that it did not seem to pain him, and he was so gentle that he took a drink of water from a cup, and even ate crumbs and seeds out of Piccola's hands. She was a proud little girl when she took her Christmas present to show the children in the garden. They had had a great many gifts,—dolls that could say "mamma," bright picture books, trains of cars, toy pianos; but not one of their playthings was alive, like Piccola's birdling. They were as pleased as she, and Rose hunted about the house until she found a large wicker cage that belonged to a blackbird she once had. She gave the cage to Piccola, and the swallow seemed to make himself quite at home in it at once, and sat on the perch winking his bright eyes at the children. Rose had saved a bag of candies for Piccola, and when she went home at last, with the cage and her dear swallow safely inside it, I am sure there was not a happier little girl in the whole country of Italy.

Christmas Stories and Legends ©1916

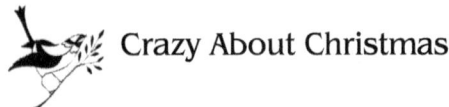 Crazy About Christmas

Cinnamon Stick Santa
Craft/Ornament

MATERIALS

- 1 cinnamon stick about 6 inches
- 2 cinnamon sticks about 1½ to 3 inches long
- glue gun
- 1 piece narrow red ribbon for hanger
- 1 small pompom
- red, white paint
- black sharpie

DIRECTIONS

1. Paint two short cinnamon sticks red to make the arms. Then add a white cuff

2. The long cinnamon stick is the body. Paint a section on the top for a hat. Leave a space for his face and pain the lower section for the body. .

3. Paint white fluffy brim on the bottom of the hat and a white beard, mustache and eyebrows.

4. Place two back dots for eyes under the eyebrows and if you want a red dot for the nose.

5. Hot-glue a short cinnamon stick to either side of Santa's head. Try and make sure that the arms are even at the top.

6. Make a loop of red ribbon and glue it to the back of Santa's head.

7. Finish by gluing the pompom on the top of Santa's hat.

St. Nicholas Day — December 6

Lebkuchen Bars
Makes 3 dozen

INGREDIENTS

1/2 cup butter, softened
1.2 cup sugar
1/3 cup packed brown sugar
2 eggs
1 cup honey or molasses
1/4 cup buttermilk
4 ½ cup all-purpose flour
1 teaspoon baking powder
1 teaspoon salt
1/4 teaspoon anise, ground
1/2 teaspoon ground cloves
1/2 teaspoon allspice
1/2 teaspoon cardamom
1/2 cup finely walnuts
1/2 cup raisins
1/2 cup pitted dates
1/2 cup candied lemon peel or citron
1/4 cup candied orange peel
3 tablespoons candied pineapple

Glaze
1/2 cup sugar
1/4 cup water
2 tablespoons confectioners' sugar

INSTRUCTIONS

1. Line a 15 inch x 10 inch x 1 inch baking pan with foil; grease the foil and set aside.
2. Put all dry ingredients into a bowl and mix well. Set aside.
3. In a large bowl, cream butter and sugars until light and fluffy.

Crazy About Christmas

4. Add eggs, one at a time, beating after each one.
5. Beat in honey (molasses if you want a stronger flavor), buttermilk and anise extract.
6. Gradually add dry ingredients to creamed mixture and mix well.
7. Stir in walnuts
8. Chop raisins, dates, candied lemon peel, orange peel, and pineapple. This can be done in a food processor by doing in small batches and pulsing so that you don't turn into a mush. Mix chopped fruits with dough.
9. Press dough into prepared pan.
10. Bake for 350° for 25-28 minutes or until lightly browned.
11. To make glaze in a small saucepan, bring water and sugar to a boil. Whisk for 1 minute. Whisk in confectioners' sugar. Spread over warm bars.
12. Cool in pan on a wire rack. Cut into bars.

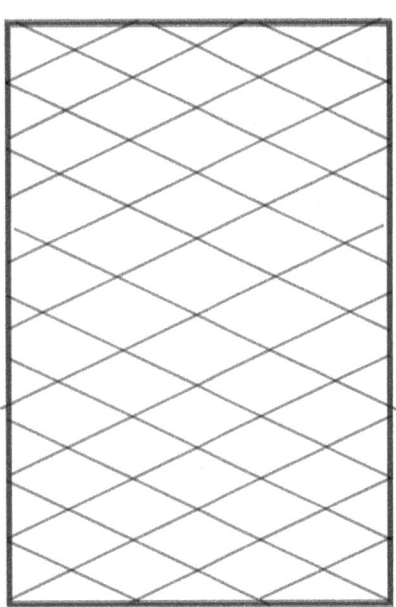

VARIATION: For fun cut cake into diamond shape and arrange on plate in the shape of a star. Add slivered almonds to the top for decoration if desired. This one is simple but you could make it as big as you wanted and make it a center piece dessert This would also make a great plated dessert to give to someone.

December 7

Why the Evergreens are Forever Green
A Cherokee Legend as told by MyLinda Butterworth

When all the trees on earth were newly made, the Great Spirit wanted to give each different species he created a gift. But first, there was a contest to see which gift would be the most useful to whom.

" I want you to stay awake and watch over the earth for seven days," said the Great Spirit to all the plants and trees.

The young plants and trees were so excited to be trusted with watching over the earth that they had no trouble staying awake the first night The trees all chatted with each other and talked about what the future held for them. They all wanted to be given a special gift from the Great Spirit and they all intended to stay awake.

During the day it was easy to stay awake because the sun was up and she was bright and warm as the second night came it became harder, and just before dawn the sourwoods could no longer keep awake and they nodded off.

Knowing that the sourwood trees had failed before dawn of the second night made all the trees aware of how easy it was to fail. So all during the daylight hours they stretched their limbs toward the sun and soaked in the sun, trying to prepare them for the next night. On the third night, the trees whispered to each other in the wind to keep themselves awake, but even so, the dogwoods dozed.

The trees began to challenge each other in ways only trees can in an effort to stay awake all seven nights. Nobody wanted to displease the Great Spirit, but it was becoming harder and harder to stay awake. On the fourth days the maples slept, on the fifth night the beeches, and, on the sixth night the mighty oaks fell asleep just as the sun peaked over the horizon.

Seven whole days had passed and only one species of trees had remained awake. They were a bristly punch with needles and spines instead of leaves. The pine, the spruce, the fir, the cedar, the holly, and the laurel stood tall when the Great Spirit arrived because they had managed to persist till the very end.

The Great Spirit was very pleased. "You have great strength," he said, "great loyalty. You shall be, for all time, the guardians of the forest."

Ever since that time, while other trees lose their leaves and sleep through the long, cold winter, the evergreens keep a vigilant watch over the earth.

Crazy About Christmas

Rustic Wood Slat Tree
Craft

Materials
4.5 feet of ¼-inch x 1 ½- inch lattice moulding
5 inch scrap of 1 ½-inch x ¾-inch wood
10 inches of quarter round
sandpaper
hot glue or wood glue
Mod Podge®
Assorted Scrapbook Paper

Directions
1. Cut the lattice moulding into the following lengths:
   - **(1)** 1 ½ inch **(2)** - 3-inches **(3)** 4 ¼-inch **(4)** 5 ¼-inch
   - **(5)** 6 ½-inch **(6)** 7 ¾ - inch **(7)** 9 inches **Tree trunk** - 15 inches
2. Base of tree: Cut a scrap of lumber that is 5 inches long. Cut two pieces of quarter round the same length.
3. Sand ends of all the wood pieces.
4. Next cut your scrapbook paper 1¼ -inches wide. Line up wood slats smallest to longest. Now place the strips of paper on them to see what paper patterns you like best, then cut the length of each strip of paper ¼-inch shorter so you will have a small border around your paper.
5. Brush Mod Podge on the back of your scrapbook paper, then place on the the slat of wood and smooth it out. Once they are dry brush on another layer of Mod Podge to seal and protect the paper. Let dry completely before the next step.
6. You are going to want to place your slats a ½ to ¾-inches apart. On the top edge of each slat mark in light pencil the center. Now using either hot glue or wood glue put on the top slat on the tree trunk slat, then continue down the tree till you have glued them all in place. Set aside and let fully dry.
7. To make the base for your tree glue one piece of the quarter round on your base piece matching the front edges. When it is dry place the remaining piece of quarter round on the opposite side this should leave a slot 1/4-inch wide for you to place your tree into. Make sure it is snug before you glue the second piece down.
8. When everything is dry you can then slide your tree trunk into the slot.

December 7

White Christmas Chili
Makes 15 servings

INGREDIENTS

8 boneless, skinless chicken breasts
2 medium onions
2 cloves, garlic, minced
1 tablespoon vegetable oil
2 cans (14-oz) chicken broth
4 cans (15.5 oz) cannellini beans, rinsed and drained
1 can (15.5 oz) cannellini beans, rinsed, drained
2 cans (4.5 oz), chopped green chilies
1 teaspoon ground cumin
3/4 teaspoon dried oregano
½ teaspoon chili powder
½ teaspoon ground black pepper
⅛ teaspoon ground red pepper
⅛ teaspon ground cloves

INSTRUCTIONS

1. Cut chicken into bite-size pieces.
2. In a large pot saute chicken, onion, and garlic in hot oil over medium-high heat for 10 minutes or until chicken is done.
3. Stir in broth, beans, green chilies, cumin, oregano, chili powder, black pepper, red pepper and cloves and bring to a boil.
4. Reduce heat and simmer uncovered for thirty minutes.
5. Serve with desired toppings.

Suggested toppings: shredded Monterey Jack cheese with jalapeno peppers, salsa, sour cream, chopped fresh cilantro.

Crazy About Christmas

Illustrations from Beatrix Potter's, *The Tailor of Gloucester, 1903* © *Frederick Warne & Co.*

December 8

The Tailor Of Gloucester
Beatrix Potter

"I'll be at charges for a looking-glass;
And entertain a score or two of tailors."
- *Richard III*
-

My Dear Freda:
Because you are fond of fairytales, and have been ill, I have made you a story all for yourself - a new one that nobody has read before.
And the queerest thing about it is - that I heard it in Gloucestershire, and that it is true - at least about the tailor, the waistcoat, and the
"No more twist!"

In the time of swords and peri wigs and full-skirted coats with flowered lappets - when gentlemen wore ruffles, and gold-laced waistcoats of paduasoy and taffeta - there lived a tailor in Gloucester.

He sat in the window of a little shop in Westgate Street, cross-legged on a table from morning till dark.

All day long while the light lasted he sewed and snippetted, piecing out his satin, and pompadour, and lutestring; stuffs had strange names, and were very expensive in the days of the Tailor of Gloucester.

But although he sewed fine silk for his neighbours, he himself was very, very poor. He cut his coats without waste; according to his embroidered cloth, they were very small ends and snippets that lay about upon the table - "Too narrow breadths for nought - except waistcoats for mice," said the tailor.

One bitter cold day near Christmastime the tailor began to make a coat (a coat of cherry-coloured corded silk embroidered with pansies and roses) and a cream-coloured satin waistcoat for the Mayor of Gloucester.

The tailor worked and worked, and he talked to himself: "No breadth at all, and cut on the cross; it is no breadth at all; tippets for mice and ribbons for mobs! for mice!" said the Tailor of Gloucester.

When the snow-flakes came down against the small leaded window-panes and shut out the light, the tailor had done his day's work; all the silk and satin lay cut out upon the table.

There were twelve pieces for the coat and four pieces for the waistcoat; and there were pocket-flaps and cuffs and buttons, all in order. For the lining of the coat there was fine yellow taffeta, and for the button-holes of the waistcoat there was cherry-coloured twist. And everything was ready to sew together in the morning, all measured and sufficient - except that there was wanting just one single skein of cherry-coloured twisted silk.

The tailor came out of his shop at dark. No one lived there at nights but little brown mice, and THEY ran in and out without any keys!

For behind the wooden wainscots of all the old houses in Gloucester, there are little mouse staircases and secret trap-doors; and the mice run from house to house through those long, narrow passages.

But the tailor came out of his shop and shuffled home through the snow. And although it was not a big house, the tailor was so poor he only rented the kitchen.

He lived alone with his cat; it was called Simpkin.

"Miaw?" said the cat when the tailor opened the door, "miaw?"

The tailor replied: "Simpkin, we shall make our fortune, but I am worn to a ravelling. Take this groat (which is our last fourpence), and, Simpkin, take a china pipkin, buy a penn'orth of bread, a penn'orth of milk, and a penn'orth of sausages. And oh, Simpkin, with the last penny of our fourpence buy me one penn'orth of cherry-coloured silk. But do not lose the last penny of the fourpence, Simpkin, or I am undone and worn to a thread-paper, for I have NO MORE TWIST."

Then Simpkin again said "Miaw!" and took the groat and the pipkin, and went out into the dark.

The tailor was very tired and beginning to be ill. He sat down by the hearth and talked to himself about that wonderful coat.

"I shall make my fortune - to be cut bias - the Mayor of Gloucester is to be married on Christmas Day in the morning, and he hath ordered a coat and an embroidered waistcoat - "

Then the tailor started; for suddenly, interrupting him, from the dresser at the other side of the kitchen came a number of little noises -

Tip tap, tip tap, tip tap tip!

"Now what can that be?" said the Tailor of Gloucester, jumping up from his chair. The tailor crossed the kitchen, and stood quite still beside the dresser, listening, and peering through his spectacles.

"This is very peculiar," said the Tailor of Gloucester, and he lifted up the tea-cup which was upside down.

Out stepped a little live lady mouse, and made a courtesy to the tailor! Then she hopped away down off the dresser, and under the wainscot.

The tailor sat down again by the fire, warming his poor cold hands. But all at once, from the dresser, there came other little noises -

December 8

Tip tap, tip tap, tip tap tip!

"This is passing extraordinary!" said the Tailor of Gloucester, and turned over another tea-cup, which was upside down.

Out stepped a little gentleman mouse, and made a bow to the tailor!

And out from under tea-cups and from under bowls and basins, stepped other and more little mice, who hopped away down off the dresser and under the wainscot.

The tailor sat down, close over the fire, lamenting: "One-and-twenty buttonholes of cherry-coloured silk! To be finished by noon of Saturday: and this is Tuesday evening. Was it right to let loose those mice, undoubtedly the property of Simpkin? Alack, I am undone, for I have no more twist!"

The little mice came out again and listened to the tailor; they took notice of the pattern of that wonderful coat. They whispered to one another about the taffeta lining and about little mouse tippets.

And then suddenly they all ran away together down the passage behind the wainscot, squeaking and calling to one another as they ran from house to house.

Not one mouse was left in the tailor's kitchen when Simpkin came back. He set down the pipkin of milk upon the dresser, and looked suspiciously at the tea-cups. He wanted his supper of little fat mouse!

"Simpkin," said the tailor, "where is my TWIST?"

But Simpkin hid a little parcel privately in the tea-pot, and spit and growled at the tailor; and if Simpkin had been able to talk, he would have asked: "Where is my MOUSE?"

"Alack, I am undone!" said the Tailor of Gloucester, and went sadly to bed.

All that night long Simpkin hunted and searched through the kitchen, peeping into cupboards and under the wainscot, and into the tea-pot where he had hidden that twist; but still he found never a mouse!

The poor old tailor was very ill with a fever, tossing and turning in his four-post bed; and still in his dreams he mumbled: "No more twist! no more twist!"

What should become of the cherry-coloured coat? Who should come to sew it, when the window was barred, and the door was fast locked?

Out-of-doors the market folks went trudging through the snow to buy their geese and turkeys, and to bake their Christmas pies; but there would be no dinner for Simpkin and the poor old tailor of Gloucester.

The tailor lay ill for three days and nights; and then it was Christmas Eve, and very late at night. And still Simpkin wanted his mice, and mewed as he stood beside the four-post bed.

But it is in the old story that all the beasts can talk in the night between Christmas Eve and Christmas Day in the morning (though there are very few folk that can hear them, or know what it is that they say).

Crazy About Christmas

When the Cathedral clock struck twelve there was an answer - like an echo of the chimes - and Simpkin heard it, and came out of the tailor's door, and wandered about in the snow.

From all the roofs and gables and old wooden houses in Gloucester came a thousand merry voices singing the old Christmas rhymes - all the old songs that ever I heard of, and some that I don't know, like Whittington's bells.

Under the wooden eaves the starlings and sparrows sang of Christmas pies; the jackdaws woke up in the Cathedral tower; and although it was the middle of the night the throstles and robins sang; and air was quite full of little twittering tunes.

But it was all rather provoking to poor hungry Simpkin.

From the tailor's shop in Westgate came a glow of light; and when Simpkin crept up to peep in at the window it was full of candles. There was a snippeting of scissors, and snappeting of thread; and little mouse voices sang loudly and gaily:

> *"Four-and-twenty tailors*
> *Went to catch a snail,*
> *The best man amongst them*
> *Durst not touch her tail;*
> *She put out her horns*
> *Like a little kyloe cow.*
> *Run, tailors, run!*
> *Or she'll have you all e'en now!"*

Then without a pause the little mouse voices went on again:

> *"Sieve my lady's oatmeal,*
> *Grind my lady's flour,*
> *Put it in a chestnut,*
> *Let it stand an hour - "*

"Mew! Mew!" interrupted Simpkin, and he scratched at the door. But the key was under the tailor's pillow; he could not get in.

The little mice only laughed, and tried another tune -

> *"Three little mice sat down to spin,*
> *Pussy passed by and she peeped in.*
> *What are you at, my fine little men?*
> *Making coats for gentlemen.*
> *Shall I come in and cut off your threads?*
> *Oh, no, Miss Pussy,*
> *You'd bite off our heads!"*

December 8

"Mew! scratch! scratch!" scuffled Simpkin on the window-sill; while the little mice inside sprang to their feet, and all began to shout all at once in little twittering voices: "No more twist! No more twist!" And they barred up the window-shutters and shut out Simpkin.

Simpkin came away from the shop and went home considering in his mind. He found the poor old tailor without fever, sleeping peacefully.

Then Simpkin went on tip-toe and took a little parcel of silk out of the tea-pot; and looked at it in the moonlight; and he felt quite ashamed of his badness compared with those good little mice!

When the tailor awoke in the morning, the first thing which he saw, upon the patchwork quilt, was a skein of cherry-coloured twisted silk, and beside his bed stood the repentant Simpkin!

The sun was shining on the snow when the tailor got up and dressed, and came out into the street with Simpkin running before him.

"Alack," said the tailor, "I have my twist; but no more strength - nor time - than will serve to make me one single buttonhole; for this is Christmas Day in the Morning! The Mayor of Gloucester shall be married by noon - and where is his cherry-coloured coat?"

He unlocked the door of the little shop in Westgate Street, and Simpkin ran in, like a cat that expects something.

But there was no one there! Not even one little brown mouse!

But upon the table - oh joy! the tailor gave a shout - there, where he had left plain cuttings of silk - there lay the most beautiful coat and embroidered satin waistcoat that ever were worn by a Mayor of Gloucester!

Everything was finished except just one single cherry-coloured buttonhole, and where that buttonhole was wanting there was pinned a scrap of paper with these words - in little teeny weeny writing -

NO MORE TWIST.

And from then began the luck of the Tailor of Gloucester; he grew quite stout, and he grew quite rich.

He made the most wonderful waistcoats for all the rich merchants of Gloucester, and for all the fine gentlemen of the country round.

Never were seen such ruffles, or such embroidered cuffs and lappets! But his buttonholes were the greatest triumph of it all.

The stitches of those buttonholes were so neat - SO neat - I wonder how they could be stitched by an old man in spectacles, with crooked old fingers, and a tailor's thimble.

The stitches of those buttonholes were so small - SO small - they looked as if they had been made by little mice!

Candy Cane Mice
Craft/Decoration/Gift Idea

MATERIALS LIST:

candy cane
2 plastic wiggly eyes
red pom pom
felt square
scissors
white glue
copy of pattern

DIRECTIONS:

1. Trace or photocopy the pattern.
2. Cut out of felt the body (A) and ears (B) of mouse.
3. Carefully cut on the dotted lines in body (A) to make slits for ears.
4. Insert ears (B) through the slits you cut in A, and fluff out the ears.
5. Glue on wiggly eyes.
6. Glue red pom pom to create a nose. If you want to give your mouse whiskers you can add a couple of strips of yarn on point of felt and then glue on the pom-pom.
7. Insert candy cane under the body of mouse and between the ears and the body leaving crooked end extending out of the back for the mouse's tail.

Fun Idea: These adorable candy cane mice are so easy to make that you won't need a lick of help! Make a box full and give them as presents or party favors or place cards on the table or fill a tree with them. They are great fun to make and you can make them in a multitude of colors.

December 8

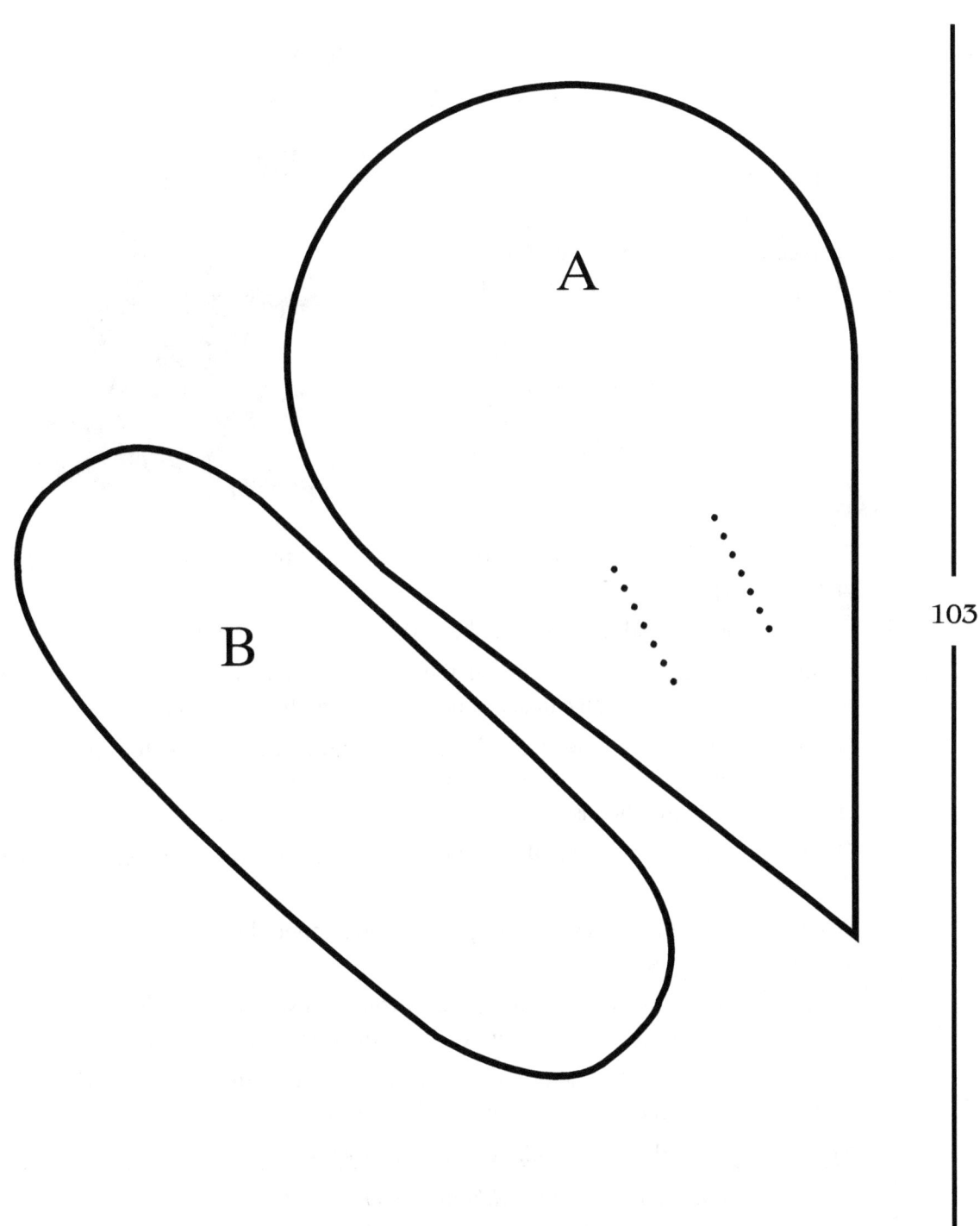

103

Chocolate Cherry Mice
Makes 24 Eatable Mice

INGREDIENTS:

- 24 Oreo cookies, split -frosted side up only
- 1 cup chocolate chips or almond bark
- 2 teaspoon shortening or coconut oil
-   cup of sliced almonds (for the ears)
- 24 maraschino cherries (for the body and tail)
- 24 chocolate kisses (for the head)
- 1 small tube red decorator icing gel
-   Red and Green Gumdrops for holly

INSTRUCTIONS:

1. Split 24 Oreo cookies. Put plain cookie aside and set the other cookies frosting side up on wax paper.
2. Drain the cherries and make sure to keep the stems intact. Set aside to dry.
3. In microwave or double boiler, melt the chocolate chips and shortening; stir until smooth - If you prefer, you can use chocolate almond bark without the shortening.
4. Holding the cherries by the stem, dip them in the melted chocolate tap on side of bowl to remove excess chocolate. Set cherry on top of Oreo with tail off one side and enough room to add the kiss.
5. Using a small spoon put a small dot of chocolate on back of kiss and gently attach to the front of the cherry.
6. While the chocolate is still soft place place sliced almonds between the cherry and the kiss to make the ears.
7. With gel icing -add two eyes and a nose to your mouse. You can also use red sugar pearls for eyes and use the gel icing or a tiny dot of chocolate to attach.
8. Cut pieces of green and red gum drops into pieces to look like holly and berries. Attach with a small drop of chocolate to one side of the mouse..
9. Now try and keep the human mice away till ready for eating.

Variation: You can make these mice without the cookies and place on a large tray to serve.

December 9

The Legend of the Christmas Robin
As told by "Grandma" Linda S. Day

"Now my little child, let me tell you the *Legend of the Christmas Robin*, and how he got his red breast." grandfather Burkey said, as I crawled upon his lap. "When I was a boy, no bigger than you, my grandfather told me this story from the old country.

Once upon a time, in a Holy land of high hills and green valleys, there was in the little town called Bethlehem, that had unexpectedly become full of people. The reason so many were in the town was that the Roman governor ordered everyone to go to the town they were born in to be taxed. People had come from everywhere down the dusty trails, walking or riding animals, and they were all looking for a place to sleep.

Behind one Inn, that was especially quiet with cool water in the well and shady trees to keep the hot sun from the courtyard, was a stable. And in the stable there were many different kinds of animals that waited while their masters were in the Inn. As they were all God's creatures, and were friendly beasts, they talked to one another about their travels and their masters until the sun had gone down, and a chill began to fill the air. Then weary with their labors of the day, the beasts in the stable settled down to rest.

A little brown robin, that had been outside on the roof, suddenly flew inside the stable and perching himself on the railing. "The night is here, the night is here, but the cloak of darkness does not cover the sky. There is a bright star in the heavens," he said," and look! Oh! Look! It shines brightest here on our little stable."

And as the animals looked, the light got brighter and brighter and an angel appeared from the heavens and said, "It is time for the Prince of Peace to be born. Tonight, in your little stable, you will be present when the Savior of the world is born. Even now, Joseph leads a donkey carrying Mary on it's back, she will be his mother." As the animals watched the angel ascend into the heavens, they noticed how extra brightly the stars in the heavens twinkled.

Then a silhouette of Joseph was at the door of the stable. As he lit a lantern and hung it from the rafter, the weary faces of Mary and Joseph reflected the long hours they had been on the road. Then Joseph spread his coat over the fresh hay and helped Mary down from the donkey, so she could rest on it. Mary's sweet face was filled with anxiety for the coming birth of her baby.

Joseph led their donkey into a stall, and did all he could to make things ready for the baby's birth. He had hoped for a better place for this special child to be born, but it was the fulfillment of prophecy.

" Ohhhhhhh! Ahhhhh! sighed the animals, as the wee babe was born.

"Heee Haaaaw, Heee Haaaw. Up! Up the hills and down I have traveled the dusty roads with this fair maiden upon my back. I am not weary for my deeds, for I know that I carried a King and his mother." The shaggy haired donkey gently brayed with a sigh, then blinked his eyes and swished his tail, as he munched on the hay in his stall.

The flutter of wings and the soft voice of the little brown robin was heard. "And what have we to give the King of Kings this Holy night?" The animals looked at the wee babe, now wrapped in swaddling clothes, and each spoke of what his gift to the Christ Child would be.

"Moooo Moooo, My new hay and this manger will I give him, to be his first cradle. The hay to pillow his head." And the black and white cow nuzzled her nose against the pile of fresh hay piled in the corner of the stable.

"Baaaa Baaaa. My wool is soft and will cradle the Babe as He lies in the manger." And her pink little nose pushed the lambs wool to the feet of Joseph, who lined the manger of straw with the soft lambs wool. Then Mary gently laid little Baby Jesus in the manger.

"Coooo Cooooo." said the doves from the rafters, high in the stable, "We will coooo a lullaby, that this blessed baby will not cry. Coooooo Coooo," they sang, as their heads nodded back and forth .

"Hummmph" said the camel, all surly and brown, as he shuffled his big feet on the ground. "I shall carry the gift of the Wise Men to this King of Kings one day." Hummmph.. Hummmph..Hummmmph..now note what I say."

And the robin cocked his head sprightly to one side and said, "Oh, what have I to give to the Babe in the manger? I have no soft wool like the sheep for him to lay on. The hay in the manger is not mine to give like the black and white cow. I could not carry them on my wings over the great hills as the shaggy haired donkey did, nor could I bring the Wise Men to this King with their gifts, as the stately camel." Sadly the little brown robin hopped over to the side of the small fire that Joseph had made to keep the chill of the night from his little family.

Fluttering his wings to smooth his feathers, the fire suddenly glowed warmer and brighter. "Yes! That's it!" said the little robin excitedly, "I shall flutter my wings here at the fires edge, so that the Babe in the manger will stay warm through the night. That will be my gift!"

And so the little brown robin fanned the fire with his wings all through the night. In the morning, as the sunlight beamed brightly into the stable, the animals all awoke.

"Baaaa, Baaaa. Wake up little robin!", but he little robin just lay lifeless beside the glowing embers of the fire. The feathers on his breast were singed black from fanning the fire all night. His gift to the Babe in the manger of warmth on that first Christmas night, had

December 9

been the willing gift of his life. When Joseph found the little brown robin and understood what he had done, he put him in his hand and gently stroked his head.

So touched by the little robin's unselfish gift, the Christ Child granted him a covering of red on his breast where it had been scorched, as a sign forever more of his love and sacrifice that first Christmas night. As the sun again broke through the clouds, the little robin redbreast stirred. Then he sat up and flew from Joseph's hand to the edge of the manger, where he cocked his head and ruffled his new red feathers. The Baby Jesus in the manger smiled and reached His hand up to the robin, as he flew high into the clouds toward heaven.

The animals looked at each other and nodded, remembering all that had happened that Holy night, in the humble stable behind the Inn at the bend of the road in Bethlehem. And today, we also remember the gift of the animals whenever we see a little Robin Redbreast hopping across the grass, perched in a tree tending its' nest, or flying high in the clouds toward heaven.

Remember the legend of the little Robin Redbreast, my child, and tell it to your children and grandchildren one day.

image by TheOtherKey from Pixabay

Story originally appeared in *Just 24 Days Till Christmas*, ©1997

Bird Bath/Feeder
Craft

MATERIALS

    3 terra cotta flower pots (12 inch, 14 inch, 16 inch)
    1 - 20" terra cotta saucer
    various shades of spray enamel or other water based paint
    clear spray enamel
    clear silicone sealer
    outdoor clear gloss spray
    acrylic paints in various colors (optional)
    paint brushes, rubber stamps, stencils

DIRECTIONS

1. Sand away any rough spots or loose clay particles on the rim, bottom edge, and outside of the pots and saucer.
2. Give the pots several coats of colored spray enamel or paint. (You don't have to paint them all the same color, you can be creative)
3. Paint the saucer inside and out, giving the inside of the saucer an extra coat.
4. Apply the sealer about 1 inch down from the rim of the each of the pots. Then run a line of glue on the inside of 14 inch pot on the inside of the pot then set it firmly on top of the 16 inch pot . Repeat the process with the 12 inch pot.
5. Place glue on the top of the 12 inch pot and firmly adhere the saucer.
6. Finish the bird bath by putting a heavy coat of sealer on the top pot.
7. Let dry for twenty-four hours, then using acrylic paints, stamp or draw on images, be creative with your design.
8. Finish with two coats of outdoor clear gloss spray.

Quicky Note: While this is supposed to be a bird bath for spring and summer in the fall and winter when the water is gone this makes a great bird feeder.

December 9

Hummingbird Cake
Serves 9-16

INGREDIENTS

- 5 cups flour
- 2 cups sugar
- 1 teaspoon baking soda
- 1 teaspoon salt
- 1 teaspoon cinnamon
- 3 eggs beaten
- 1½ cup oil
- 1½ teaspoon vanilla
- 1 12 oz. can crushed pineapple, undrained
- 1 cup pecans or walnuts, chopped
- 2 cups chopped bananas

INSTRUCTIONS

1. Preheat oven to 350°F.
2. Grease and flour (3) round 9 inch cake pans or one large layer pan and set aside.
3. Combine flour, sugar, soda, salt and cinnamon in a large bowl; add eggs and oil stirring until all dry ingredients are moistened. Do not beat.
4. Stir in vanilla, pineapple, nuts and bananas. Make sure batter is blended well, but don't beat.
5. Spoon batter into pans, bake at 350° for 25 to 30 minutes. Cool for 10 minutes in pan, remove from pans, let cool completely.
6. Frost with Cream Cheese Frosting and sprinkle with 1 cup of chopped nuts.

Cream Cheese Frosting

- 1 8 oz package cream cheese, softened
- ½ cup butter/margarine, softened
- 1 pound powdered sugar
- 1 teaspoon vanilla

1. Combine cream cheese and butter and mix until smooth.
2. Add box of powdered sugar and vanilla, beat until light and fluffy.
3. Makes enough frosting to cover a 3 layer cake.

There are two ways to live:
you can live as if nothing is a miracle;
or you can live as if everything
is a miracle"
— Albert Einstein —

December 10

The Miracle
Author unknown

"Tess was a precocious eight year old when she heard her Mom and Dad talking about her little brother, Andrew. All she knew was that he was very sick and they were completely out of money. They were moving to an apartment complex next month because Daddy didn't have the money for the doctor bills and the house.

Only a very costly surgery could save him now and it was looking like there was no-one to loan them the money.

She heard Daddy say to her tearful Mother with whispered desperation, "Only a miracle can save him now."

Tess went to her bedroom and pulled a glass jelly jar from its hiding place in the closet. She poured all the change out on the floor and counted it carefully. Three times, even. The total had to be exactly perfect. No chance here for mistakes. Carefully placing the coins back in the jar and twisting on the cap, she slipped out the back door and made her way six blocks to the drug store. She waited patiently for the pharmacist to give her some attention but

he was to busy at this moment. Tess twisted her feet to make a scuffing noise. Nothing. She cleared her throat with the most disgusting sound she could muster. No good.

Finally she took a quarter from her jar and banged it on the glass counter. That did it!

And what do you want?" the pharmacist asked in an annoyed tone of voice. "I'm talking to my brother from Chicago whom I haven't seen in ages," he said without waiting for a reply to his question.

"Well, I want to talk to you about my brother," Tess answered back in the same annoyed tone. "He's really, really sick... and I want to buy a miracle."

"I beg your pardon?" said the pharmacist.

"His name is Andrew and he has something bad growing inside his head and my Daddy says only a miracle can save him now. So how much does a miracle cost?"

"We don't sell miracles here, little girl. I'm sorry but I can't help you," the pharmacist said, softening a little.

"Listen, I have the money to pay for it. If it isn't enough, I will get the rest. Just tell me how much it costs."

The pharmacist's brother was a well dressed man. He stooped down and asked the little girl, "What kind of a miracle does you brother need?"

Crazy About Christmas

"I don't know," Tess replied with her eyes welling up. "I just know he's really sick and Mommy says he needs an operation. But my Daddy can't pay for it, so I want to use my money.

"How much do you have?" asked the man from Chicago.

"One dollar and eleven cents," Tess answered barely audibly. "And it's all the money I have, but I can get some more if I need to. "Well, what a coincidence," smiled the man. "A dollar and eleven cents--the exact price of a miracle for little brothers." He took her money in one hand and with the other hand he grasped her mitten and said "Take me to where you live. I want to see your brother and meet your parents. Let's see if I have the kind of miracle you need."

That well dressed man was a surgeon, specializing in Neurosurgery. The operation was completed without charge and it wasn't long until Andrew was home again and doing well. Mom and Dad were happily talking about the chain of events that had led them to this place. "That surgery," her Mom whispered. "was a real miracle. I wonder how much it would have cost?"

Tess smiled. She knew exactly how much a miracle cost... One dollar and eleven cents —plus the faith of a little child.

Is this story true? I will leave that up to you to determine.

December 10

Holiday Coasters
Craft/Gift

MATERIALS

4½ inch ceramic tile
Recycled cards, napkins or decorative paper
sticky back stiffened felt or cork
Mod Podge®
sponge brush
clear acrylic sealer

DIRECTIONS

1. Make sure your tiles are clean and have no grease on them, rubbing alcohol will make them squeaky clean.
2. Find old Christmas Cards, napkins or decorative paper and cut them into 4 inch squares.
3. With a sponge brush apply a thin layer of Mod Podge glue on the back of your image..
4. Place image onto tile, adjusting to make sure the border is the same all around, when you are happy with placement use a credit card or other smooth edged object to squeegee out any air bubbles. Let dry.
5. When dry apply another layer of Mod Podge over the image and let dry.
6. To make sure it survives wet or hot cups being put on it put several layers of clear acrylic sealer over the image, letting dry between layers.
7. After the sealer is completely dry turn the tile over and attach a 4-inch square of sticky backed stiffened felt or cork. These often come with the adhesive already attached.
8. Make a set of four for gift giving or more for a party or just to use around home.

If you want a coaster with a high glass-like, stain-proof finish then try a two-part epoxy like Envirotex,. It is used to coat bar-tops in bars and restaurants so it's designed to be durable. One coat of Envirotex is equivalent to 50 coats of regular varnish. If you want to make a gift that will last for years, then it's worth using. Best place to find it is on Amazon or at your craft store.

Savory Toasted Cheese with Noodles
aka Macaroni and Cheese

INGREDIENTS:
1 pound wide egg noodles or fresh noodles
1 Tbsp oil
Large pinch salt
½ pound crisp bacon, crumbled

SAUCE:
½ pound butter
½ pound cream cheese
½ pound Brie or sharp cheddar cheese, grated
¼ tsp white pepper
dash of Cayenne pepper (optional)

Calorie Rich Calorie Counting Not Advised!

INSTRUCTIONS
1. Boil noodles in water* with oil & salt until al dente (tender-crisp). Drain well.
2. While noodles are boiling make sauce
3. To make the sauce melt the butter over medium heat. Cut the cream cheese into cubes and place grated cheese over butter.
4. Whisk or mix continually to blend the ingredients and keep the sauce from separating (which it is very much inclined to do). If it gets too thick you can add a little milk. When you have a uniform, creamy sauce you are done. Before serving add white pepper and a dash of Cayenne.
5. In a serving bowl or platter place some sauce. Lay noodles on top and add more sauce. Continue to layer noodles and sauce ending with a layer of sauce. Top with crumbled bacon. Serve immediately, or place in a oven to keep warm till ready to serve.

Serves 8

NOTE: This recipe is based on a Medieval recipe for *Savory Toasted Cheese* and was originally served over toast or over vegetables. I like it anyway you want to serve it, even just with a spoon

December 11

The Stranger Child
Translated by Count Franz Pocci

There once lived a laborer who earned his daily bread by cutting wood. His wife and two children, a boy and girl, helped him with his work. The boy's name was Valentine, and the girl's, Marie. They were obedient and pious and the joy and comfort of their poor parents.

One winter evening, this good family gathered about the table to eat their small loaf of bread, while the father read aloud from the Bible. Just as they sat down there came a knock on the window, and a sweet voice called, "O let me in! I am a little child, and I have nothing to eat, and no place to sleep in. I am so cold and hungry! Please, good people, let me in!"

Valentine and Marie sprang from the table and ran to open the door, saying:--

"Come in, poor child, we have but very little ourselves, not much more than thou hast, but what we have we will share with thee."

The stranger Child entered, and going to the fire began to warm his cold hands.

The children gave him a portion of their bread, and said:--

"Thou must be very tired; come, lie down in our bed, and we will sleep on the bench here before the fire."

Then answered the stranger Child: "May God in Heaven reward you for your kindness."

They led the little guest to their small room, laid him in their bed, and covered him closely, thinking to themselves:--

"Oh! how much we have to be thankful for! We have our nice warm room and comfortable bed, while this Child has nothing but the sky for a roof, and the earth for a couch."

When the parents went to their bed, Valentine and Marie lay down on the bench before the fire, and said one to the other:--

"The stranger Child is happy now, because he is so warm! Good-night!"

Then they fell asleep.

They had not slept many hours, when little Marie awoke, and touching her brother lightly, whispered:--

"Valentine, Valentine, wake up! wake up! Listen to the beautiful music at the window."

Valentine rubbed his eyes and listened. He heard the most wonderful singing and the sweet notes of many harps.

Crazy About Christmas

"Blessed Child,
Thee we greet,
With sound of harp
And singing sweet.

"Sleep in peace,
Child so bright,
We have watched thee
All the night.

"Blest the home
That holdeth Thee,
Peace, and love,
Its guardians be."

The children listened to the beautiful singing, and it seemed to fill them with unspeakable happiness. Then creeping to the window they looked out.

They saw a rosy light in the east, and, before the house in the snow, stood a number of little children holding golden harps and lutes in their hands, and dressed in sparkling, silver robes.

Full of wonder at this sight, Valentine and Marie continued to gaze out at the window, when they heard a sound behind them, and turning saw the stranger Child standing near. He was clad in a golden garment, and wore a glistening, golden crown upon his soft hair. Sweetly he spoke to the children:--

"I am the Christ Child, who wanders about the world seeking to bring joy and good things to loving children. Because you have lodged me this night I will leave with you my blessing."

As the Christ Child spoke He stepped from the door, and breaking off a bough from a fir tree that grew near, planted it in the ground, saying:--

"This bough shall grow into a tree, and every year it shall bear Christmas fruit for you."

Having said this He vanished from their sight, together with the silver-clad, singing children-- the angels.

And, as Valentine and Marie looked on in wonder, the fir bough grew, and grew, and grew, into a stately Christmas Tree laden with golden apples, silver nuts, and lovely toys. And after that, every year at Christmas time, the Tree bore the same wonderful fruit.

And you, dear boys and girls, when you gather around your richly decorated trees, think of the two poor children who shared their bread with a stranger child, and be thankful.

from *Stories for Little Children,*, ©1920

December 11

Holiday Pillow Cases
Sewing/Gift

Materials

1   yard of holiday fabric (standard pillowcase)
1¼ yard of holiday fabric (king size pillowcase)
     Matching thread
     Sewing machine

Directions

1. Cut fabric down to 41 inches wide.
2. Open fabric up and lay flat. Fold top edge down 1/2 inch and iron flat. Then fold the top edge over another 4 inches and iron in place. (*This applies for either sizes*)
3. Now top stitch that flap down, about 1/4 inch away from the bottom fold.
4. We are now going to make a "French Seam". Now fold in half with print side up or with wrong sides together.
5. Sew 1/4 inch seam allowance on the right side and bottom. You should have a pillowcase with the seams on the outside.
6. Clip the corner off the bottom right hand corner...but don't clip though the threads.
7. Trim about 1/8 inch off the right raw edge and the bottom raw edge.
8. Turn inside out and press flat, poking out the bottom corners and making the edges as flat and even as possible.
9. Sew a 1/4 inch seam allowance over the seams you just made to encase the raw edges.
10. Turn the entire thing right side out and poke your corners out, and iron flat.

To make a pillowcase with a different color hem you only have to make a couple of changes. First you will need to cut your fabric 41 inches wide and 27 inches long. Follow all the directions from 4-10. For the cuff you will need 1/3 yard of contrasting fabric and either wide bias tape or a decorative ribbon to cover the seam. Make your French seam like above in directions 3-5. Now fold wrong sides together and press flat. You will now have a big loop. Next place fabric loop on inside of pillowcase. Pin loop and wide bias tape together. Sew together according to bias tape directions. Open flat and press seam so that you have a full sized pillowcase. Stitch down loose edge of bias tape either by hand or machine. If you want you can top stitch both sides of the bias tape. That's it.

Spicy Sausage and Bean Soup
Serves 6

INGREDIENTS

- 1 pound hot Italian sausage (if you have links take the casing off first)
- 1 medium onion diced
- 2 cans (15½ ounces each) great northern beans, rinsed and drained
- 1 package (16 ounce) coleslaw mix
- 1 jar (24 ounce) garlic and herb spaghetti sauce
- 3 cups water

INSTRUCTIONS

1. In a large pot brown sausage with the onion. Cook sausage until it is no longer pink. Drain
2. Rinse and drain great northern beans. Add to sausage.
3. Add spaghetti sauce, coleslaw mix, and water. Stir.
4. Bring to the soup to a boil then turn down the heat and let simmer for 20 minute to allow flavors to deepen. Then ladle u a bowl and enjoy with a piece of crusty bread.

December 12

The Wooden Shoes of Little Wolff
François Coppée

Once upon a time—so long ago that the world has forgotten the date—in a city of the North of Europe—the name of which is so hard to pronounce that no one remembers it—there was a little boy, just seven years old, whose name was Wolff. He was an orphan and lived with his aunt, a hard-hearted, avaricious old woman, who never kissed him but once a year, on New Year's Day; and who sighed with regret every time she gave him a bowlful of soup.

The poor little boy was so sweet-tempered that he loved the old woman in spite of her bad treatment, but he could not look without trembling at the wart, decorated with four gray hairs, which grew on the end of her nose.

As Wolff's aunt was known to have a house of her own and a woolen stocking full of gold, she did not dare to send her nephew to the school for the poor. But she wrangled so that the schoolmaster of the rich boys' school was forced to lower his price and admit little Wolff among his pupils. The bad schoolmaster was vexed to have a boy so meanly clad and who paid so little, and he punished little Wolff severely without cause, ridiculed him, and even incited against him his comrades, who were the sons of rich citizens. They made the orphan their drudge and mocked at him so much that the little boy was as miserable as the stones in the street, and hid himself away in corners to cry—when the Christmas season came.

On the Eve of the great Day the schoolmaster was to take all his pupils to the midnight mass, and then to conduct them home again to their parents' houses.

Now as the winter was very severe, and a quantity of snow had fallen within the past few days, the boys came to the place of meeting warmly wrapped up, with fur-lined caps drawn down over their ears, padded jackets, gloves and knitted mittens, and good strong shoes with thick soles. Only little Wolff presented himself shivering in his thin everyday clothes, and wearing on his feet socks and wooden shoes.

His naughty comrades tried to annoy him in every possible way, but the orphan was so busy warming his hands by blowing on them, and was suffering so much from chilblains, that he paid no heed to the taunts of the others. Then the band of boys, marching two by two, started for the parish church.

It was comfortable inside the church, which was brilliant with lighted tapers. And the pupils, made lively by the gentle warmth, the sound of the organ, and the singing of the choir, began to chatter in low tones. They boasted of the midnight treats awaiting them at home. The son of the Mayor had seen, before leaving the house, a monstrous goose larded with truffles so that it looked like a black-spotted leopard. Another boy told of the fir tree waiting for him, on the branches of which hung oranges, sugar-plums, and punchinellos. Then they talked about what the Christ Child would bring them, or what he would leave in their shoes which they would certainly be careful to place before the fire when they went to bed. And the eyes of the little rogues, lively as a crowd of mice, sparkled with delight as they thought of the many gifts they would find on waking, -- the pink bags of burnt almonds, the bonbons, lead soldiers standing in rows, menageries, and magnificent jumping-jacks, dressed in purple and gold.

Little Wolff, alas! knew well that his miserly old aunt would send him to bed without any supper; but as he had been good and industrious all the year, he trusted that the Christ Child would not forget him, so he meant that night to set his wooden shoes on the hearth.

The midnight mass was ended. The worshipers hurried away, anxious to enjoy the treats awaiting them in their homes. The band of pupils, two by two, following the schoolmaster, passed out of the church.

Now, under the porch, seated on a stone bench, in the shadow of an arched niche, was a child asleep, -- a little child dressed in a white garment and with bare feet exposed to the cold. He was not a beggar, for his dress was clean and new, and -- beside him upon the ground, tied in a cloth, were the tools of a carpenter's apprentice.

Under the light of the stars, his face, with its closed eyes, shone with an expression of divine sweetness, and his soft, curling blond hair seemed to form an aureole of light about his forehead. But his tender feet, blue with the cold on this cruel night of December, were pitiful to see!

The pupils so warmly clad and shod, passed with indifference before the unknown child. Some, the sons of the greatest men in the city, cast looks of scorn on the barefooted one. But little Wolff, coming last out of the church, stopped deeply moved before the beautiful, sleeping child.

"Alas!" said the orphan to himself, "how dreadful! This poor little one goes without stockings in weather so cold! And, what is worse, he has no shoe to leave beside him while he sleeps, so that the Christ Child may place something in it to comfort him in all his misery."

And carried away by his tender heart, little Wolff drew off the wooden shoe from his right foot, placed it before the sleeping child; and as best as he was able, now hopping, now limping, DREW OFF THE WOODEN SHOE and wetting his sock in the snow, he returned to his aunt.

"You good-for-nothing!" cried the old woman, full of rage as she saw that one of his shoes was gone. "What have you done with your shoe, little beggar?"

December 12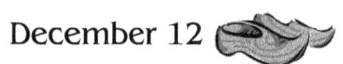

Little Wolff did not know how to lie, and, though shivering with terror as he saw the gray hairs on the end of her nose stand upright, he tried, stammering, to tell his adventure.

But the old miser burst into frightful laughter. "Ah! the sweet young master takes off his shoe for a beggar! Ah! master spoils a pair of shoes for a barefoot! This is something new, indeed! Ah! well, since things are so, I will place the shoe that is left in the fireplace, and tonight the Christ Child will put in a rod to whip you when you wake. And tomorrow you shall have nothing to eat but water and dry bread, and we shall see if the next time you will give away your shoe to the first vagabond that comes along."

And saying this the wicked woman gave him a box on each ear, and made him climb to his wretched room in the loft. There the heartbroken little one lay down in the darkness, and, drenching his pillow with tears, fell asleep.

But in the morning, when the old woman, awakened by the cold and shaken by her cough, descended to the kitchen, oh! wonder of wonders! she saw the great fireplace filled with bright toys, magnificent boxes of sugar-plums, riches of all sorts, and in front of all this treasure, the wooden shoe which her nephew had given to the vagabond, standing beside the other shoe which she herself had placed there the night before, intending to put in it a handful of switches.

And as little Wolff, who had come running at the cries of his aunt, stood in speechless delight before all the splendid Christmas gifts, there came great shouts of laughter from the street.

The old woman and the little boy went out to learn what it was all about, and saw the gossips gathered around the public fountain. What could have happened? Oh, a most amusing and extraordinary thing! The children of all the rich men of the city, whose parents wished to surprise them with the most beautiful gifts, had found nothing but switches in their shoes!

Then the old woman and little Wolff remembered with alarm all the riches that were in their own fireplace, but just then they saw the pastor of the parish church arriving with his face full of perplexity.

Above the bench near the church door, in the very spot where the night before a child, dressed in white, with bare feet exposed to the great cold, had rested his sleeping head, the pastor had seen a golden circle wrought into the old stones. Then all the people knew that the beautiful, sleeping child, beside whom had lain the carpenter's tools, was the Christ Child himself, and that he had rewarded the faith and charity of little Wolff.

from *Good Stories for Great Holidays* ©1914

Spinning Whirligig Toy
Craft/Toy

This toy has been around since Medieval times. It is very addictive.

MATERIALS

A large button or wooden disc
20-22 inches of yarn or string
Markers or paint
drill

DIRECTIONS

1. Start with a large button, wooden disc with two holes drilled in the center and a piece of sturdy string or yarn about 20-22 inches long.

2. If you are using a wooden disc/circle you can paint a spiral or design on each side of the disc.

3. Thread the string through one hole and back through the second hole. Tie the ends of the string together in a tight knot.

4. Place index fingers through the ends of the string.

5. Wind up the string and begin to pull your hands outwards. The string and button should begin to pulsate and create a "whirling" sound. The trick is to wind it up enough that as let the button wind and unwind that it will wind back on itself after you pull it out and keep going as long as you can keep the rhythm going.

NOTE: When I was a kid we took tree limbs and cut them about 1/4 to 1/2 inch thick and made lots of wooden discs. After the discs were drilled and sanded part of the fun was to make wild patterns on each side. When you get the whirligig spinning the pattern changes before your eyes. Hours of fun!

HINT: You can find assorted solid wood disks at most craft stores.

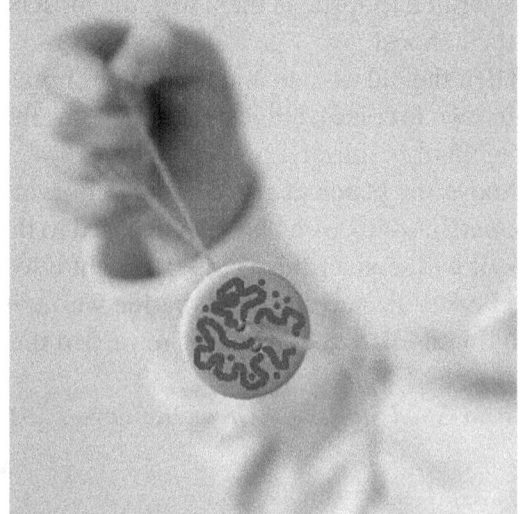

December 12

Gingerdoodles
makes 3½ dozen cookies

INGREDIENTS

Gingersnap dough
1   cup packed brown sugar
¾   cup shortening
¼   cup molasses
1   egg
2 ⅓ all-purpose flour
2   teaspoons baking soda
1   teaspoon ground cinnamon
1   teaspoon ground ginger
½   teaspoon ground cloves
¼   teaspoon salt

Snickerdoodle Dough
½   cup butter or margarine, softened
½   cup shortening
1½ cups sugar
2   eggs
2 ¾ cups all purpose flour
2   teaspoons cream of tartar
1   teaspoon baking soda
¼   teaspoon salt

¼   cup granulated sugar
2   teaspoons cinnamon

INSTRUCTIONS
1. Heat oven to 375°. Line cookie sheet with cooking parchment paper.
2. To make Gingersnaps mix in a large bowl brown sugar, shortening, molasses and egg.
3. Add flour, baking soda, cinnamon, ginger, cloves and salt and mix well. Set dough aside.

Crazy About Christmas

4. To make Snickerdoodles Mix thoroughly butter, shortening, sugar and the eggs.
5. Blend in flour, cream of tartar, soda and salt. Set dough aside.
6. For each cookie, shape a level tablespoon of gingersnap and snickerdoodle dough and roll into a ball. Mix 1/4 granulated sugar and cinnamon in small bowl. Roll dough balls in cinnamon sugar mix and place on cookie sheet.
7. Bake 9-11 minutes or until light golden brown around edges. Cool 2 minutes on cookie sheet. Remove to cooking rack to cool completely.
8. *Variation* to make these more like swirls roll out snickerdoodle recipe then roll out gingersnap dough. Place one on top of the other and roll the two layers together. Then slice and bake.

December 13

A Sweet Reminder
MyLinda Butterworth

My mother's family settled in Indiana when they arrived from the old country and with them came many glorious stories. But it was a story that my Great Grandma Pearl always told me around Christmas that has stayed with me for a lifetime. I'm sure that you have heard it too, for it is a story of a man's desire to give people sweet reminders of the **reason for the season** of Christmas.

It was Christmas time and my world was covered in a blanket of newly fallen snow. Everywhere windows were adorned with garlands of holly and berries of red, Christmas trees were laden with beautiful decorations, and people were smiling even under their heavy coats and arms full of parcels. Yes, it's Christmas! A wonderful time of year, a time when we forget about ourselves and remember our friends, neighbors and those who are less fortunate than we are. I was nearly twelve and it seemed to me there had to be more to this holiday than bright tinsel and packages under a tree.

My father was a candy maker by trade, so of course, Christmas was a very busy time of year in his candy shop, especially the week before the great event. When everyone else was out sledding, I was busy helping Papa make truffles, or toffee, or waiting on customers, so I got very little time to play with my friends. Not that I minded, but there were other things I would rather be doing than spending all my time stuck in the candy shop.

One evening after the door had been latched and the closed sign hung in place, I went to the back of the shop to walk home with Papa for dinner. He was standing at one of the marble tables with his head down.

"Papa, what's wrong?" I asked.

Without looking up he beckoned to me, "Come here Hannah." As I reached his side, he looked up and asked, "Do you know why we celebrate Christmas?"

"Sure, everyone knows that!" I said, with a big smirk on my face, "It is the day when Kris Kringle brings presents to all the good little boys and girls, and the day when Jesus was born. Right?" I asked, half cocky and half questioning.

Papa took my face in his hands and looked deep into my eyes, for what seemed an eternity and quietly, yet firmly said, "Hannah, the birth of the Savior is the **only** reason for Christmas. Kris Kringle was a game we played with you when you were young to help you to be good. On Christmas Eve when you put your shoes out to see whether you received a present or a lump of coal, that was all part of the game. But don't you remember our reading the story of Jesus' birth every Christmas morning before we opened any presents?"

Crazy About Christmas

I did of course and shook my head to acknowledge the fact. Papa is a very religious man and my whole family had been raised to be the same. I should have been a little more careful with my answer, but as usual I spoke before I thought about it.

I could tell that something was really bothering my Papa. Something that went much deeper than the fact that I didn't take his question seriously. "Papa, what's bothering you? Did I say something wrong? If I did I'm sorry, I didn't mean it. I ...". But before I could finish my sentence, Papa put his arms around me and gave me a big hug, "My little one," he said excitedly, "how could I have been so blind? It is not you that has done anything wrong, but you who has given me an idea!"

Then Papa took me by the shoulders and gave me a little shake, his eyes were twinkling with excitement and then he danced me around the kitchen until I was dizzy with the spinning. "I know what to do," he shouted, " I know what to do! I will make a special candy. It will only be available during Christmas time! What do you think Hannah? Do you think it will work?"

My head was still spinning and my eyes were just beginning to focus again, but I understood what my Papa was getting at. "Yes!" I exclaimed, "It's a wonderful idea, but ... what kind of candy will it be and how will it help people remember what Christmas is all about?"

My Papa stopped and said thoughtfully, "I don't know, but I am sure once I've eaten your mother's fine dinner tonight and talked with the rest of the family it will come to me. Let's go home!" And with that we put on our coats, hats and mittens, and arm and arm we walked, no, I would say we nearly floated home.

When we reached home, mother as usual had the table set and the food waiting and ready for us to sit and eat. After grace had been said, I attacked the food on the table. I was simply ravenous since I missed lunch, due to the shop being so busy. The evening meal was always the highlight of my day, because the whole family was together at one time and we got to share whatever was on our minds and relate the events of the day. Tonight my head was reeling after my talk with Papa in the shop, and I was anxious for him to bring up the subject of the special Christmas candy. Mother was about to clear the dishes from the table, when Papa asked her to sit down. "Tonight, family," Papa began and everyone cringed because such a statement usually meant someone was in trouble, "Hannah and I were discussing the meaning of Christmas. We decided a special Christmas candy needed to be created that will help people remember that Christmas is about Christ's birth, not presents, or Kris Kringle, or music, or friends, or any of those things but simply the Saviors birth. Will you help me come up with some ideas for my new candy creation?" With that the room was suddenly a buzz with an abundance of suggestions, filling the air with excitement, and there at the end of the table was Papa smiling with great contentment.

December 13

I don't remember half of the ideas that flowed across the dinner table that evening, but there were some good ones that Papa said he would think about. My younger brother Hans said it should be a candy that lasts a long time and my sister Evette suggested that it should be in the shape of a "J" for Jesus. Christian, age three, thought it should be shaped like a baby just like him at which the whole family burst into laughter. After about an hour of discussion, Papa announced that his brain could hold no more suggestions and recommended we all help mother clean up from dinner and retire for the evening.

It was hard to go to sleep that night with so many things floating around my head, and I wondered what Papa was going to do. I knew that when he said his evening prayers he would ask God to help him, and being the kind of man my Papa was, God would surely help him find the answer.

The next morning I arose as usual to the smell of bread baking in the oven and sausage sizzling in the pan. I dressed myself for the day and headed downstairs for breakfast. When I arrived at the table, mother told me that Papa had left for the candy shop at daybreak and wanted me to hurry along when I was ready because he would need my help again today. Normally I would have tried to beg off, saying that Evette could go today, but I knew that Papa would be busy creating a special Christmas treat and I wanted to be there when it was finished. I gulped down my food, kissed my mother and ran out the door, forgetting all my outside winter clothes. It only took one step into the cold crisp morning air to remind me that I needed all those winter trappings or be ready to turn into an icicle.

I ran all the way to the candy shop, not stopping to slide across the frozen creek as I usually did, or even throw snowballs at the cats in the street. I knew that today was going to be special and I didn't want to miss a thing. When I reached the back door of the shop, I could smell the familiar scent of peppermint in the air. I loved peppermint, and wondered what kind of candy Papa was making this morning. I tossed my hat, coat, scarf and mittens on the rack and scurried over to where Papa was busily shaping candy on the cold marble. I threw my arms around him, planted a big kiss on his check, and said, "Good Morning Papa, any special candy visions during the night?" He simply smiled and said, "Yes! Would you like to see it?"

I thought to myself what kind of silly question is that to ask me after sending me to bed with my mind reeling with visions of sweet confections dancing in my head. "Of course I do, show me quick."

"First close your eyes and open your mouth." I quickly closed my eyes and opened my mouth and Papa placed a small piece of candy in my mouth. The taste was peppermint but the consistency was hard. I let the candy dissolve in my mouth and it was not only tasty, but refreshing. When I opened my eyes Papa stepped aside and I saw a whole table of white and red striped candy, formed in the shape of a J. I threw my arms around my Papa,

Crazy About Christmas

knowing that he had truly been inspired by our Maker, and gave him a great big bear hug. "It is wonderful," I exclaimed, "surely it will be everything you want it to be."

Papa pinched my cheek and winked at me, "I couldn't have done it without you. For it was you that inspired me to want to shout to the people in the streets that Jesus's birth is the reason we celebrate Christmas. Now I can let my candy creation shout it for me. Help me display them in the window and make a sign for our latest candy the 'Christmas Candy Cane'."

As it turned out, my father's candy was a success, not just in our little town in Indiana, but all over the world. People may not always remember the reason he made it, or what it symbolizes. I know that some people see his creation as simply the candy cane, a colorful, meaningless decoration that is edible. But every Christmas when Papa puts up his "Christmas Candy Cane" sign, he always explains the symbolism. It reads:

Linda S. Day

The Christmas Candy Cane
Christmas is a season that we all celebrate. I want to add my witness to the celebration. So I created this simple confection. Each part of the candy represents something special.
The pure white candy represents the virgin birth and sinless nature of Christ.
The hardness of the candy represents the solid rock on which His church is founded.
The small red stripes represent the scourging Jesus received by which we are healed.
The large red stripes are for the blood shed by the Savior for us all.
The candy is shaped in the form of the letter "J" to denote the precious name of Jesus.
I hope this special Christmas Candy will help us remember why we are celebrating this time of year.

Many Thanks .... Jules

Each year at Christmas I buy candy canes. Some are used as decorations and some are gobbled up by my family. But at least once each year I remember the story that my Great Grandmother Pearl told me about the creation of the candy cane and the reason for its existence. I don't know if the story is true, but the candy and its legend are part of my life. Perhaps now that you have heard this tale it will cause you to reflect on the **reason for the season** in a different way too.

December 13

Candy Cane Vase
Craft/Decoration

MATERIALS

40 candy canes (any color)
tin can
strong rubber band
ribbon
craft glue
flowers or spruce trimmings

DIRECTIONS

1. Place the rubber band around the middle of the tin can. You will need an empty can for this project. Make sure that the can is completely clean and dry inside and out and that the label is removed.
2. Insert the candy canes under the rubber band. They should all be positioned so that the hooks on the top are facing out. Put them as close together as possible so that the can is not visible behind the candy canes. As you insert more and more, you will see your vase start to take shape. Be gentle so that they do not break. You can stop when the tin can is completely covered.
3. Place a piece of ribbon around the rubber band in tie it into a pretty bow. You may wish to use wire edged ribbon to make the bow larger and fluffier. You can use a drop or two of glue to hold the ribbon in place. It should cover the rubber band completely.
4. Snip the ends of the ribbon on a diagonal to prevent fraying. This makes the vase a little more festive and gives it the air of a Christmas present.
5. Fill the vase with the flowers, spruce trimmings or even a small rosemary plant. Your vase will scent the whole house with the wonderful, winter aroma of spruce. It will also help everyone get in the holiday mood.

Winter-Mint Crunch
Makes about 1/2 pound

INGREDIENTS

1   6 ounce package white baking morsels
6-8 candy canes (crushed)

INSTRUCTIONS

1. Melt white chocolate according to your favorite method. Mix chocolate until smooth.
2. Put candy canes in a zipper bag and hit with a hammer to crush. Remember you want chips not dust so do not break into to small a pieces.
3. Add crushed candy canes and mix well.
4. Line a cookie sheet with wax paper. Pour melted chocolate mix on to wax paper and spread out until thin and it covers entire surface.
5. Place cookie sheet in freezer for a few minutes or until chocolate is set.
6. Remove from freezer and break into desired pieces. (This mix may also be molded if candy canes are broken into small enough pieces).

December 14

The Christmas Fairy of Strasburg
A Tale of Germany
as told by J. Stirling Coyne

Once, long ago, there lived near the ancient city of Strasburg, on the river Rhine, a young and handsome count, whose name was Otto. As the years flew by he remained unwed, and never so much as cast a glance at the fair maidens of the country round; for this reason people began to call him "Stone-Heart."

It chanced that Count Otto, on one Christmas Eve, ordered that a great hunt should take place in the forest surrounding his castle. He and his guests and his many retainers rode forth, and the chase became more and more exciting. It led through thickets, and over pathless tracts of forest, until at length Count Otto found himself separated from his companions.

He rode on by himself until he came to a spring of clear, bubbling water, known to the people around as the "Fairy Well." Here Count Otto dismounted. He bent over the spring and began to lave his hands in the sparkling tide, but to his wonder he found that though the weather was cold and frosty, the water was warm and delightfully caressing. He felt a glow of joy pass through his veins, and, as he plunged his hands deeper, he fancied that his right hand was grasped by another, soft and small, which gently slipped from his finger the gold ring he always wore. And, lo! when he drew out his hand, the gold ring was gone.

Full of wonder at this mysterious event, the count mounted his horse and returned to his castle, resolving in his mind that the very next day he would have the Fairy Well emptied by his servants.

He retired to his room, and, throwing himself just as he was upon his couch, tried to sleep; but the strangeness of the adventure kept him restless and wakeful.

Suddenly he heard the hoarse baying of the watch-hounds in the courtyard, and then the creaking of the drawbridge, as though it were being lowered. Then came to his ear the patter of many small feet on the stone staircase, and next he heard indistinctly the sound of light footsteps in the chamber adjoining his own.

Count Otto sprang from his couch, and as he did so there sounded a strain of delicious music, and the door of his chamber was flung open. Hurrying into the next room, he found himself in the midst of numberless Fairy beings, clad in gay and sparkling robes. They paid no heed to him, but began to dance, and laugh, and sing, to the sound of mysterious music.

In the center of the apartment stood a splendid Christmas Tree, the first ever seen in that country. Instead of toys and candles there hung on its lighted boughs diamond stars, pearl necklaces, bracelets of gold ornamented with colored jewels, aigrettes of rubies and sapphires, silken belts embroidered with Oriental pearls, and daggers mounted in gold and studded with the rarest gems. The whole tree swayed, sparkled, and glittered in the radiance of its many lights.

Count Otto stood speechless, gazing at all this wonder, when suddenly the Fairies stopped dancing and fell back, to make room for a lady of dazzling beauty who came slowly toward him.

She wore on her raven-black tresses a golden diadem set with jewels. Her hair flowed down upon a robe of rosy satin and creamy velvet. She stretched out two small, white hands to the count and addressed him in sweet, alluring tones: --

"Dear Count Otto," said she, "I come to return your Christmas visit. I am Ernestine, the Queen of the Fairies. I bring you something you lost in the Fairy Well."

And as she spoke she drew from her bosom a golden casket, set with diamonds, and placed it in his hands. He opened it eagerly and found within his lost gold ring.

Carried away by the wonder of it all, and overcome by an irresistible impulse, the count pressed the Fairy Ernestine to his heart, while she, holding him by the hand, drew him into the magic mazes of the dance. The mysterious music floated through the room, and the rest of that Fairy company circled and whirled around the Fairy Queen and Count Otto, and then gradually dissolved into a mist of many colors, leaving the count and his beautiful guest alone.

Then the young man, forgetting all his former coldness toward the maidens of the country round about, fell on his knees before the Fairy and besought her to become his bride. At last she consented on the condition that he should never speak the word "death" in her presence.

The next day the wedding of Count Otto and Ernestine, Queen of the Fairies, was celebrated with great pomp and magnificence, and the two continued to live happily for many years.

Now it happened on a time, that the count and his Fairy wife were to hunt in the forest around the castle. The horses were saddled and bridled, and standing at the door, the company waited, and the count paced the hall in great impatience; but still the Fairy Ernestine tarried long in her chamber. At length she appeared at the door of the hall, and the count addressed her in anger.

"You have kept us waiting so long," he cried, "that you would make a good messenger to send for Death!"

Scarcely had he spoken the forbidden and fatal word, when the Fairy, uttering a wild cry, vanished from his sight. In vain Count Otto, overwhelmed with grief and remorse, searched the castle and the Fairy Well, no trace could he find of his beautiful, lost wife but the imprint of her delicate hand set in the stone arch above the castle gate.

December 14

Years passed by, and the Fairy Ernestine did not return. The count continued to grieve. Every Christmas Eve he set up a lighted tree in the room where he had first met the Fairy, hoping in vain that she would return to him.

Time passed and the count died. The castle fell into ruins. But to this day may be seen above the massive gate, deeply sunken in the stone arch, the impress of a small and delicate hand. And such, say the good folk of Strasbourg, was the origin of the Christmas Tree.

Olcott, Frances Jenkins, *Good Stories for Great Holidays*, Houghton Miflin Company, 1914.

Christmas Fairy
Craft/Decoration

MATERIALS

card stock
copy paper
scissors

DIRECTIONS

1. Trace the pattern to your right on to card stock.
2. To make the skirt follow the directions on page 241 to make a snowflake.
3. Cut a slit large enough to slide snowflake up to waist. You may want to gently fold the skirt area in half so you don't have to cut such a big slit. Once in place tape closed the slit on the backside and adjust skirt.

December 14

Cranberry Raspberry Jam
makes 8 half-pints

INGREDIENTS

- 2   10 oz packages frozen raspberries, thawed
- 1   cup water
- 1   pound (4 cups) fresh cranberries
- 5   cups sugar
- 1   package (1¾ ounces) powdered fruit pectin

INSTRUCTIONS

1. Put water, raspberries, cranberries and pectin into a large heavy saucepan Mix well.
2. Bring to a full rolling boil for one minute, stirring constantly.
3. Stir in sugar and return to a full rolling boil for an additional minute, make sure to keep stirring. Remove from heat, skim off any foam.
4. Pour into hot half-pint jars, leaving ¼ inch head space. Wipe off rims and adjust lids.
5. Process in the boiling water bath canner for 15 minutes.

Note: If you want a smoother jam you can put the fruit in a blender and pulse to the consistency you want before you put it in the pan to cook. You can also use a potato masher to the cooked fruit as an option to the blender process.

Crazy About Christmas

Illustration from the 1853 U.S. edition of The Nutcracker and the Mouse King
published by D. Appleton, New York

December 15

The Nutcracker and the Mouse King
A summary of E.T.A. Hoffman's novella

CHRISTMAS EVE

It's a cozy Christmas Eve at the Stahlbaum's house.

Their house is decorated with Christmas ornaments, wreaths, stockings, mistletoe and in the center of it all, a majestic Christmas tree. As the Stahlbaum's prepare for their annual Christmas party, their children, Fritz and Marie, wait anxiously for their family and friends to arrive.

When the guests finally appear, the party picks up with dancing and celebration. A mysterious guest arrives dressed in dark clothing, nearly frightening Fritz, but not Marie. Marie knows he is Godfather Drosselmeyer, the toymaker. His surprise arrival is warmly accepted and all the children dance and carry on with laughter.

The celebration is interrupted again when Drosselmeyer reveals to the children that he has brought them gifts. The girls receive beautiful china dolls and the boys receive bugles. Fritz is given a beautiful drum, but Marie is given the best gift of all, the Nutcracker. Fritz grows jealous, snatches the Nutcracker from Marie and plays a game of toss with the other boys.

It isn't long until the Nutcracker breaks. Marie is upset, but Drosselmeyer fixes it with a handkerchief. Drosselmeyer's nephew offers Marie a small make-shift bed under the Christmas tree for her injured Nutcracker.

The party grows late and the children become sleepy. Everyone generously thanks the Stahlbaum's before they leave.

As Marie's family retires to bed, she checks on her Nutcracker one last time and ends up falling asleep under the Christmas tree with the Nutcracker in her arms.

At the stroke of midnight, Marie wakes up to a frightening scene. The house, the tree, and the toys seem to be getting larger. Is she shrinking? Out of nowhere large mice dressed in army uniforms, led by the Mouse King, begin to circle the room while the toys and Christmas tree come to life. Marie's Nutcracker groups the soldier toys into battle formation and fights the mouse army.

The Mouse King traps the Nutcracker in the corner, but the Nutcracker can't overcome the Mouse King's strength. Marie makes a desperate move to save her Nutcracker from defeat and throws her slipper at the Mouse King. She hits him directly in the head! The Nutcracker is able to overcome the stunned Mouse King and claims victory. The mice army quickly carries away their King.

Marie falls onto the Nutcracker's bed, overwhelmed by the moment. As angels and delightful music hover over their heads, the bed turns into a magical sleigh, floating higher

Crazy About Christmas

and higher. The Nutcracker is transformed into a human prince (who looks very much like Drosselmeyer's nephew).

He gets on Marie's sleigh and drives through a snowy forest where the snowflakes turn into dancing maidens.

After their magical journey through the snow forest, they come to their destination in the Land of Sweets. Marie can't believe her eyes; ladyfinger mountains topped with whipped cream whiter than snow, sweetly glazed flowers and butter cream frosting everywhere she looks. Upon their arrival, they are greeted by the Sugar Plum Fairy. As they reenact the night's events, the Sugar Plum Fairy becomes impressed with Marie's bravery and the Nutcracker's heroism. In their honor, the Sugar Plum Fairy takes them inside the Candy Castle and throws a lavish festival. They are treated like royalty and presented with every imaginable sweet. Shortly thereafter, the dancing begins.

Hot Cocoa dances to the lively music of trumpets and castanets of the Spanish fandango.

The women of coffee dance in veils and move their bodies like rising steam to an Arabian song, while Mandarin tea dances to an exotic Asian flute chorus. Matryoshkas (Russian dolls) follow the Mandarin tea leaping and dancing to an invigorating Russian Trepak.

To Marie's enjoyment, there is still more to be seen. A giant gingerbread house, known as Mother Ginger, dances onto the Sugar Plum Fairy's court. She opens her skirt and eight little gingerbread children come dancing out circling around her. After the Mirliton dance is over, the children quickly file back into the large gingerbread house and Mother Ginger leaves the room. Soon after Mother Ginger exits, the dancing flowers enter to the tune of the harp. Perhaps the most beautiful waltz she has ever heard, Marie and the Nutcracker Prince watch with amazement. The flowers dance in beautiful mesmerizing patterns as a single Dewdrop floats above them.

Silence quickly follows the end of their dance. Marie doesn't know what to expect next. A handsome Cavalier enters the scene and escorts the Sugar Plum Fairy to the center of the room. They dance to the most recognizable song in the entire work. The captivating pair dance lighter than air. This beautiful dance completes Marie's most perfect evening. The festival concludes when everyone comes together on the court and bids Marie and the Nutcracker Prince farewell. She tells the Nutcracker she wishes the adventure would never end and he tells her it won't for those who have an eye to see it.

Christmas Day

When Marie wakes up the next morning under the Christmas she tells her mother all about her adventures. Her mother dismisses it all as a beautiful dream. But Marie insists that it really happened and that the Nutcracker was really Uncle Drosselmeyer's nephew, with that everyone begins laughing and the more Marie tried to explain about the Marzipan Castle and all the wonderful dancers the harder they all laughed. Just as Marie is about to

December 15

run away from all the jesting there is a loud knock at the door and who should enter but her Uncle Drosselmeyer and his nephew.

The young man was handsome, polite and well-mannered. He gave Marie all sorts of toys and replaced the marzipan and sugar dolls that the Mouse King had destroyed. To Fritz he gave a beautiful saber. At the table he cracked nuts for everyone.

After dinner Marie and the nephew walked into the living room where he knelt and asked Marie to become his queen and to reign with him at the Marzipan Castle. She accepted immediately.

When she was a bit older they married and there were twenty-two thousand of the most brilliant dancers dressed in earls and diamonds to entertain at the wedding. Marie became the queen of a country in which shimmering Christmas forests and glazed marzipans castles, She lived in a marvelous place and enjoyed the sweetness of life with her Nutcracker.

Note: This story was written as a novella in 1816 by German author E.T.A. Hoffman, a simplified version of the story by Alexandre Dumas in 1892 is said to have influenced the Russian composer Pyotr Ilyich Tchaikovsky and choreographers Marius Petipa and Lev Ivanov who turned the story into the ballet The Nutcracker, which became one of Tchaikovsky's most famous compositions, and one of the most popular ballets in the world.

Linda S. Day 1997

 Crazy About Christmas

Holiday Cone Boxes
Craft/Ornament/Gift Idea

MATERIALS:

Old Christmas cards at least 5" x 6"or scrapbook card stock
Scissors
Pencil
Ruler
Bread knife or orange stick or scoring tool
Glue, double-stick tape or hot glue
Cord for loops

DIRECTIONS:

1. Copy or trace cone pattern from the next page. Cut out pattern. Lay pattern over the area on the card or paper you want the image to be. At this point you can either tape the pattern into place or trace it on.
2. Cut around outline of box.
3. On the plain side of the box fold or score on the dotted lines. You can score with a ruler and a bread knife. Start by folding the flap in first, then fold in half to meet the edge of folded flap, Now fold each side to the middle. If you did it right you will have four equal sides.
4. With the card folded in half spread either glue or double sided tape to the flap and press to seal. When dry open up box adjust folds and fold in the flaps.
5. Poke or punch a small hole in the center of the lid. Take a 8-inch piece of cord knot it at the bottom and thread loop through the hole. Secure knot with a small piece of tape. .
6. Fill the box with sweet treats, candied nuts or small treasures. Hang on your tree or give as gifts. You can enlarge this pattern to make larger boxes.

Variation: Use fancy scrapbook card stock to have a more Victorian look and then add lace and other embellishments. Fold the lid and flaps inside and fill with flowers.
Suggestions: Tired of advent calendars, make and number twenty-four cone boxes and fill them with special treats and hang them on the tree. Allow the children to take off one cone each day till Christmas. Lots more fun than opening windows on an oversized card.

December 15

——————— Cut lines

— — — — Fold lines

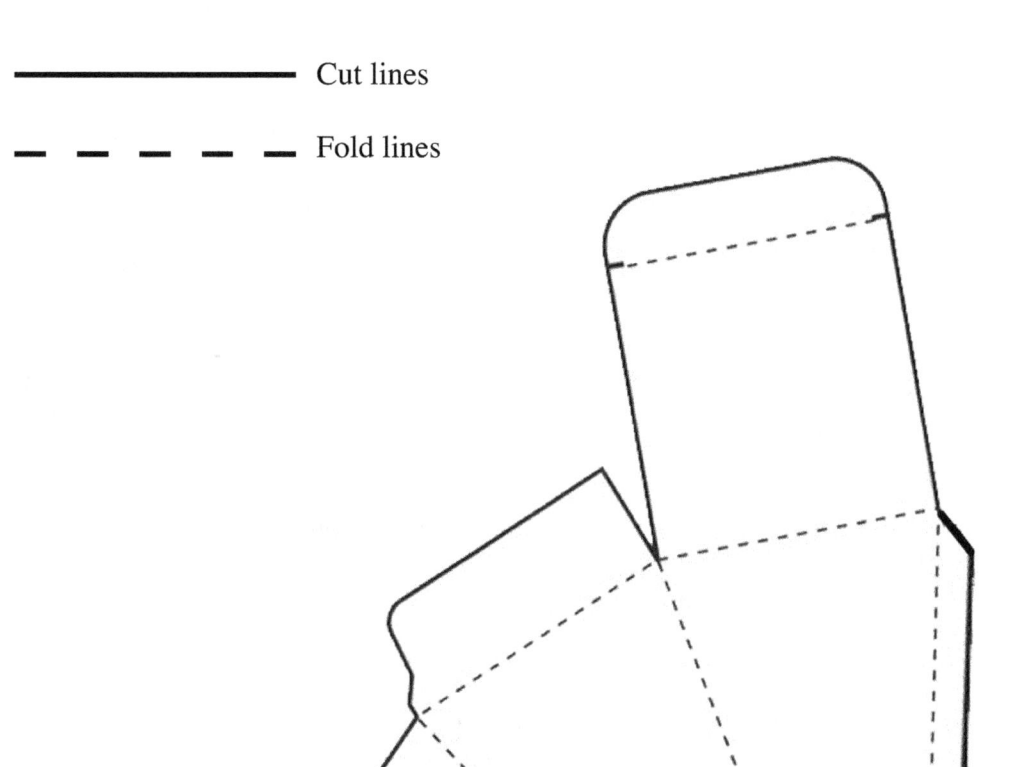

141

Crazy About Christmas

Spiced Candied Pecans

INGREDIENTS

- 2 ½ cups raw pecans
- 1 large egg white, lightly beaten
- ¼ cup sugar
- 2 teaspoon cinnamon
- ½ teaspoon allspice
- ½ teaspoon salt

INSTRUCTIONS

1. Preheat oven to 300F. Line a baking sheet with parchment paper.
2. In a large bowl, stir the pecans with the egg white.
3. In a small bowl, stir together the sugar, cinnamon, allspice and salt. Pour over the nuts and stir until evenly coated.
4. Spread in a single layer on the baking sheet and bake for 30 minutes.
5. Slide parchment paper (with nuts still on it) off of the baking sheet and onto a wire rack (or the counter) to cool.
6. Break nuts up into a bowl to serve or store at room temperature in an airtight container.

Did I say addictive? Watch out these are simple and addictive.

Gift Idea: Take some of these tasty nuts and put into our pretty cone boxes on the previous page and give as gifts.

Variation: While I love pecans these are also great made with almonds. Honestly any nut you love or a mix of nuts will work just fine.

December 16

The Worker in Sandalwood
By Marjorie L. C. Pickthall

The good curé of Terminaison says that this tale of Hyacinthe's is all a dream. But then Madame points triumphantly to the little cabinet of sandalwood in the corner of her room. It had stood there for many years now, and the dust has gathered in the fine lines of the little birds' feathers, and softened the petals of the lilies carved at the corners. And the wood has taken on a golden gleam like the memory of a sunset.

"What of that, my friend?" says Madame, pointing to the cabinet. And the old curé bows his head.

"It may be so. God is very good," he says gently. But he is never quite sure what he may believe.

On that winter day long ago, Hyacinthe was quite sure of one thing and that was that the workshop was very cold. There was no fire in it, and only one little lamp when the early dark drew on. The tools were so cold they scorched his fingers, and feet were so cold he danced clumsily in the shavings to warm them. He was a great clumsy boy of fourteen, dark-faced, dull-eyed, and uncared for. He was clumsy because it is impossible to be graceful when you are growing very fast and have not enough to eat. He was dull-eyed because all eyes met his unlovingly. He was uncared for because no one knew the beauty of his soul. But his heavy young hands could carve things like birds and flowers perfectly. On this winter evening he was just wondering if he might lay aside the tools, and creep home to the cold loft where he slept, when he heard Pierre L'Oreillard's voice shouting outside.

"Be quick, be quick, and open the door, thou imbecile. It is I, thy master."

"Oui, mon maitre," said Hyacinthe, and he shambled to the door and opened it.

"Slow worm!" cried Pierre, and he cuffed Hyacinthe as he passed in. Hyacinthe rubbed his head and said nothing. He was used to blows. He wondered why his master was in the workshop at that time of day instead of drinking brandy at the Cinq Chateaux.

Pierre L'Oreillard had a small heavy bundle under his arm, wrapped in sacking, and then in burlap, and then in fine soft cloths. He laid it on a pile of shavings, and unfolded it carefully; and a dim sweetness filled the dark shed and hung heavily in the thin winter sunbeams.

"It is a piece of wood," said Hyacinthe in slow surprise. He knew that such wood had never been seen in Terminaison.

Pierre L'Oreillard rubbed the wood respectfully with his knobby fingers.

"It is sandalwood," he explained to Hyacinthe, pride of knowledge making him quite amiable, "a most precious wood that grows in warm countries, thou great goblin. Smell it, idiot. It is sweeter than cedar. It is to make a cabinet for the old Madame at the big house."

Crazy About Christmas

"Oui, mon maitre," said the dull Hyacinthe.

"Thy great hands shall shape and smooth the wood, and I will render it beautiful," said Pierre, puffing out his chest.

"Yes, Master," answered Hyacinthe humbly, "and when is it to be ready for Madame?"

"Madame will want it perhaps next week, for that is Christmas. It is to be finished and ready on the holy festival, great sluggard. Hearest thou?" and he cuffed Hyacinthe's ears again furiously.

Hyacinthe knew that the making of the cabinet would fall to him, as most of the other work did. When Pierre L'Oreillard was gone he touched the strange sweet wood and at last laid his cheek against it, while the fragrance caught his breath. "How it is beautiful!" said Hyacinthe, and for a moment his eyes glowed, and he was happy. Then the light passed and with bent head he shuffled back to his bench through a foam of white shavings curling almost to his knees.

"Madame will want the cabinet for Christmas," repeated Hyacinthe to himself, and fell to work harder than ever, though it was so cold in the shed that his breath hung in the air like a little silvery cloud. There was a tiny window on his right, through which, when it was clear of frost, one looked on Terminaison; and that was cheerful, and made him whistle. But to the left, through the chink of the ill-fitting door, there was nothing to be seen but the forest, and the road dying under the snow.

Brandy was good at the Cinq Chateaux and Pierre L'Oreillard gave Hyacinthe plenty of directions, but no further help with the cabinet.

"That is to be finished for Madame at the festival, sluggard," said he every day, cuffing Hyacinthe about the head, "finished, and with a prettiness about the corners, hearest thou, bear-cub?"

"Yes, Monsieur," said Hyacinthe in his slow way; "I will try to finish it. But if I hurry I shall spoil it."

Pierre's little eyes flickered. "See that it is done, and done properly. I suffer from a delicacy of the constitution and a little feebleness of the legs these days, so that I cannot handle the tools properly. I must leave this work to thee, bungler. Now stand up and touch a hand to thy cap when I speak to thee, slow-worm."

"Yes, monsieur," said Hyacinthe wearily.

It is hard to do all the work and to be beaten into the bargain. And fourteen is not very old. Hyacinthe worked on at the cabinet with his slow and exquisite skill. But on Christmas eve he was still at work, and the cabinet unfinished.

"The master will beat me," thought Hyacinthe, and he trembled a little, for Pierre's beatings were cruel. "But if I hurry, I shall spoil the wood, and it is too beautiful to be spoiled."

But he trembled again when Pierre came into the workshop, and he stood up and touched his cap.

December 16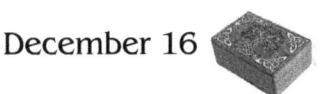

"Is the cabinet finished, imbecile?" asked Pierre. And Hyacinthe answered in a low voice, "No, it is not finished yet, monsieur."

"Then work on it all night, and show it to me completed in the morning, or thy bones shall mourn thine idleness," said Pierre, with a wicked look in his little eyes. And he shut Hyacinthe into the shed with a smoky lamp, his tools, and the sandalwood cabinet.

It was nothing unusual. He had been often left before to finish a piece of work overnight while Pierre went off to his brandies. But this was Christmas eve, and he was very tired. Even the scent of the sandalwood could not make him fancy he was warm. The world seemed to be a black place, full of suffering and despair.

"In all the world, I have no friend," said Hyacinthe, staring at the flame of the lamp. "In all the world, there is no one to care whether I live or die. In all the world, no place, no heart, no love. O kind God, is there a place, a love for me in another world?"

I hope you feel very sorry for Hyacinthe, lonely, and cold, and shut up in the workshop on the eve of Christmas. He was but an overgrown, unhappy child. And I think with old Madame that for unhappy children, at this season, no help seems too divine for faith.

"There is no one to care for me," said Hyacinthe. And he even looked at the chisel in his hand, thinking that by a touch of that he might lose it all, and be at peace, somewhere, not far from God. Only it was forbidden. Then came the tears, and great sobs that shook him, so that he scarcely heard the gentle rattling of the latch.

He stumbled to the door, opening it on the still woods and the frosty stars. And a lad who stood outside in the snow said, "I see you are working late, comrade. May I come in?"

Hyacinthe brushed his ragged sleeve across his eyes and nodded "Yes." Those little villages strung along the great river see strange wayfarers at times. And Hyacinthe said to himself that surely here was such a one. Blinking into the stranger's eyes, he lost for a flash the first impression of youth, and received one of incredible age or sadness. But the wanderer's eyes were only quiet, very quiet, like the little pools in the wood where the wild does went to drink. As he turned within the door, smiling at Hyacinthe and shaking some snow from his cap, he did not seem to be more than sixteen or so.

"It is very cold outside," he said. "There is a big oak tree on the edge of the fields that had split in the frost and frightened all the little squirrels asleep there. Next year it will make an even better home for them. And see what I found close by!" He opened his fingers and showed Hyacinthe a little sparrow lying unruffled in the palm.

"Poor thing!" said the dull Hyacinthe. "The poor thing! Is it then dead?" He touched it with a gentle forefinger.

"No," answered the strange boy, "it is not dead. We will put it here among the shavings, not far from the lamp, and it will be well by the morning."

He smiled at Hyacinthe again, and the shambling lad felt dimly as if the scent of the sandalwood were sweeter, and the lamp-flame clearer. But the stranger's eyes were only quiet.

Crazy About Christmas

"Have you come far?" asked Hyacinthe. "It is a bad season for traveling, and the wolves are out."

"A long way," said the other. "A long, long way. I heard a child cry—"

"There is no child here," put in Hyacinthe. "Monsieur L'Oreillard says children cost too much money. But if you have come far, you must need food and fire, and I have neither. At the Cinq Chateaux you will find both."

The stranger looked at him again with those quiet eyes, and Hyacinthe fancied that his face was familiar. "I will stay here," he said; "you are late at work, and you are unhappy."

"Why as to that," answered Hyacinthe, rubbing his cheeks and ashamed of his tears, "most of are sad at one time or another, the good God knows. Stay here and welcome if it pleases you; and you may take a share of my bed, though it is no more than a pile of balsam boughs and an old blanket in the loft. But I must work at this cabinet, for the drawers must be finished and the handles put on and the corners carved, all by the holy morning; or my wages will be paid with a stick."

"You have a hard master," put in the other, "if he would pay you with blows upon the feast of Noel."

"He is hard enough," said Hyacinthe, "but once he gave me a dinner of sausages and white wine; and once, in the summer, melons. If my eyes will stay open, I will finish this by morning. Stay with me an hour or so, comrade, and talk to me of your travels, so that the time may pass more quickly."

And while Hyacinthe worked, he told,—of sunshine and dust, of the shadow of vine-leaves on the flat white walls of a house; of rosy doves on the roof; of the flowers that come out in the spring, anemones crimson and blue, and white cyclamen in the shadow of the rocks; of the olive, the myrtle, and the almond; until Hyacinthe's fingers ceased working, and his sleepy eyes blinked wonderingly.

"See what you have done, comrade," he said at last; "you have told me of such pretty things that I have done but little work for an hour. And now the cabinet will never be finished, and I shall be beaten."

"Let me help you," smiled the other. "I also was bred a carpenter."

At first Hyacinthe would not, fearing to trust the sweet wood out of his own hands. But at length he allowed the stranger to fit in one of the drawers. And so deftly was it done that Hyacinthe pounded his fists on the bench in admiration. "You have a pretty knack," he cried. "It seemed as if you did but hold the drawer in your hands a moment, and hey! it jumped into its place."

"Let me fit in the other little drawers while you rest awhile," said the stranger. So Hyacinthe curled up among the shavings, and the other boy fell to work upon the little cabinet of sandalwood.

December 16

Hyacinthe was very tired. He lay still among the shavings, and thought of all the boy had told him, of the hillside flowers, the laughing leaves, the golden bloom of the anise, and the golden sun upon the roads until he was warm. And all the time the boy with the quiet eyes was at work upon the cabinet, smoothing, fitting, polishing.

"You do better work than I," said Hyacinthe once, and the stranger answered, "I was lovingly taught." And again Hyacinthe said, "It is growing towards morning. In a little while I will get up and help you."

"Lie still and rest," said the other boy. And Hyacinthe lay still. His thoughts began to slide into dreams, and he woke with a little start, for there seemed to be music in the shed; though he could not tell whether it came from the strange boy's lips, or from the shabby tools as he used them, or from the stars.

"The stars are much paler," thought Hyacinthe. "Soon it will be morning, and the corners are not carved yet. I must get up and help this kind one in a little moment. Only the music and the sweetness seem to fold me close, so that I may not move."

Then behind the forest there shone a pale glow of dawn, and in Terminaison the church bells began to ring. "Day will soon be here," thought Hyacinthe, "and with day will come Monsieur L'Oreillard and his stick. I must get up and help for even yet the corners are not carved."

But the stranger looked at him, smiling as though he loved him, and laid his brown finger lightly on the four empty corners of the cabinet. And Hyacinthe saw the squares of reddish wood ripple and heave and break, as little clouds when the wind goes through the sky. And out of them thrust forth the little birds, and after them the lilies, for a moment living; but even as Hyacinthe looked, settling back into the sweet reddish-brown wood. Then the stranger smiled again, laid all the tools in order, and, opening the door, went away into the woods.

Hyacinthe crept slowly to the door. The winter sun, half risen, filled all the frosty air with splendid gold. Far down the road a figure seemed to move amid the glory, but the splendor was such that Hyacinthe was blinded. His breath came sharply as the glow beat on the wretched shed, on the old shavings, on the cabinet with the little birds and the lilies carved at the corners.

He was too pure of heart to feel afraid. But "Blessed be the Lord," whispered Hyacinthe, clasping his slow hands, "for He hath visited and redeemed His people. But who will believe?"

Then the sun of Christ's day rose gloriously, and the little sparrow came from his nest among the shavings and shook his wings to the light.

published by *Everyland*, ©1914

Crazy About Christmas

Christmas Card Boxes
Recycled Project/Gift Wrap

MATERIALS LIST:

last years' Christmas cards
double-sided tape or hot glue
pencil
butter knife or orange stik
scissors
ruler

DIRECTIONS:

1. Pick out a Christmas card that has a design that is fairly centered. Cut it apart at the fold.

2. Take inside of card (the part with the greeting on it) and cut off a tiny amount (about 1/16", not more than 1/8") off two sides (one short side, and one long side), this will become the bottom of the box.

3. Turn over card front (box top). Now with a pencil draw a line one inch from the card edge (this will make a one inch deep box). Do this on all four sides.

4. Repeat the process on the card section with the greeting, but draw the lines on the same side as the greeting. This will put the words on the inside of your box.

5. Now line up your ruler on each line and use a butter knife or orange stik to score each line (that means press down hard on the line to make an impression). Do this to both halves of the card.

6. Now with your scissors cut to where the lines intersect on both sides of the short edge.

7. Fold on the lines, toward the center of box.

8. Put tape on one of the short edges (the box ends). Fold up the long edge, folding in the extensions. Tape extension to inside of short edge. Do one end of the box at a time. Repeat process on the other end. .

9. Repeat instruction number 8 for bottom of box.

December 16

8. Put tape on one of the short edges (the box ends). Fold up the long edge, folding in the extensions. Glue extension to inside of short edge. Do one end of the box at a time. Repeat process on the other end. If you are in a hurry use double-stick tape instead.

9. Repeat instruction number 8 for bottom of box.

10. Now place top of box over bottom.

VARIATION 1: If you want to change the depth of the box, simply change the amount you measure (i.e. change 1 inch to 1 1/2 inch or 3/4 inch, etc.).

VARIATION 2: For a little more fun skip the gluing and fold each edge in half (mark and score before folding). Then fold the extensions in on both sides of one end and fold the short end over both extensions. You now have a folded box with no glue and have decreased the depth of the box by half.

Super Gift Idea!
Line box with plastic wrap and pour your fudge into the bottom of box.
Fudge for One™

VARIATION 3: You don't have to use old Christmas cards. If you want to create your own boxes simple cut out two identical pieces of index weight paper and color your own design on one side. Then follow the directions above.

VARIATION 4: Buy a piece of poster board and make a really big box. Just determine how deep you need your box, then mark, score and fold according to the directions above.

Variation 5: *If I am going to make a lot of these boxes I will cut them all apart, trim, stack and then score them all at once keeping the sets together. Then I will use a hot glue gun to get the job done quickly.*

Once you get started you won't want to stop!

TIP 1: Score before folding: Scoring before folding gives a much cleaner, sharper fold and makes the folding easier.

TIP 2: You must make sure that you do not cut more than 1/8 inch off the two edges of greeting section of the card or your bottom will fit too loosely. Just think no wider than the width of your scissor blade.

Pumpkin Pie Fudge
makes 48 one inch squares

INGREDIENTS:

- 1½ cups granulated sugar
- 2/3 cup evaporated milk
- 1/2 cup mashed pumpkin (canned)
- 2 tablespoons butter or margarine
- 1/4 teaspoon salt
- 1½ teaspoons pumpkin pie spice
- 1 package (12 ounces) white baking morsels
- 2 cups miniature marshmallows
- 1/3 cup chopped nuts (optional)
- 1¼ teaspoons vanilla extract

INSTRUCTIONS:

1. Using butter or margarine, lightly grease the sides and bottom of a medium saucepan.
2. Line an 8-inch square pan with foil and lightly grease. Set aside.
3. Put pumpkin, sugar and spices in pan, mix until all are incorporated.
4. Add evaporated milk, butter, salt, into the pumpkin mix in the saucepan. Stirring constantly over medium heat, bring the mixture to a boil and boil for 12 minutes.
5. Remove from the heat and stir in the baking chips and marshmallows until melted.
6. Stir in the nuts and vanilla.
7. Pour into your prepared 8-inch square pan.
8. Chill mixture until set.
9. Using the foil to lift out fudge. Cut into small squares to serve. Does not have to be refrigerated but most be covered to keep it soft.

December 17

The Most Beautiful Thing
Author Unknown

The sides of the path were covered with rings of white snow. But, in the center its whiteness was crushed and churned into a foaming brown by the tramp, tramp of hundreds of hurrying feet. It was the day before Christmas.

People rushed up and down the path carrying armloads of bundles. They laughed and called to each other as they pushed their way through the crowds.

Above the path, the long arms of an ancient tree reached upward to the sky. It swayed and moaned as a strong wind grasped its branches, and bent them toward the earth. Down below a haughty laugh sounded, and a lovely fir tree stretched and preened its thick green branches, sending a fine spray of snow shimmering downward to the ground.

"I should think," said the fir, in a high smug voice, "that you'd try a little harder to stand still. Goodness knows you're ugly enough with the leaves you've already lost. If you move around any more, you'll be quite bare."

"I know," answered the old tree. "Everything has put on its most beautiful clothes for the celebration of the birth of Christ. Even from here I can see the decorations shining from each street corner. And yesterday some men came and put the brightest, loveliest lights on every tree along the path—except me, of course." He sighed softly, and a flake of snow melted in the form of a teardrop and ran down his gnarled trunk.

"Oh, indeed! And did you expect they'd put lights upon you so your ugliness would stand out even more?" smirked the fir.

"I guess you're right," replied the old tree in a sad voice. "If there were only somewhere I could hide until after the celebrations are over, but here I stand…the only ugly thing among all this beauty. If they would only come and chop me down," and he sighed sorrowfully.

"Well, I don't wish you any Ill will," replied the fir, "but you are an eyesore. Perhaps it would be better for us all if they came and chopped you down." Once again he stretched his lovely thick branches. "You might try to hold onto those three small leaves you still have. At least you wouldn't be completely bare."

"Oh, I've tried so hard," cried the old tree. "Each fall I say to myself, 'this year I won't give up a single leaf, no matter what the cause', but someone always comes along who seems to need them more than I," and he sighed once again.

"I told you not to give away so many to that dirty little paper boy," said the fir. "Why you even lowered your branches a little, so that he could reach them. You can't say I didn't warn you then."

"Yes, you did at that," the old tree replied. "But they made him so happy. I heard him say he would pick some for his invalid mother."

"Oh they all had good causes," mocked the fir. "That young girl, for instance, colored leaves for her party, indeed! They were your leaves!"

"She took a lot, didn't she?" said the old tree, and he seemed to smile.

Just then a cold wind blew down the path and a tiny brown bird fell to the ground at the foot of the old tree and lay there shivering, too cold to lift its wings. The old tree looked down in pity, and then quickly he let go of his last three leaves. The golden leaves fluttered down and settled softly over the shivering little bird, and it lay there quietly under the warmth of them.

"Now you've done it!" shrieked the fir. "You've given away every single leaf! Christmas morning you'll make our path the ugliest sight in the whole city!"

The old tree said nothing. Instead, he stretched out his branches to gather what snowflakes he could that they might not fall on the tiny bird.

The young fir turned away in anger, and it was then he noticed a painter sitting quietly a few feet from the path, intent upon his long brushes and his canvas. His clothes were old and tattered, and his face wore a sad expression. He was thinking of his loved ones and the empty, cheerless Christmas morning they would face, for he had sold not a single painting in the last few months.

But the little tree didn't see this. Instead, he turned his back to the old tree and said in a haughty voice, "At least keep those bare branches as far away from me as possible. I'm being painted and your hideousness will mar the background."

"I'll try," replied the old tree. And he raised his branches as high as possible.

It was almost dark when the painter picked up his easel and left. And the little fir was tired and cross from all his preening and posing.

Christmas morning he awoke late, and as he proudly shook away the snow from his lovely branches, he was amazed to see a huge crowd of people surrounding the old tree, ah-ing and oh-ing as they stood back and gazed upward. And even those hurrying along the path had to stop for a moment to sigh before they went on.

"Whatever could it be?" thought the haughty fir, and he too looked up to see if perhaps the top of the old tree had been broken off during the night.

Just then a paper blew away from the hands of an enraptured newsboy and sailed straight into the young fir. The fir gasped in amazement, for there on the front page was a picture of the painter holding his painting of a great white tree whose leafless branches, laden with snow, stretched upward into the sky. While below lay a tiny brown bird almost covered by three golden leaves. And beneath the picture were the words, "The Most Beautiful Thing Is That Which Hath Given All."

The young fir quietly bowed its head beneath the great beauty of the humble old tree.

December 17

Kissmas Trees
Table Decoration/Craft/Ornament

Materials

Scrapbook paper
Hershey's kisses® or Rollo®
glue stick
scissors
toothpicks
tape

Directions:

1. Flat Tree
   Fold paper in half vertically and trace pattern. Cut two identical trees on fold.
   Tape toothpick to the inside bottom of one tree to make trunk
   Using glue stick cover second tree with glue and match together.
   Stick toothpick into top of kiss to use as pot to stand up your tree.
2. For 3-D tree
   Fold paper in half horizontally and trace pattern. Cut out four identically trees on fold.
   With paper still folded place glue on one side of tree. Attach second piece to the first, keeping folded in half. Keep moving around tree.
   Before you glue the final side down you can attach a couple of fancy beads or a star by attaching beads to wire and taping wire to the inside. If you want tree to have a base tape toothpick to the center fold on the bottom.
   Glue final side of tree. Make sure it is good and dry before you fan it out and stick it into the kiss.

Crazy About Christmas

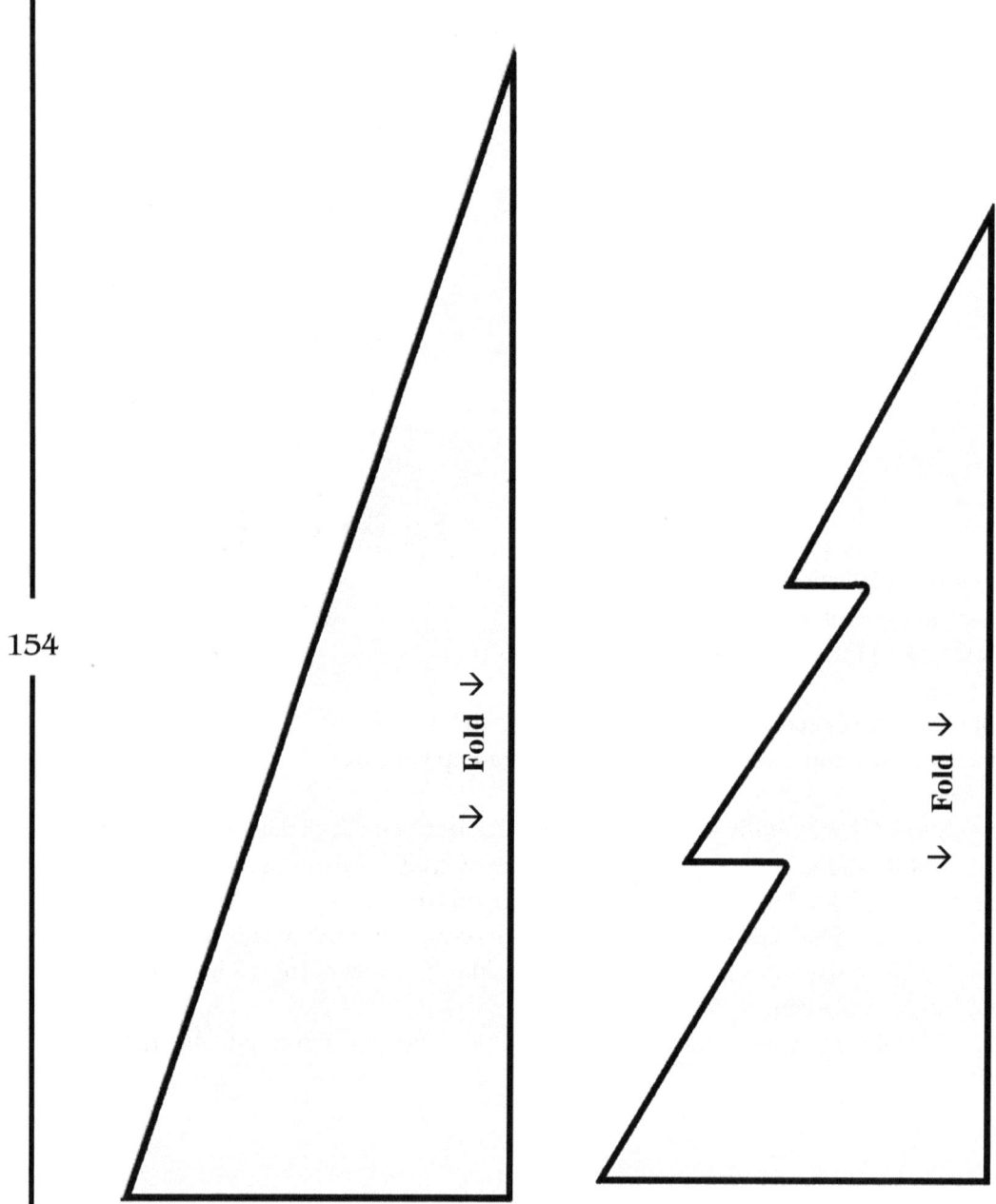

Flat Tree pattern - Cut 2 on fold

3-D Tree pattern - Cut 8 on fold

December 17

Hot Fudge Pudding Cake
serves 9

INGREDIENTS

1	cup all purpose flour
½	cup granulated sugar
¼	cup cocoa powder
2	teaspoons baking powder
¼	teaspoon salt
¾	cup milk
¼	cup unsalted butter, melted
1	teaspoon vanilla
1	cup finely chopped nuts (optional)

FUDGE SAUCE

½	cup granulated sugar
½	cup packed brown sugar
3	tablespoons cocoa powder
1¼	cups of hot water
	whipped cream or vanilla ice cream (optional)

INSTRUCTIONS

1. Heat oven to 350°F. Lightly grease a 9-inch square pan. Boil water while making cake.
2. For the cake measure flour,sugar, cocoa powder, baking powder and salt into bowl.
3. Blend in milk, vanilla and butter whisk until smooth.
4. Fold in nuts if you want at this time.
5. Pour batter into your pre-greased square pan..
6. To make the sauce Stir together white and brown sugar and 3 tablespoons of cocoa; sprinkle over evenly over batter. Slowly pour boiling water over batter. IMPORTANT that you do NOT stir or mix into batter, just lett the water sit on top.
7. Bake for 35 minutes; or until the center is almost set. Remove from oven and let cool for 15 minutes before serving. Serve in dessert dishes, spooning sauce from bottom of pan over top.
8. Serve with a scoop of vanilla ice cream or whipped cream, if desired.

Note: If this cake becomes cold, not likely, the sauce turns into a cold pudding.

One of the most glorious messes in the world is the mess created in the living room on Christmas

Day.
 Don't clean it up too quickly.
—Andy Rooney—

December 18

Christmas Humor

RIDDLE ME THIS

What comes at the end of Christmas Day? (*The letter Y*)

    What goes OH, OH, OH? (*Santa walking backwards*)

What do elves learn in school? (*The elf-abet*)

    What do snowmen eat for breakfast? (*Frosted Flakes*)

Which of Santa's reindeer has bad manners? (*Rude-olph*)

    What did Adam say on the day before Christmas? (*It's Christmas, Eve*)

Who is never hungry at Christmas? (*The turkey – he's always stuffed*)

    If athletes get athlete's food, what do elves get? (*Mistle-toes*)

Why did the elves ask the turkey to join the band? (*Because he had the drumsticks*)

    What do you call a letter sent up the chimney on Christmas Eve? (*Black mail*)

What do you get when you cross a snowman with a vampire? (*Frostbite*)

    What fall's but never gets hurt? (*Snow*)

Why are Christmas trees like bad knitters? (*They both drop their needles*)

    What do you call people who are scared of Santa Claus? (*Claustrophobic*)

What do you call Santa when he has no money? (*Saint "Nickel"-less*)

    What do you get if you cross Santa with a flying saucer? (*A UF ho, ho, ho*)

What do you call someone who doesn't believe in Father Christmas? (*A rebel without a Claus*)

 ## Crazy About Christmas

What do snowmen eat for lunch? (*Icebergers* !)

How do snowmen travel around? (*By icicle*!)

How do snowmen greet each other? (*Ice to meet you*!)

What do you call a snowman in the summer? (*A puddle*)

What's a snowman's favorite Mexican food? (*Brrrrrr-itos*!)

What do you get if you cross an apple with a Christmas tree? (*A pineapple*)

What do you give a train driver for Christmas? (*Platform shoes*)

What did the big candle say to the little candle? (*I'm going out tonight*.)

What do you get if you cross Father Christmas with a detective? (*Santa Clues*)

What is Sherlock's favorite Christmas song? (*"I'll be Holmes for Christmas"*)

How do sheep in Mexico say Merry Christmas? (*Fleece Navidad*)

What is green, covered with tinsel and goes "ribbet ribbet"? (*A mistle-"toad"*)

What did the grape say to the peanut butter? (*'Tis the season to be jelly'*)

Why did the gingerbread man go to the doctor? (*Because he was feeling crummy*.)

What did the Christmas bell say to the other Christmas bell? (*Give me a ring sometime*.)

What kind of money do they use at the North Pole? (*Cold cash*)

What kind of music do elves like best? (*'Wrap' music*)

How did the chickens dance at the Christmas party? (Chick to chick)

December 18

KNOCK-KNOCK JOKES

Knock-Knock.
—Who's there? Mary.
—Mary who?
—Mary Christmas!

Knock. Knock.
—Who's there?
—Hanna.
—Hanna who?
—Hanna partridge in a pear tree!

Knock Knock.
—Who's there?
—Wayne.
—Wayne who?
—Wayne in a manger!

Knock Knock.
—Who's there?
—Donut.
—Donut who?
—Donut open 'til Christmas!

Knock Knock.
—Who's there?
—Elf.
—Elf who?
—Elf me wrap this present for Santa!

Knock Knock.
—Who's there?
—Yule.
—Yule who?
—Yule be sorry if you don't Holly up and Elf me wrap this present for Santa!

159

 *Crazy About Christmas*

Tongue Tied at Christmas

Ten tiny tin trains toot ten times.
Seven Santa's sang silly songs.
Tiny Timmy trims the tall tree with tinsel.
Ten tiny tin trains toot ten times.
Snow slows Santa's sleigh.
Candy cane cookies keep kids coming
Chilly chipper children cheerfully chant.
Pretty packages perfectly packed in paper.
Molly merrily mixes mincemeat.

Jokes

Do you know what would have happened if there had been Three Wise WOMEN instead of Three Wise MEN? The WOMEN would have:
– Asked directions,
– Arrived on time,
– Helped deliver the baby,
– Cleaned the stable,
– Made a casserole, and
– Brought practical gifts (like diapers!)

You know it's a tough Christmas when you get batteries with a note attached saying "Toy not included."

• • • • • • • • • •

"Last Christmas, Grandpa was feeling his age and found that shopping for Christmas gifts had become too difficult. So he decided to send checks to everyone instead.

"In each card he wrote, 'Buy your own present!' and mailed them early.

"He enjoyed the usual flurry of family festivities, and it was only after the holiday that he noticed that he had received very few cards in return. Puzzled over this, he went into his study, intending to write a couple of his relatives and ask what had happened. It was then, as he cleared off his cluttered desk that he got his answer. Under a stack of papers, he was horrified to find the gift checks which he had forgotten to enclose with the cards."

• • • • • • • • • •

It was a cold and misty Christmas morning in the very depth of Winter after a heavy fall of snow and only one farmer and the minister managed to arrive at the church for the morning service. "Well", said the clergyman "'I guess there's no point in having a service today." "Well that's not how I see it," said the farmer. "If only one cow turns up at feeding time, I still feed it.'

December 18

Cookie Cutter Gift Bags
Craft/Gift Wrap Idea

Materials

brown paper bag
gift wrap or cellophane or tissue paper
cookie cutters
pencil
scissors
ribbon
paper punch
glue

Directions

1. Lay paper bag flat on table.
2. Trace around your favorite cookie cutter with a pencil.
3. Carefully cut out the shape you traced.
4. Take a piece of wrapping paper, cellophane, or tissue paper and cut it out 2 inches bigger than the shape you just cut out.
5. Open up the bag and put glue on the inside edges of the design. Now place your paper or cellophane over the shape you cut out from the inside of the bag. Feel free to embellish your bag if you want to.
6. Fold the top of the bag over at least three inches.
7. Punch two holes about 2-3 inches apart on the flap.
8. Thread ribbon through the holes and tie a bow.

Quicky Tip: Brown paper bags are a great canvas for making gift bags. You don't have to cut out the images if you don't want to. You can rubber stamp on them or even paste an old Christmas card to the front of the bag. Whatever you do will be an original piece of art that will be appreciated it shows caring on the outside of the bag and on the inside..

Glazed Popcorn

A collected recipe from my college days. It was always a hit.

INGREDIENTS:

¼ cup butter/margarine
¼ cup light corn syrup/honey
½ cup sugar
1 package (3 oz) gelatin, any flavor
10 cups popped popcorn

INSTRUCTIONS:

1. Combine butter & corn syrup in a microwave safe bowl. Microwave until melted.
2. Add sugar & Jello powder. Stir. Put in microwave and cook until it comes to a rolling boil (doubles in size), about 2 to 3 minutes.
3. Pour over popcorn in a large bowl. Stir to coat.
4. Place on greased baking sheet and bake at 250° F for ½ hour, stirring every 10 minutes.
5. Cool & break apart. Store in airtight container.

Variation: Make several batches of this yummy popcorn in different flavors. Then layer the popcorn in a glass jar or mix together in a big bowl for a rainbow of colors and flavors.

Gift Suggestion: Decorate brown lunch bags (page 58) and fill with our sweet glazed popcorn.

December 19

The Legend Of The White Gifts
Phebe A. Curtiss

A great many years ago in a land far away from us there was a certain king who was dearly beloved by all of his people. Men admired him because he was strong and just. In all of his dealings they knew they could depend upon him. Every matter that came to his consideration was carefully weighed in his mind and his decisions were always wise. Women trusted him because he was pure and true, with lofty thoughts and high ambitions, and the children loved him because of his gentleness and tenderness toward them. He was never so burdened with affairs of state that he could not stop to speak a pleasant word of greeting to the tiniest child, and the very poorest of his subjects knew they could count upon his interest in them.

This deep-seated love and reverence for their king made the people of this country wish very much for a way in which to give expression to it so that he would understand it. Many consultations were held and one after another the plans suggested were rejected, but at last a most happy solution was found. It was rapidly circulated here and there and it met with the most hearty approval everywhere.

It was a plan for celebrating the King's birthday.

Of course, that had been done in many lands before, but there were certain features about this celebration which differed materially from anything that had ever been tried. They decided that on the King's birthday the people should all bring him gifts, but they wanted in some way to let him know that these gifts were the expression of a love on the part of the giver which was pure and true and unselfish, and in order to show that, it was decided that each gift should be a "White Gift."

The King heard about this beautiful plan, and it touched his heart in a wonderful way. He decided that he would do his part to carry out the idea and let his loving subjects know how much he appreciated their thoughtfulness.

You can just imagine the excitement there was all over the land as the King's birthday drew near. All sorts of loving sacrifices had been made and everyone was anxious to make his gift the very best he had to offer. At last the day dawned, and eagerly the people came dressed in white and carrying their white gifts. To their surprise they were ushered into a great, big room—the largest one in the palace. They stood in silence when they first entered it, for it was beautiful beyond all expression. It was a *white* room;--the floor was white marble; the ceiling looked like a mass of soft, white fluffy clouds; the walls were hung with beautiful white silken draperies, and all the furnishings were white. In one end of the room stood a stately white throne, and seated upon it was their beloved ruler and he was clad in shining white robes, and his attendants—all dressed in white—were grouped around him.

Then came the presentation of the gifts. What a wealth of them there was—and how different they were in value. In those days it was just as it is now—here were many people who had great wealth, and they brought gifts which were generous in proportion to their wealth.

One brought a handful of pearls, another a number of carved ivories. There were beautiful laces and silks and embroideries, all in pure white, and even splendid white chargers were brought to his majesty.

But many of the people were poor—some of them very poor—and their gifts were quite different from those I have been telling about. Some of the women brought handfuls of white rice, some of the boys brought their favorite white pigeons, and one dear little girl smilingly gave him a pure white rose.

It was wonderful to watch the King as each one came and kneeled before him as he presented his gift. He never seemed to notice whether the gift was great or small; he regarded not one gift above another so long as all were white. Never had the King been so happy as he was that day and never had such real joy filled the hearts of the people. They decided to use the same plan every year, and so it came to pass that year after year on the King's birthday the people came from here and there and everywhere and brought their white gifts—the gifts which showed that their love was pure, strong, true and without stain, and year after year the King sat in his white robes on the white throne in the great white room and it was always the same—he regarded not one gift above another so long as all were *white*.

Found in *Christmas Stories and Legends* ©1916

December 19

White Elephant Exchange
Game/Gift Exchange

What Christmas party would be complete without a white elephant game? This is a party pleaser, doubles as a party favor, all while allowing you to off load some poor unloved item in the hopes of getting something you will love, or at least tolerate.

Getting the gifts: There are a variety of rules that apply when selecting the type of gifts you will use in the white elephant game. Be sure all participants are on the same page. If you plan on having a white elephant game, it might be wise to specify what type of exchange it will be. It can be gag gifts, used items (or the re-gift), pamper me gifts, books, etc. Just be sure you do name it. If the gifts are to be purchased set a price limit to keep things fair. At my house you can't buy the gift it has to be something you already own that is nice, but not for you, like a tie or a game you never play.

How to play: One person goes first and play passes clockwise around the circle. The play consists of selecting and opening a wrapped gift, or stealing a gift that has been opened by a previous player. If your gift is stolen you get to open a new gift or take one from another player. (You can't take the gift that was stolen from you back.) Play continues around the circle with each player having one chance to steal a gift or keep the one they already have. Each gift can only be stolen twice. The third person to take it gets it, period. It is permissible to encourage people to steal your gift if you don't like it.

In my home when people arrive they take a number off the door as they enter that is used for various games all night, but when we start the white elephant we draw numbers at random. Then the person who drew first has one more chance to either play by drawing from the pile (I always add one more gift than people) or the last chance to steal. Then the game is over. Final rule you have to take home the gift you won or I will rewrap it for next year.

 Crazy About Christmas

Finger Food Party Night

Every year we have a holiday party. Our guest bring with them a white elephant gift and some type of food munchie to share.

A party should be something you enjoy too. Don't do it all yourself.

Below are a couple of simple recipes for the night.

Mistletoe Punch
30 servings

INGREDIENTS

- 1   6 ounce can frozen lemonade concentrate, thawed
- 1   6-ounce can frozen orange juice concentrate, thawed
- 6   cups water
- ½   cup grenadine syrup
- 1   quart ginger ale, chilled

INSTRUCTIONS

Combine lemonade, orange juice, water and grenadine syrup in a punch bowl. Just before serving add ginger ale.

I suggest making an ice ring earlier in the day with wafer-thin lemon slices and maraschino cherries. To make the ice ring fill a bundt or large muffin tin about half way up with water. Then drop in the cherries and lemon slices. It will keep your punch cool and look festive at the same time.

December 19

Herb and Garlic Cheese
Similar to Alouette®

INGREDIENTS

8 ounces cream cheese
1 tablespoon herb and garlic salad dressing mix
2 tablespoons milk

INSTRUCTIONS

1. In a food processor with a steel blade place cream cheese and 1 tablespoon of herb and garlic salad dressing mix and 1 tablespoon milk.

2. Blend until smooth. Check for consistency. Cheese should be spreadable. If it is still to thick add another tablespoon of milk.

3. Serve with a variety of crackers, sliced vegetables, or sliced French bread.

Ham Pinwheels

INGREDIENTS

2 (8 ounce) packages cream cheese
10 slices boiled ham
10 green onions

INSTRUCTIONS

1. Pat the ham slice with a paper towel to take off excess moisture

2. Spread softened cream cheese out to the edges of ham slice.

3. Place a clean and trimmed green onion across short end and roll up. Trim ends of onions and pack ham roll with extra cheese if necessary.

4. Repeat with each ham slice.

5. Refrigerate about one hour.

6. Cut each roll into slices about one inch long. Arrange with cut side up on a platter.

Amazing Crustless Quiche
Serves 8-10

INGREDIENTS

- 2¼ cups evaporated milk
- 3 eggs
- 4 egg whites
- ½ cup unbleached flour
- 2 teaspoons onion flakes or dehydrated onions
- ¼ teaspoon marjoram, dried and crushed
- ¾ cup shredded Monterey jack cheese
- ⅓ cup Parmesan cheese
- 4 slices Canadian bacon, diced

INSTRUCTIONS

1. Spray a 10-inch pie plate* or quiche pan with vegetable spray.
2. In blender combine milk, eggs, flour onion, marjoram, and a dash of salt. Cover; blend 15 seconds.
3. Pour into pie plate.
4. Dice up 4 slices of Canadian bacon and sprinkle over egg mix.
5. Top with cheeses.
6. Bake in a 400° F oven for 20 to 25 minutes or till a knife inserted near-center comes out clean.
7. Let stand 5 minutes.

VARIATION: You can make 24 mini quiches by pouring the egg mix into greased mini-muffin tin and then adding diced ham and cheese to each cup. Bake these for 10-12 minutes or until knife inserted near-center comes out clean. After they cool they can be removed from tin and placed on a plate. Now you have true finger food.

Note: You can add other items to the filling, like mushrooms, spinach, different cheeses, artichokes, the list goes on and on. Just know that watery vegetables should be pre-cooked before adding to allow quiche to set up properly.

December 19

Chicken Nut Puffs
Makes about 6 dozen puffs

Ingredients

- 1½ cups finely chopped cooked rotisserie chicken or 9.75 ounces can chicken drained
- 3 cup chopped almonds, toasted
- 1 cup chicken broth
- ½ cup vegetable oil
- 2 teaspoons Worcestershire sauce
- 1 tablespoon dried parsley flakes
- 1 teaspoon seasoned salt
- ½ teaspoon celery seed
- ⅛ teaspoon cayenne pepper
- 1 cup all-purpose flour
- 4 eggs

Instructions

1. Combine the chicken and almonds, set aside.
2. In a large saucepan, combine broth, oil, Worcestershire sauce, parsley, seasoned salt, celery, and cayenne pepper. Bring to a boil
3. Add flour all at once, stir until a smooth ball forms.
4. Remove from heat and let rest for 5 minutes.
5. Add eggs, one at a time, beating well after each addition. Beat until smooth.
6. Stir in chicken and almonds.
7. Drop by heaping teaspoonfuls onto a greased baking sheet.
8. Bake at 450° for 12-14 minutes or until golden brown.
9. Serve warm.

Streusel Linzer Squares
Serves 12

INGREDIENTS

- 1½ cups flour
- ¼ teaspoon salt
- 1¼ cups ground almonds (about 5 ounces)
- ¾ cup unsalted butter, softened (1½ sticks)
- 1 cup powdered sugar
- 2 egg yolks
- 1 teaspoon vanilla extract
- 2 teaspoon almond extract
- 1 (12-ounce) jar seedless, red raspberry preserves
- 1 tablespoon lemon juice

INSTRUCTIONS

1. Preheat oven to 350° F. Lightly grease a 9-inch square baking pan.
2. In a medium bowl, combine flour, salt, and 1 cup almonds. Mix lightly
3. In another medium bowl, using a hand-held electric mixer, mix butter and ¾ cup powdered sugar until light and fluffy. Add egg yolks, vanilla, and almond extract and beat until well combined. Add flour mixture and stir until just blended.
4. Press two-thirds of dough onto bottom of pan. In a small bowl, stir together preserves and lemon juice. Spread preserves evenly over dough.
5. Add ¼ cup almonds to remaining dough and with your hands blend together. Mixture will be crumbly. Scatter over preserves.
6. Bake until golden brown, 35 to 40 minutes.
7. Let cool in pan on wire rack.
8. When cool sprinkle remaining powdered sugar over top and cut into 12 squares. For parties I often cut these into two-inch squares so that they last a little longer.

December 20

The First Christmas Rose
An Old Legend

The sun had dropped below the western hills of Judea, and the stillness of night had covered the earth. The heavens were illumined only by numberless stars, which shone the brighter for the darkness of the sky. No sound was heard but the occasional howl of a jackal or the bleat of a lamb in the sheepfold. Inside a tent on the hillside slept the shepherd, Berachah, and his daughter, Madelon. The little girl lay restless,--sleeping, waking, dreaming, until at last she roused herself and looked about her.

"Father," she whispered, "oh, my father, awake. I fear for the sheep."

The shepherd turned himself and reached for his staff. "What nearest thou, daughter! The dogs are asleep. Hast thou been burdened by an evil dream?"

"Nay, but father," she answered, "seest thou not the light? Hearest thou not the voice?"

Berachah gathered his mantle about him, rose, looked over the hills toward Bethlehem, and listened. The olive trees on yonder slope were casting their shadows in a marvellous light, unlike daybreak or sunset, or even the light of the moon. By the camp-fire below on the hillside the shepherds on watch were rousing themselves. Berachah waited and wondered, while Madelon clung to his side. Suddenly a sound rang out in the stillness. Madelon pressed still closer.

"It is the voice of an angel, my daughter. What it means I know not. Neither understand I this light." Berachah fell on his knees and prayed.

"Fear not: for, behold, I bring you good tidings of great joy, which shall be to all people. For unto you is born this day in the city of David a Saviour, which is Christ the Lord. And this shall be a sign unto you; Ye shall find the babe wrapped in swaddling clothes, lying in a manger."

The voice of the angel died away, and the air was filled with music. Berachah raised Madelon to her feet. "Ah, daughter," said he, "It is the wonder night so long expected. To us hath it been given to see the sign. It is the Messiah who hath come, the Messiah, whose name shall be called Wonderful, Counselor, the mighty God, the Everlasting Father, the Prince of Peace. He it is who shall reign on the throne of David, he it is who shall redeem Israel."

Slowly up the hillside toiled the shepherds to the tent of Berachah, their chief, who rose to greet them eagerly.

 Crazy About Christmas

"What think you of the wonder night and of the sign?" he queried. "Are we not above all others honored, thus to learn of the Messiah's coming!"

"Yea, and Berachah," replied their spokesman, Simon, "believest thou not that we should worship the infant King! Let us now go to Bethlehem, and see this thing which has come to pass."

A murmur of protest came from the edge of the circle, and one or two turned impatiently away, whispering of duty toward flocks, and the folly of searching for a new-born baby in the city of Bethlehem. Hardheaded, practical men were these, whose hearts had not been touched by vision or by song.

The others, however, turned expectantly toward Berachah, awaiting his decision. "Truly," said Jude, "the angel of the Lord hath given us the sign in order that we might go to worship Him. How can we then do otherwise? We shall find Him, as we have heard, lying in a manger. Let us not tarry, but let us gather our choicest treasures to lay at His feet, and set out without delay across the hills toward Bethlehem."

"Oh, my father," whispered Madelon, "permit me to go with thee." Berachah did not hear her, but turned and bade the men gather together their gifts.

"I, too, father?" asked Madelon. Still Berachah said nothing. Madelon slipped back into the tent, and throwing her arms around Melampo, her shepherd dog, whispered in his ear. Soon the shepherds returned with their gifts. Simple treasures they were,--a pair of doves, a fine wool blanket, some eggs, some honey, some late autumn fruits. Berachah had searched for the finest of his flock,--a snow-white lamb. Across the hills toward Bethlehem in the quiet, star-lit night they journeyed. As they moved silently along, the snow beneath their feet was changed to grass and flowers, and the icicles which had dropped from the trees covered their pathway like stars in the Milky Way.

Following at a distance, yet close enough to see them, came Madelon with Melampo at her heels. Over the hills they travelled on until Madelon lost sight of their own hillside. Farther and farther the shepherds went until they passed David's well, and entered the city. Berachah led the way.

"How shall we know?" whispered Simon. And the others answered, "Hush, we must await the sign."

When at last they had compassed the crescent of Bethlehem's hills, they halted by an open doorway at a signal from their leader. "The manger," they joyfully murmured, "the manger! We have found the new-born King!"

One by one the shepherds entered. One by one they fell on their knees. Away in the shadow stood the little girl, her hand on Melampo's head. In wonder she gazed while the shepherds presented their gifts, and were permitted each to hold for a moment the new-born Saviour.

December 20

Melampo, the shepherd dog, crouched on the ground, as if he too, like the ox and the ass within, would worship the Child. Madelon turned toward the darkness weeping. Then, lifting her face to heaven, she prayed that God would bless Mother and Baby. Melampo moved closer to her, dumbly offering his companionship, and, raising his head, seemed to join in her petition. Once more she looked at the worshipping circle.

"Alas," she grieved, "no gift have I for the infant Saviour. Would that I had but a flower to place in His hand."

Suddenly Melampo stirred by her side, and as she turned again from the manger she saw before her an angel, the light from whose face illumined the darkness, and whose look of tenderness rested on her tear-stained eyes.

"Why grievest thou, maiden?" asked the angel.

"That I come empty-handed to the cradle of the Saviour, that I bring no gift to greet Him," she murmured.

"The gift of thine heart, that is the best of all," answered the angel.

"But that thou mayst carry something to the manger, see, I will strike with my staff upon the ground."

Wonderingly Madelon waited. From the dry earth wherever the angel's staff had touched sprang fair, white roses. Timidly she stretched out her hand toward the nearest ones. In the light of the angel's smile she gathered them, until her arms were filled with flowers. Again she turned toward the manger, and quietly slipped to the circle of kneeling shepherds.

Closer she crept to the Child, longing, yet fearing, to offer her gift.

"How shall I know," she pondered, "whether He will receive this my gift as His own?"

Berachah gazed in amazement at Madelon and the roses which she held. How came his child there, his child whom he had left safe on the hillside? And whence came such flowers! Truly this was a wonder night.

Step by step she neared the manger, knelt, and placed a rose in the Baby's hand. As the shepherds watched in silence, Mary bent over her Child, and Madelon waited for a sign. "Will He accept them?" she questioned. "How, oh, how shall I know?" As she prayed in humble silence, the Baby's eyes opened slowly, and over His face spread a smile.

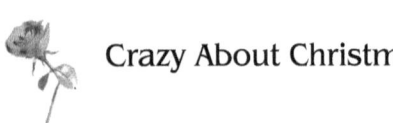 Crazy About Christmas

Stained Glass Jars
Craft/Gift

MATERIALS

white glue
food coloring
liquid lead paint or black fabric paint
printed rose pattern
glass jar
plastic or disposable cups
brush or craft sticks

DIRECTIONS:

1. Copy or trace the rose pattern and make it the size that will fit on your jar.
2. Tape the printed pattern inside the jar, Trace the pattern outlines with liquid lead or fabric paint and let dry.
3. Put about a tablespoon of white glue in a disposable container and add a drop or two of food coloring, mixing well with a craft stick. Don't overdo the food coloring because you want the glue part of the mixture to dry clear, leaving behind a color similar to stained glass.
4. Make pots of other colors in the same way, mixing the food coloring if necessary to obtain different shades i.e. blue and red for a mauve color, or red and yellow for orange.
5. Using a brush or craft stick to spread the glue coloring in a thick layer, almost as thick as the lead outlines, filling in the empty space of your design with different colors. If the area is tiny, use a toothpick to spread the glue mixture. If you want a marbled look in your paint add a drop of different color and use a toothpick to swirl it around.
6. Let the rose dry overnight on the glass. To wash this jar you will need to use just a damp cloth. Remember even if it looks like stain glass if you try to wash it the glue will dissolve.

December 20

VARIATION: *If you think you will have trouble working on the jar directly. Use a picture frame with glass in it for your workspace. Place the design under the glass and tape in place, then follow the directions above. When the paint is sufficiently dry, slowly peel the window decal off the glass. Now you can stick it easily to a jar, house window, car window, mirror or almost anything made of glass. When you want to change the look, just take it off and make a new one. Enjoy!*

TIP: If you want to use different patterns try looking for clip art with simple lines.

NOTE: Plaid makes regular stain glass window paint called Galaxy Glass if you are interested in something a little more permanent.

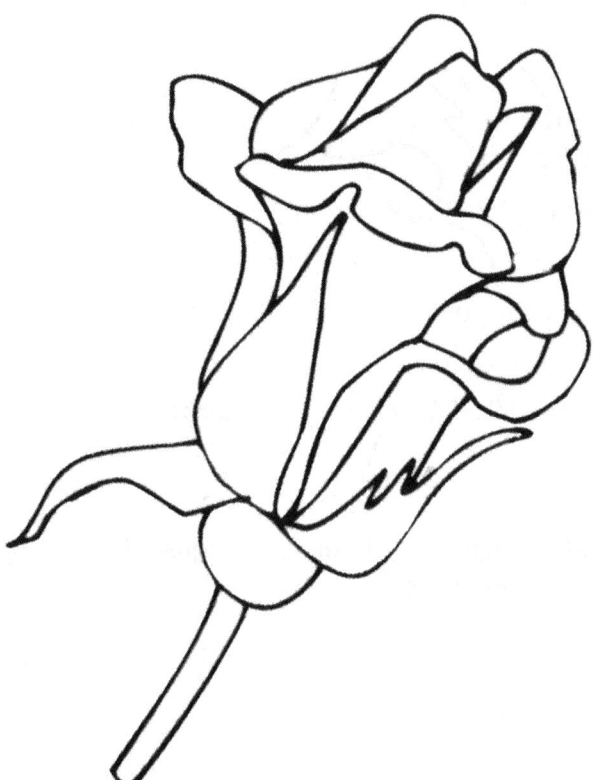

Sand Art Brownies
Gift Jar or 12 brownies

INGREDIENTS

- ⅔ teaspoon salt
- ½ cup + 2 tablespoons flour
- 1/3 cup cocoa
- ½ cup flour
- ⅔ cup brown sugar
- ⅔ cup sugar
- ½ cup semi-sweet chocolate chips
- ½ cup vanilla flavored baking chips
- ½ cup walnuts (or to fill balance of jar space)

INSTRUCTIONS

1. If you are putting this in a gift jar make sure that it is a wide mouth quart jar. Place ingredients in jar in the order given and tamp down between layers.
2. Attach the following directions to the jar.

> Combine the contents of this jar with 1 teaspoon vanilla extract
>
> 2/3 cups vegetable oil and 3 eggs.
>
> Pour into a greased 9x9 square pan and bake at 350°F for 25-30 minutes.

3. You can skip putting ingredients in the jar and just place all the ingredients in bowl and follow the directions above.

December 21

THE STAR
By Florence M. Kingsley

Once upon a time in a country far away from here, there lived a little girl named Ruth. Ruth's home was not at all like our houses, for she lived in a little tower on top of the great stone wall that surrounded the town of Bethlehem. Ruth's father was the hotel-keeper—the Bible says the "inn keeper." This inn was not at all like our hotels, either. There was a great open yard, which was called the courtyard. All about this yard were little rooms and each traveler who came to the hotel rented one. The inn stood near the great stone wall of the city, so that as Ruth stood, one night, looking out of the tower window, she looked directly into the courtyard. It was truly a strange sight that met her eyes. So many people were coming to the inn, for the King had made a law that every man should come back to the city where his father used to live to be counted and to pay his taxes. Some of the people came on the backs of camels, with great rolls of bedding and their dishes for cooking upon the back of the beast. Some of them came on little donkeys, and on their backs too were the bedding and the dishes. Some of the people came walking—slowly; they were so tired. Many miles some of them had come. As Ruth looked down into the courtyard, she saw the camels being led to their places by their masters, she heard the snap of the whips, she saw the sparks shoot up from the fires that were kindled in the courtyard, where each person was preparing his own supper; she heard the cries of the tired, hungry little children.

Presently her mother, who was cooking supper, came over to the window and said, "Ruthie, thou shalt hide in the house until all those people are gone. Dost thou understand?"

"Yes, my mother," said the child, and she left the window to follow her mother back to the stove, limping painfully, for little Ruth was a cripple. Her mother stooped suddenly and caught the child in her arms.

"My poor little lamb. It was a mule's kick, just six years ago, that hurt your poor back and made you lame."

"Never mind, my mother. My back does not ache today, and lately when the light of the strange new star has shone down upon my bed my back has felt so much stronger and I have felt so happy, as though I could climb upon the rays of the star and up, up into the sky and above the stars!"

Her mother shook her head sadly. "Thou art not likely to climb much, now or ever, but come, the supper is ready; let us go to find your father. I wonder what keeps him."

They found the father standing at the gate of the courtyard, talking to a man and woman who had just arrived. The man was tall, with a long beard, and he led by a rope a snow-white mule, on which sat the drooping figure of the woman. As Ruth and her mother came near,

 Crazy About Christmas

they heard the father say, "But I tell thee that there is no more room in the inn. Hast thou no friends where thou canst go to spend the night?" The man shook his head. "No, none," he answered. "I care not for myself, but my poor wife." Little Ruth pulled at her mother's dress. "Mother, the oxen sleep out under the stars these warm nights and the straw in the caves is clean and warm; I have made a bed there for my little lamb."

Ruth's mother bowed before the tall man. "Thou didst hear the child. It is as she says—the straw is clean and warm." The tall man bowed his head. "We shall be very glad to stay," and he helped the sweet-faced woman down from the donkey's back and led her away to the cave stable, while the little Ruth and her mother hurried up the stairs that they might send a bowl of porridge to the sweet-faced woman, and a sup of new milk, as well.

That night when little Ruth lay down in her bed, the rays of the beautiful new star shone through the window more brightly than before. They seemed to soothe the tired aching shoulders. She fell asleep and dreamed that the beautiful, bright star burst and out of it came countless angels, who sang in the night:

"Glory to God in the highest, peace on earth, good will to men." And then it was morning and her mother was bending over her and saying, "Awake, awake, little Ruth. Mother has something to tell thee." Then as the eyes opened slowly—"The angels came in the night, little one, and left a Baby to lay beside your little white lamb in the manger."

That afternoon, Ruth went with her mother to the fountain. The mother turned aside to talk to the other women of the town about the strange things heard and seen the night before, but Ruth went on and sat down by the edge of the fountain. The child, was not frightened, for strangers came often to the well, but never had she seen men who looked like the three who now came towards her. The first one, a tall man with a long white beard, came close to Ruth and said, "Canst tell us, child, where is born he that is called the King of the Jews?"

"I know of no king," she answered, "but last night while the star was shining, the angels brought a baby to lie beside my white lamb in the manger." The stranger bowed his head. "That must be he. Wilt thou show us the way to Him, my child?" So Ruth ran and her mother led the three men to the cave and "when they saw the Child, they rejoiced with exceeding great joy, and opening their gifts, they presented unto Him gold, and frankincense and myrrh," with wonderful jewels, so that Ruth's mother's eyes shone with wonder, but little Ruth saw only the Baby, which lay asleep on its mother's breast.

"If only I might hold Him in my arms," she thought, but was afraid to ask.

After a few days, the strangers left Bethlehem, all but the three—the man, whose name was Joseph, and Mary, his wife, and the Baby. Then, as of old, little Ruth played about the courtyard and the white lamb frolicked at her side. Often she dropped to her knees to press the little woolly white head against her breast, while she murmured: "My little lamb, my very, very own. I love you, lambie," and then together they would steal over to the entrance of the cave to peep in at the Baby, and always she thought, "If I only might touch his hand," but was afraid to ask. One night as she lay in her bed, she thought to herself: "Oh, I wish I had a beautiful gift for him, such as the wise men brought, but I have nothing at all to offer and I love him so much." Just then the light of the star, which was nightly fading, fell across the foot of the bed and shone full upon the white lamb which lay asleep at her feet—and then she thought of something. The next morning she arose with her face shining with joy. She dressed carefully and with the white lamb held close to her breast, went slowly and painfully down the stairway and over to the door of the cave. "I have come," she said, "to worship Him, and I have brought Him—my white lamb." The mother smiled at the lame child, then she lifted the Baby from her breast and placed Him in the arms of the little maid who knelt at her feet.

A few days after, an angel came to the father, Joseph, and told him to take the Baby and hurry to the land of Egypt, for the wicked King wanted to do it harm, and so these three—the father, mother and Baby—went by night to the far country of Egypt. And the star grew dimmer and dimmer and passed away forever from the skies over Bethlehem, but little Ruth grew straight and strong and beautiful as the almond trees in the orchard, and all the people who saw her were amazed, for Ruth was once a cripple.

"It was the light of the strange star," her mother said, but little Ruth knew it was the touch of the blessed Christ-Child, who was once folded against her heart.

Linda S. Day ©1997

Found in *Christmas Stories And Legends*, compiled by
PHEBE A. CURTISS, ©1916

Dishtowel Angel
Craft/ Gift/Decoration

MATERIALS:

1 dishtowel
1 washcloth
1 Pot holder
Ribbon

DIRECTIONS

1. Fanfold the dishtowel lengthwise. Fold in half. Tie a ribbon about 2 to 3 inches from fold, to form the head.

2. Fanfold the washcloth. This forms the arms.

3. Gather the potholder with the loop along top edge. This forms the wings.

4. Place the washcloth on top of the potholder and secure in the center with a ribbon

5. Lay body (towel) on top of potholder and washcloth. Bring the arms (washcloth) around the neck and tie arms together 1 inch from ends to form the hands and hold all the pieces together.

6. Take excess ribbon from potholder and tie in a bow around neck for added security or tie ends together and form a loop for hanging.

7. Add a wooden spoon, or flowers at her hands.

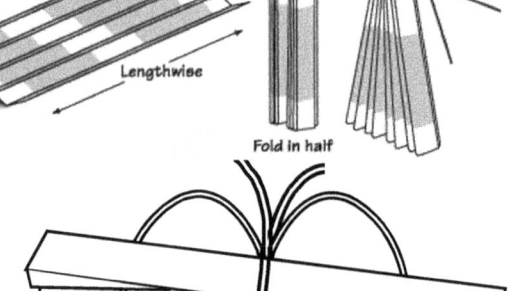

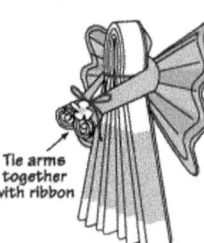

December 21

Cream Puffs
Serves 12

INGREDIENTS

1	cup water
½	cup butter
1	cup all-purpose flour
4	eggs
	pudding -any flavor, whipped cream, ice cream or fruit filling

INSTRUCTIONS

1. Heat oven to 400° Heat water and butter to a rolling boil.
2. Add flour and mix vigorously over heat for about 1 minute or until mixture forms a ball.
3. Remove from heat. Beat in eggs *one* at a time, until smooth.
4. Drop dough by scant ¼ cupfuls 3 inches apart onto ungreased baking sheet.
5. Bake for 35-40 minutes or until puffed and golden brown.
6. Cool away from draft.
7. Cut off tops. Pull out any soft dough.
8. Carefully fill puffs with pudding or whipped cream just before serving.
9. Replace tops, dust with confectioners' sugar
10. Refrigerate until time to serve.

Variation: Poke a hole in the side with a knife or your finger and then fill the inside with anything that can go through a pastry bag with a plain tip.

Variation 2: If you shape the dough into fingers or make them about 4 inches long and 1½ wide you will have the shape for an Eclair. Then we they are cool and filled you can frost them with chocolate icing.

The magical dust of
Christmas glittered on
the cheeks of humanity
ever so briefly,
reminding us of what is
worth having and what
we were intended to be.
— Max Lucado —

December 22

Two Babes in a Manger
Author unknown

In 1994, two Americans answered an invitation from the Russian Department of Education to teach morals and ethics (based on biblical principles) in the public schools. They were invited to teach at prisons, businesses, the fire and police departments and a large orphanage. About 100 boys and girls who had been abandoned, abused, and left in the care of a government-run program were in the orphanage. They relate the following story in their own words:

It was nearing the holiday season, 1994, time for our orphans to hear, for the first time, the traditional story of Christmas. We told them about Mary and Joseph arriving in Bethlehem. Finding no room in the inn, the couple went to a stable, where the baby Jesus was born and placed in a manger.

Throughout the story, the children and orphanage staff sat in amazement as they listened. Some sat on the edges of their stools, trying to grasp every word. Completing the story, we gave the children three small pieces of cardboard to make a crude manger. Each child was given a small paper square, cut from yellow napkins I had brought with me. No colored paper was available in the city.

Following instructions, the children tore the paper and carefully laid strips in the manger for straw. Small squares of flannel, cut from a worn-out nightgown an American lady was throwing away as she left Russia, were used for the baby's blanket. A doll-like baby was cut from tan felt we had brought from the United States.

The orphans were busy assembling their manger as I walked among them to see if they needed any help. All went well until I got to one table where little Misha sat. He looked to be about 6 years old and had finished his project. As I looked at the little boy's manger, I was startled to see not one, but two babies in the manger. Quickly, I called for the translator to ask the lad why there were two babies in the manger. Crossing his arms in front of him and looking at this completed manger scene, the child began to repeat the story very seriously.

For such a young boy, who had only heard the Christmas story once, he related the happenings accurately...until he came to the part where Mary put the baby Jesus in the manger. Then Misha started to ad-lib. He made up his own ending to the story as he said,

"And when Maria laid the baby in the manger, Jesus looked at me and asked me if I had a place to stay.

I told him I have no mamma and I have no papa, so I don't have any place to stay. Then Jesus told me I could stay with him. But I told him I couldn't, because I didn't have a gift to give him like everybody else did. But I wanted to stay with Jesus so much, so I thought about what I had that maybe I could use for a gift. I thought maybe if I kept him warm, that would be a good gift.

So I asked Jesus, "If I keep you warm, will that be a good enough gift?"

And Jesus told me, "If you keep me warm, that will be the best gift anybody ever gave me."

"So I got into the manger, and then Jesus looked at me and he told me I could stay with him...for always."

As little Misha finished his story, his eyes brimmed full of tears that splashed down his little cheeks. Putting his hand over his face, his head dropped to the table and his shoulders shook as he sobbed and sobbed.

The little orphan had found someone who would never abandon nor abuse him, someone who would stay with him...FOR ALWAYS. I've learned that it's not what you have in your life, but who you have in your life that counts.

December 22

Fruity Playdough
Craft

MATERIALS

- 2 cups flour
- 1 cup salt
- 4 teaspoons cream of tarter
- 2 cups water
- 2 tablespoons oil
- 3 packs unsweetened powdered drink mix

DIRECTIONS

1. Place flour, salt, cream of tartar, and drink mix into medium size saucepan and mix together.
2. Add water and oil and mix well.
3. Cook on low heat. Stir constantly to avoid burning until mixture becomes a ball and follows the spoon, cleaning the side of the pan.
4. Remove, mixture and place on counter top.
5. Knead dough (it will be hot) on counter ten to twelve times or until smooth.
6. When cool store in air tight containers or zipper bags. .

> *Quicky Tip:* This dough is the best recipe I have ever used. It stays soft for a really long time if stored properly. It smells good and best of all if the kids eat it they won't get sick. Your going to want to make several batches in different colors/flavors.
>
> *Variation:* For a little sparkle, put glitter in one batch of dough.
> *Variation 2:* Don't add the unsweetened drink mix and add a 1 tbsp ground cinnamon, 2 tsp ground ginger, 1 tsp ground nutmeg, 1 tsp ground cloves and mix as usual to make Gingerbread Playdough.

Gingerbread Muffins
Makes 24

INGREDIENTS

1	teaspoon baking soda	½	cup dark corn syrup
½	cup buttermilk	2	cups flour
¼	cup shortening	2	teaspoons ground ginger
½	cup granulated sugar	1½	teaspoon cinnamon
½	cup packed dark brown sugar	½	teaspoon ground allspice
2	eggs	½	teaspoon ground cloves

INSTRUCTIONS

1. In a small bowl, dissolve baking soda in buttermilk, stirring to blend.
2. Beat shortening, sugar, brown sugar together with an electric mixer until light and fluffy, about 5 minutes. Continue mixing while you add the eggs one at a time, Finish by mixing in the corn syrups.
3. In a medium bowl sift together flour, ginger, cinnamon, allspice, and cloves. Add to butter mixture, alternating with buttermilk mixture, beating well after each addition, until well blended. Cover and refrigerate 24 hours or as long as 2 days.
4. Preheat oven to 350°F. Grease 24 muffin tins. Fill tins about three-fourths full. Bake 20 to 25 minutes or until only moist crumbs cling to a toothpick or knife inserted into the muffins.

QUICKY TIPS: Make the batter one or two days in advance of Christmas and put it in the refrigerator so that you can just put them in the oven in the morning and enjoy the heavenly aroma wafting through the house as the kids are opening presents.

VARIATION: Place chopped walnuts on top of batter before baking or chopped candied ginger...

December 23

A Christmas Orange
Author unknown

In the very early 1800s, a young boy about fourteen years old named John lived in an orphanage, in England along with several other children. Orphanages were dreaded. "Orphan" meant unwanted and unloved. The orphanage was administered by a master and his wife, they were short on love but high on discipline. No child-like play, no expressions of compassion, no understanding.

Every day of the year was spent working. They worked in gardens, cleaned, sewed, and cooked sometimes for wealthy children. They were up at dawn and worked until dark and usually received only one meal a day. However hey were very grateful because they were taught to be hard workers. John had absolutely nothing to call his own. None of the children did.

Christmas was the one-day of the year when the children did not work and received a gift. There was a gift for children—something to call their own. This special gift was an orange. John had been in the orphanage long enough to look forward with delight and anticipation of this special day of Christmas and to the orange he would receive.

In England, and to John and his orphan companions, an orange was a rare and special gift. It h ad an unusual aroma of something they smelled only at Christmas. The children prized it so much that they kept in for several days, weeks and even months—protecting it, smelling it, touching it, and loving it. Usually they tried to savor and preserve it for so long that it rotted before they ever peeled it to enjoy the sweet juice.

Many thoughts were expressed this year as Christmastime approached. The children would say, "I will keep mine the longest." They always talked about how big their last orange was how long they had kept it. John usually slept with his next to his pillow. He would put it right by his nose and smell of its goodness, holding it tenderly and carefully as not to bruise it. He would dream of children all over the world smelling the sweet aroma of oranges. It gave him security and a sense of well being, hope and dreams of a future filled with good food and a life different from this meager existence.

This year John was overjoyed by the Christmas season. He was becoming a man. He knew he was becoming stronger and soon he would be old enough to leave. He was excited by this anticipation and excited about Christmas. He would save his orange until his birthday in July. If he preserved it very carefully, kept it cool, and did not drop it, he might be able to eat it on h is birthday.

Christmas Day finally came. The children were so excited as they entered the big dining hall. John could smell the unusual aroma of meat. In his excitement and because of his oversized feet, he tripped, causing a disturbance. Immediately the master roared, "John, leave the hall and there will be no orange for you this year." John's heart broke wide open. He began to cry. He turned and ran back to the cold room and his corner so the small children would not see his anguish.

A little while later, he heard the door open, and each of the children entered. Little Elizabeth, with her hair falling over her shoulders, a smile on her face, and tears in her eyes, held out a piece of rag to John. "Here, John," she said, "this is for your." Her sweet and innocent face touched John as he reached for the tiny package.

As he lifted back the edges of the rag, he saw a big juicy orange all peeled and quartered…and then he realized what they had done. Each had sacrificed a quarter of their own orange to create a big, beautiful orange for John.

John never forgot the sharing, love and personal sacrifice his friends had shown him that Christmas Day. John's beginning was meager; however, his growth to manhood was rewarded by wealth and success. In memory of that day, every year he would send oranges all over the world to children everywhere. His desire was that no child would ever spend Christmas without a special Christmas orange.

December 23

Pomander Ball
Traditional Craft/Air Freshener

MATERIALS

2 unblemished oranges
   (or try lemons or lime)
Push pin or toothpick
Whole cloves
Tissue paper
4 feet of Ribbon

Spice Mixture:
3 tablespoons. ground cinnamon
3 tablespoons ground cloves
3 tablespoons ground nutmeg
3 tablespoons. ground ginger
3 tablespoons Orris root powder (a herb fixative that holds the scent of the spices) *optional*

DIRECTIONS

1. Making a Pomander Ball is easy, but can take some time! Simply stick a clove directly into an orange (or any of the other fruits listed above). You may want to use a toothpick or push pin to make the first punctures so that the cloves are easier to insert. It seems that everyone has his or her own method when it comes to filling a ball! You don't have to fill the entire ball though—try a pattern or design if you feel inspired.
2. Once the ball is completely studded with cloves, roll it in the spice mixture, wrap it in tissue paper and set it aside for a couple of weeks in a cool dry spot so that it will dry.
3. Once dried, tie a ribbon around the ball for hanging. Multiple pomander balls also look beautiful displayed together in a large decorative bowl.

Orris root powder is generally found in shops that carry dried herbs or online. Orris root is only used to preserve the scent of the spices you can make them without it if you can't find any.

 Crazy About Christmas

Caramelized Orange Flan
Serves 8

INGREDIENTS

2 ¼   cups freshly squeezed orange juice
6   large egg yolks
3   large eggs
¾   cup granulated sugar
1   pinch salt
1   cinnamon stick
3   cups heavy cream

Caramel
¾   cup granulated sugar
¼   cup water

INSTRUCTIONS

1. To prepare the caramel: In a small heavy bottomed pan, mix together the sugar and water. Cook the sugar over medium heat until it dissolves. Increase to high heat and cook until it is golden amber. Remove caramel from the heat and pour into individual ramekins or custard cups Set them aside to harden.

2. Preheat the oven to 300 degrees.

3. In a small heavy bottomed sauce pan reduce the orange juice over medium heat to one cup.

4. In a mixing bowl whisk together the egg yolks, eggs, sugar and salt. Stir in the reduced orange juice.

5. In a separate sauce pan, warm the cream along with the cinnamon until scalded. Take off of the heat and whisk into the orange mixture. Remove the cinnamon stick.

6. Fill the ramekins with the orange flan mixture. Place them in a large baking pan. Place in the middle of the oven and carefully fill pan half way up the ramekin with water. Cover with foil. Bake until just set 45- 50 minutes. Remove from pan and refrigerate until cooled. To unmold, run a small knife around the inside edge of each ramekin, turning it over on to the plate.

December 24

A Different Kind of Christmas
Author Unknown

Martha had tried to ignore the approach of Christmas. She would have kept it almost entirely out of her thoughts if Jed had not come eagerly into the cabin one day, stomping the snow from his cold feet as he said in an excited voice. "Martha, we're going to have a Christmas tree this year. I spotted a cedar on the rise out south of the wheat field, over near the Norton's place. It's a scrubby thing, but it will still be the kind of Christmas we used to have."

As she shook her head, Martha noticed that Daniel glanced quickly up from the corner where he was playing, patiently tying together some sticks with bits of string left over from the quilt she had tied a few days earlier. She drew Jed as far away from the boy as possible.

"I don't want a tree," she said. "We won't be celebrating Christmas. Even a tree couldn't make it the kind of Christmas we used to have."

"Martha, we've got to something for the boy at least. Children set such store by Christmas."

Don't you think I know? All those years of fixing things for Maybelle and Tella. I know all about the kids and Christmas." She stopped and drew a deep breath, glancing over to see Daniel was occupied and not listening. "But I can't do those things for him. It would be like a knife in the heart, fixing a tree and baking cookies and making things for another woman's child when my own girls are back there on that prairie."

"Martha, Martha," Jed said softly. "It has been almost a year and half. That's over, and Danny needs you. He needs a Christmas like he remembers." She turned her back to his pleading face. "I can't, I just can't," she said.

Jed touched her shoulder gently. "I know how hard it is for you, Martha, but think of the boy." He turned and went back out into the snowy weather.

Think of the boy. Why should she think of them, when her own children, her two blue-eyed, golden-curled daughters, had been left in a shallow grave beside the trail back there on that endless, empty prairie? The boy came to her not because she had wanted him, but because she couldn't say "no" to the bishop back in Salt Lake City last April before they came to settle in the valley.

Bishop Clay had brought Daniel to her and Jed one day and asked for them to care for Daniel because his mother had died on the trek to the valley last summer and his pa had passed away just a week before and he need a good home.

Jed had gripped the bishop's hand and with tears in his eyes, thanked him, but Martha had turned away from the sight of the thin, ragged, six-year-old boy who stood before them, not fast enough however, to miss the sudden brief smile he flashed at her, a smile that should have caught her heart and opened it wide. Her heart was closed, though, locked tightly around the memory of the two gentle little girls. She didn't want a noisy, rowdy boy hanging around, disturbing those memories, filling the cabin with a boy's loud games.

Yet she had taken him, because she felt like she had no choice. Faced with the bishop's request and Jed's obvious joy, she couldn't refuse. He came with them out to the new valley west of the Salt Lake settlement and had proved himself a great help to Jed, despite his young age. Sometimes Martha felt pity for him, but she didn't love him. With Jed, it was different. He had accepted Daniel immediately as his own son and enjoyed having a boy with him. They had a special relationship.

Daniel mentioned Christmas only once. One day it was too cold and snowy to play outside and he had been humming softly to himself as he played in his corner. Suddenly, he looked up at Martha and asked, "Can you sing, Aunt Martha?"

Martha paused and straightened up from the table where she was kneading bread. She used to sing for her girls all the time. "No, I can't Daniel," she said. "Not anymore."

"My mother used to sing a pretty song at Christmas," he said. "I wish I could remember it."

On the day before Christmas, Jed went through the deep snow to do some chores for their neighbor, who was ill. Daniel was alone outside most of the day, although he made several rather furtive trips in and out of the cabin. On one trip, he took the sticks he had been tying together.

Toward evening, Martha went out to the stable to milk Rosie, since Jed had not yet returned. As she approached, she saw there was a light inside. Opening the door softly, she peered within. Daniel had lit the barn lantern, and with its glow, he knelt in the straw by Rosie's stall. In front of him were the sticks he had tied together, which Martha recognized now as a crude cradle. It held Stella's rag doll, all wrapped up in the white shawl Martha kept in her trunk. Her first impulse was to rush in and snatch it, but she stopped because the scene was strangely beautiful in the soft light from the lantern. Rosie and the two sheep stood close by, watching Daniel. He seemed to be addressing them when he spoke.

"The shepherds came following the star," he was saying. "And they found the baby Jesus who had been born in a stable." He paused for a moment, then went on. "And his mother loved him."

Martha felt suddenly that she couldn't breathe. Another mother, another day, had loved her boy, and had told him the beautiful story of the Christ Child with such love that he hadn't forgot it, young as he was. And she, Martha, had failed that mother.

In the silence, she began to sing, "Silent Night, she sang. "Holy Night."

Daniel didn't move until the song was finished. Then he turned with that quick heart-melting smile. "That's the one," he whispered. "That's the song that my mother used to sing to me."

December 24

Martha ran forward and gathered the boy into her arms. He responded immediately, clasping his arms tightly around her.

"Danny," she said, sitting on the edge of Rosie's manger, "Let's go in and get the cabin ready for Christmas. Maybe it isn't too late for Jed...for pa-to get that tree. It might be a little different kind of Christmas, but it will still be a little like the Christmases we used to know."

"Do you mind it being different? Danny asked. "I mean with a boy instead of your girls?"

Martha wondered how long it would take her to make up to him for the hurt she had inflicted these many months. "No," she said. "After all, the Baby Jesus was a boy."

"That's right," he said wonderingly.

She set him down on the floor and put her arms around his shoulders. "Merry Christmas," she said. "Merry Christmas, Danny." He looked up at her with a smile that did not fade quickly away this time, a sweet smile, full of the love he had been waiting to give her. "Merry Christmas," he said, and then added softly, "Mother."

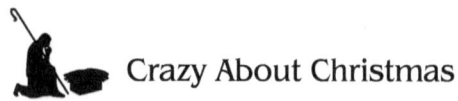 Crazy About Christmas

Stained Glass Manger
Decoration/Craft

MATERIALS

Black construction paper
Silhouette pattern (on next page)
Clear contact paper
Assorted colors of tissue paper

DIRECTIONS

1. Cut one piece of construction paper into 1 inch wide strips. Then cut two strips to 8 inches and 2 pieces to 10 inches. Set aside.

2. Cut two pieces of contact paper to 9 x 11 inches

3. Either trace nativity pattern onto construction paper with a pencil or copy out pattern on next page or any other silhouette you want and tape to paper and cut out image.

4. Take one piece of contact paper and carefully peel off backing.

5. We are now going to make a frame. Place one 10 inch strip of construction paper 1/2-inch away from edge. Place 8-inch pieces below the either end. Finally place the other 10-inch piece below the side pieces to make a full frame.

6. Place your cutout image inside the frame where you want it to be. Remember it is difficult to remove the paper once it is pressed down onto the contact paper.

7. Cut or tear different colors of tissue paper in to small pieces. Stick the tissue to the paper to create a stained glass look.

8. When you are finished adding the tissue paper, remove the backing to the other piece of contact paper and carefully line up with your finished art and press into place.

9. Hang in window for a true stain glass look or put into a picture frame to place as art on the wall.

Note: While this craft is specifically for Christmas I have used this technique with a variety of different images and no matter what you place down the kids love to do this type of art and will want to do multiples. Also don't discount the idea of cutting 1/2-inch wide strips of paper and placing them at different angles on the contact paper and just filling in the blanks or adding to your image for a true stained glass piece of art.

December 24

 Crazy About Christmas

Bacon Baklava
Makes about 28 pieces

INGREDIENTS

For the filling:
- 2 teaspoons ground cinnamon
- 3-4 teaspoons ground allspice
- 1 pound blanched almonds
- 1½ pound bacon
- ⅔ cup sugar
- ¼ cup water
- 1 teaspoon rose water (optional)
- 1 pound phyllo dough, thawed
- 8 ounces clarified unsalted butter, melted or ghee melted

For the syrup:
- 1¼ cups honey
- 1¼ cups water
- 1¼ cups sugar
- 1 cinnamon stick
- ½ lemon, juiced

INSTRUCTIONS

1. Heat the oven to 350 degrees F.
2. Fry bacon. Place on paper towel to drain. Crumble into pieces
3. Place the almonds, sugar and spices into the bowl of a food processor and pulse until finely chopped, but not paste or powder, approximately 15 quick pulses. Now add crumbled bacon and toss together. Set aside.
4. Combine the water and rose water in a small spritz bottle and set aside.
5. Trim the sheets of phyllo to fit the bottom of a 13 by 9 by 2-inch metal pan. Brush the bottom and sides of the pan with butter; lay down a sheet of phyllo and brush with butter. Repeat this step 9 more times for a total of 10 sheets of phyllo. Top with 1/3 of the nut mixture and spread thinly. Spritz thoroughly with the rose water. Layer 6 more sheets of phyllo with butter in between each of them, followed by another third of the nuts and spritz with rose water. Repeat with another 6 sheets of phyllo, butter, remaining nuts, and rose water. Top with 8 sheets of phyllo brushing with butter in between each sheet. Brush the top generously with butter.
6. Place in the oven and bake for 30 minutes. Remove pan from the oven and cut into 28 squares. Return pan to the oven and continue to bake for another 30 minutes. Remove pan from the oven, place on a cooling rack, and cool for 2 hours before adding the syrup.
7. Make the syrup during the last 30 minutes of cooling. Combine the honey, water, sugar, and cinnamon stick in a 4-quart saucepan and set over high heat. Stir occasionally until the sugar has dissolved. Once boiling, boil for 10 minutes, stirring occasionally. Remove

December 24

    from the heat and discard the cinnamon stick and stir in lemon juice.
8. After the baklava has cooled for 2 hours, re-cut the entire pan following the same lines as before. Pour the hot syrup evenly over the top of the baklava, allowing it to run into the cuts and around the edges of the pan.
9. Allow the pan to sit, uncovered until completely cool. Cover and store at room temperature for at least 8 hours and up to overnight before serving. Store, covered, at room temperature for up to 5 days (if it lasts that long).

Note: I was terrified to make Baklava the first time, but found it is not difficult to make it just takes time to butter every layer, now I make it a couple times a year.
This recipe is a twist on a classic baklava that I devised for a competition and was declared the winner of Bacon Wars at Trial by Fire. While the idea of bacon in this sweet dish sounds odd the combination of sweet and salty is very satisfying. To serve I often use cupcake papers to place my baklava in for easy consumption and dry fingers.

 Crazy About Christmas

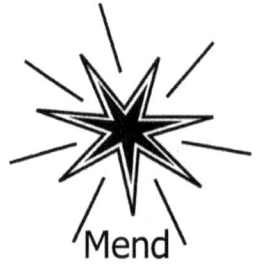

This Christmas

Mend a quarrel.
Seek out a forgotten friend.
DISMISS SUSPICION AND REPLACE IT WITH TRUST.
Write a letter.
Give a soft answer. Encourage youth.
Manifest your loyalty in word and deed.
Keep a promise. Forgo a grudge.
FORGIVE AN ENEMY. APOLOGIZE.
Try to understand. Examine your demands on others.
Think first of someone else.
BE KIND. BE GENTLE.
Laugh a little more. Express your gratitude.
Welcome a stranger. Gladden the heart of a child.
Take pleasure in the beauty and wonder of the earth.
Speak your love, and then speak it again.

President Howard W. Hunter

Christmas Day—December 25

The Story of Christmas
Nora A. Smith

Christmas Day, you know, dear children, is Christ's day, Christ's birthday, and I want to tell you why we love it so much, and why we try to make every one happy when it comes each year.

A long, long time ago—more than eighteen hundred years—the baby Christ was born on Christmas Day; a baby so wonderful and so beautiful, who grew up to be a man so wise, so good, so patient and sweet that, every year, the people who know about Him love Him better and better, and are more and more glad when His birthday comes again. You see that He must have been very good and wonderful; for people have always remembered His birthday, and kept it lovingly for eighteen hundred years.

He was born, long years ago, in a land far, far away across the seas.

Before the baby Christ was born, Mary, His mother, had to make a long journey with her husband, Joseph. They made this journey to be taxed or counted; for in those days this could not be done in the town where people happened to live, but they must be numbered in the place where they were born.

In that far-off time the only way of traveling was on a horse, or a camel, or a good, patient donkey. Camels and horses cost a great deal of money, and Mary was very poor; so she rode on a quiet, safe donkey, while Joseph walked by her side, leading him and leaning on his stick. Mary was very young, and beautiful, I think, but Joseph was a great deal older than she.

People dress nowadays, in those distant countries, just as they did so many years ago, so we know that Mary must have worn a long, thick dress, falling all about her in heavy folds, and that she had a soft white veil over her head and neck, and across her face. Mary lived in Nazareth, and the journey they were making was to Bethlehem, many miles away.

They were a long time traveling, I am sure; for donkeys are slow, though they are so careful, and Mary must have been very tired before they came to the end of their journey.

They had traveled all day, and it was almost dark when they came near to Bethlehem, to the town where the baby Christ was to be born. There was the place they were to stay,—a kind of inn, or lodging-house, but not at all like those you know about.

They have them today in that far-off country, just as they built them so many years ago.

It was a low, flat-roofed, stone building, with no windows and only one large door. There were no nicely furnished bed rooms inside, and no soft white beds for the tired travelers;

there were only little places built into the stones of the wall, something like the berths on steamboats nowadays, and each traveler brought his own bedding. No pretty garden was in front of the inn, for the road ran close to the very door, so that its dust lay upon the door sill. All around the house, to a high, rocky hill at the back, a heavy stone fence was built, so that the people and the animals inside might be kept safe.

Mary and Joseph could not get very near the inn; for the whole road in front was filled with camels and donkeys and sheep and cows, while a great many men were going to and fro, taking care of the animals. Some of these people had come to Bethlehem to pay their taxes, as Mary and Joseph had done, and others were staying for the night on their way to Jerusalem, a large city a little further on.

The yard was filled, too, with camels and sheep; and men were lying on the ground beside them, resting and watching and keeping them safe. The inn was so full and the yard was so full of people that there was no room for anybody else, and the keeper had to take Joseph and Mary through the house and back to the high hill, where they found another place that was used for a stable. This had only a door and front, and deep caves were behind, stretching far into the rocks.

This was the spot where Christ was born. Think how poor a place!—but Mary was glad to be there, after all; and when the Christ-child came, He was like other babies, and had so lately come from heaven that He was happy everywhere.

There were mangers all around the cave, where the cattle and sheep were fed, and great heaps of hay and straw were lying on the floor. Then, I think, there were brown-eyed cows and oxen there, and quiet, woolly sheep, and perhaps even some dogs that had come in to take care of the sheep.

And there in the cave, by and by, the wonderful baby came, and they wrapped Him up and laid Him in a manger.

All the stars in the sky shone brightly that night, for they knew the Christ-child was born, and the angels in heaven sang together for joy. The angels knew about the lovely child, and were glad that He had come to help the people on earth to be good.

There lay the beautiful baby, with a manger for His bed, and oxen and sheep all sleeping quietly round Him. His mother watched Him and loved Him, and by and by many people came to see Him, for they had heard that a wonderful child was to be born in Bethlehem. All the people in the inn visited Him, and even the shepherds left their flocks in the fields and sought the child and His mother.

But the baby was very tiny, and could not talk any more than any other tiny child, so He lay in His mother's lap, or in the manger, and only looked at the people. So after they had seen Him and loved Him, they went away again.

Christmas Day—December 25

After a time, when the baby had grown larger, Mary took Him back to Nazareth, and there He lived and grew up.

And He grew to be such a sweet, wise, loving boy, such a tender, helpful man, and He said so many good and beautiful things, that everyone who knew Him, loved Him. Many of the things He said are in the Bible, you know, and a great many beautiful stories of the things He used to do while He was on earth.

He loved little children like you very much, and often used to take them up in His arms and talk to them.

And this is the reason we love Christmas Day so much, and try to make everybody happy when it comes around each year. This is the reason; because Christ, who was born on Christmas Day, has helped us all to be good so many, many times, and because He was the best Christmas present the world ever had!

From "*The Story Hour*," by Kate Douglas Wiggins and Nora A. Smith., 1891.

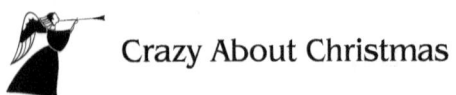
Crazy About Christmas

The Christmas Carol Game II
Family Activity

MATERIALS

copy of clues   *card stock*
scissors   *timer and or watch*
candy cane   *whistle*

This is a game to test your knowledge of Christmas music (this includes carols, traditional music as well as new holiday songs). The clues are shown in bold text and the answers are in parenthesis. You will note that the clues are a play on words and sometimes merely the names of each song with a worded twist.

OBJECTIVE: Be the first person to collect three cards. A card is collected by answering correctly the last song on a card.

GAME SETUP: To play the game photocopy the clues below on card stock. Cut apart on dotted lines . There should be three clues/answers on each card. Prepare the cards well in advance and keep hidden until you are ready to play. Identify an individual to be the Clue Master; the one to read the clues and run the timer. Identify an individual to be the Time Keeper; this person should have access to a watch (digital preferred) or some other time keeping device. The Time Keeper needs to be able to alert players to the 10 seconds time play by a short blow on his/her whistle. The purpose of the Time Keeper is to limit players time to answer each clue. You will also need a candy cane which is used to identify who the current player is. Select first player and give them the candy cane.

DIRECTIONS FOR GAME:
1. The Clue Master reads the first clue from the first card, starting the timer as they read the clue. (Hint: The Clue Master should read over each card silently before giving them, some of the clues are real tongue twisters and you want to give each player their full time to answer.) The person with the candy cane is the current player and is the one authorized to answer the question, they may give as many answers as want within the 10 second time frame. If they answer the clue correctly the Clue Master then proceeds to the next clue on the card and the current player again tries to answer the clue correctly. Note the timer needs to be reset for 10 seconds for each clue before it is read. If the ten seconds run out before the current player gives the correct answer then it becomes all play, which means any

Christmas Day—December 25

player can try to answer the clue. All players still only have 10 seconds to answer the clue. The player that answered the clue correctly is the player that receives the next clue and has a chance to answer. If it was the last clue on the card the Clue Master gives the card to the player who answered correctly. If nobody gives the right answer to the last clue on the card, the Clue Master keeps that card. The candy cane is passed onto the next player when no one has answered the clue correctly or a card has been given to a player. Play continues until one player has collected three cards. That player is then dubbed the Christmas Song Master and they get to eat the candy cane. In case of a tie, use the tie breaker question for the parties in question, the player who first answers the question right ... wins.

2. Team Play: A team is two or more players. All regular rules still apply with the exception that any member of the team may answer the clues.

Sample Question:
Rapture to the Planet
(Joy to the World)

_____

TIE BREAKER QUESTION

Exclamatory remark concerning a diminutive municipality in Judea southwest of Jerusalem
(O Little Town of Bethlehem)

Crazy About Christmas

Listen to the Celestial Choir
(Hark the Herald Angels Sing)

O Yuletide Tall woody plant
(O Christmas Tree)

Junket over naturally occurring surface aquifer and timberlands
(Over the River & through the Woods)

A dozen times of light between one Yuletide nocturnal period and the next.
(Twelve Days of Christmas)

Firmament dwellers apprehend by the ear by first person plural
(Angels We Have Heard on High)

The edible part of a tree of the Beech family toasting on a phenomenon of combustion manifested in light
(Chestnuts Roasting on an Open Fire)

Christmas Day—December 25

Female parental unit observed caressing with the lips gift bearing Yuletide figure by first person singular
(I saw Mommy Kissing Santa Claus)

Age challenged sleigh driving person is advancing to municipality
(Santa Claus is Coming to Town)

Chilly crystalline precipitation non-female being
(Frosty the Snow Man)

At the Peak of the Domicile
(Up on the House Top)

Duel Noel wish for upper Incisor
(All I want for Christmas is my Two Front Teeth)

Rudimentary start of mature appearance of last calendar Holiday
(It's Beginning to look a lot like Christmas)

Crazy About Christmas

Clinking Carillons
(Jingle Bells)

Swing back and forth surrounding the Yuletide tall woody plant
(Rockin' Around the Christmas Tree)

Carillons apprehended by ear during December 25th
(I Heard the Bells on Christmas Day)

Toys R Us
(Toyland)

Move hitherward the entire assembly of those who are loyal in their belief
(O Come All Ye Faithful)

Embellish interior passageways
(Deck the Halls)

Christmas Day—December 25

Vertically challenged adolescent percussionist
(Little Drummer Boy)

Natal Celebration devoid of color as a hallucinatory phenomenon for me
(I'm Dreaming of a White Christmas)

Majestic triplet referred to in the first person plural
(We Three Kings)

Arrival Time 2400 hours—Weather Cloudless
(It Came Upon A Midnight Clear)

Soundless nocturnal period
(Silent Night)

The Yuletide occurrence preceding all others
(The First Noel)

Crazy About Christmas

Precious metal musical devices
(Silver Bells)

Omnipotent supreme being who elicits respite to ecstatic distinguished males
(God Rest Ye Merry Gentlemen)

Caribou with vermilion olfactory appendage
(Rudolph the Red Nosed Reindeer)

Allow crystalline formations to descend, Allow crystalline formations to descend, Allow crystalline formations to descend
(Let it Snow, Let it Snow, Let it Snow)

Jovial Yuletide desired for the second person singular or plural by us
(We Wish You a Merry Christmas)

Bipedal traveling through an amazing acreage during the period between December 21st and March 21st
(Walking Through A Winter Wonderland)

Christmas Day—December 25

Melancholy Yuletide
(Blue Christmas)

By a long distance in a trough
(Away in a Manger)

Did you apprehend by the ear the same thing I did?
(Do You Hear What I Hear?)

Transportation over snow and ice
(Sleigh Ride)

A female ancestor trampled by a northern antlered wild mammal.
(Grandma Got Run Over by a Reindeer)

Clinking Carillons swing back and forth
(Jingle Bell Rock)

Crazy About Christmas

Not a thing for Yuletide celebration
(Nuttin' for Christmas)

Move hitherward the entire assembly of those who are loyal in their belief
(Oh, Come All Ye Faithful)

Full of high spirits, age challenged, gift bearing religious person
(Jolly Old Saint Nicholas)

Query Regarding Identity of one recently born.
(What Child is This?)

O Sacred Nocturnal Period
(O Holy Night)

First person singular, to return to natal area from a distance.
(I'll Be Home for Christmas)

Christmas Day—December 25

Breakfast

Overnight Eggnog French Toast
Orange slices sprinkled with Sugar
Hot Chocolate

Overnight Eggnog French Toast
Makes 12 slices

Ingredients

5	eggs	1½	cups half-and-half or milk
¼	cup sugar	¼	teaspoon nutmeg
1	teaspoons vanilla	¾	teaspoons rum extract
12	¾ inch thick slices French bread		
	Powdered sugar		jam, jelly, syrup (optional)

Instructions

1. Grease a 15x10x1 inch baking pan.
2. In large bowl, combine eggs, half and half, sugar, nutmeg, vanilla and rum extract; beat until well blended.
3. Arrange bread slices in greased baking pans. Pour egg mixture over bread in pans. Lift and move bread slices until all egg mixture is absorbed. Cover with foil; refrigerate overnight or freeze up to one week.
4. Heat oven to 500° F. Remove bread slices from refrigerator or freezer (do not thaw); remove foil. Bake 1 pan at 500° F. for 15 minutes or until golden brown. Sprinkle with powdered sugar.

Christmas Feast

*Ham • Cheesy Potatoes
Corn • Green Beans • Sweet Potato Casserole
Broccoli Cauliflower Salad • 90 Minute Rolls
Pumpkin Pie Crunch Cake*

Sweet Potato Casserole

A favorite recipe from my friend Lucy Casablanca

Ingredients

1 large can of yams, drained and mashed
½ cup granulated sugar
2 eggs
1 teaspoon vanilla
¼ cup butter or margarine, softened
1 can evaporated milk

Topping:
1 cup pecans, chopped
1 cup brown sugar, packed
¼ cup self-rising flour
⅓ cup butter or margarine

Instructions

1. Butter a 10 inch pan. Heat oven to 350°F.
2. In a medium sized bowl dump can of drained yams and mash with potato masher. Add sugar, eggs, vanilla, butter and milk. Mix together and pour into pan.
3. To make the topping mix the butter, flour and sugar together with a pastry blender till it begins to crumble then by hand mix in the pecans. Crumble the topping over the yam mixture. Place on center rack in oven and bake for 30 minutes. Topping will be golden and yams will be bubbling.

Christmas Day—December 25

Cheesy Potatoes

INGREDIENTS
4 cups cubed potatoes or 32 ounce bag southern style hash browns
1 can condensed cream of chicken soup
4 oz cream cheese
4 tablespoons butter
½ cup milk
½ cup sour cream
1 ½ cup sharp cheddar cheese, shredded
½ onion, shredded or finely chopped
½ teaspoon ground black pepper
1 teaspoon salt
½ teaspoon garlic powder

A family favorite all year long.

1. Preheat oven to 350F, and lightly spray a 9 x 13 baking dish with cooking spray.
2. In a large pot, bring to a boil salted water for potato cubes and boil about 8-10 minutes or until just softened.
3. While potatoes are cooking, in a glass bowl place cream cheese, milk, and butter an microwave (you can also do this on the stove) for about 1 minute or until melted. Remove from microwave and whisk until smooth.
4. Add onions, sour cream, can of soup, salt, pepper, garlic powder and cheese and stir until mixed.
5. Drain potatoes and place into baking dish. Pour cheesy mixture over potatoes and mix until coated. Spread out.
6. At this point you can decide if you want a crunchy top on your potatoes and sprinkle them over the top evenly, I say this because some of my kids prefer it naked. Bake for 15-20 minutes or until warmed all the way through, and the topping is nicely browned.

Crunchy topping options, use 2-3 cups:
Corn Flakes   Crushed Ritz Crackers™   French Fried Onions
Crushed Kettle Chips (like Jalapeno)   Crushed Butter & Garlic Croutons

VARIATION: Sometimes I like to add diced ham, bacon, or chicken to the potatoes and make it a whole meal. I mean really how can you resist nice creamy, cheesy potatoes and meat?

Broccoli Cauliflower Salad
Serves 6

INGREDIENTS

- 3 cups broccoli (cut up in small pieces- no stems)
- 3 cups cauliflower (cut into small pieces)
- 1/2 cup red onion, finely chopped
- 1 cup cheddar cheese, shredded
- 6 bacon, cooked and chopped
- 1/4 cup sunflower seeds or sliced almonds
- 1/3 cup raisins or dried cranberries

DRESSINGS

- 1/3 cup granulated sugar
- 1 cup mayonnaise
- 2 tablespoon cider vinegar
- 2 tablespoon red wine vinegar

DIRECTIONS

1. Cut broccoli and cauliflower into bite size pieces and place in large bowl. Add red onion, nuts, and fruit and mix together

2. To make dressing whisk sugar, mayonnaise and vinegars together in small bowl. Pour over vegetables and mix well. Place in refrigerator.

3. Just before you serve mix in the bacon and the cheddar cheese and mix well.

Christmas Day—December 25

90 Minute Dinner Rolls
Makes 1 dozen rolls

INGREDIENTS

- 2 cups all-purpose flour
- 2 tablespoons granulated sugar
- 1 package (¼ ounce) quick-rise yeast
- ½ teaspoon salt
- ½ cup milk
- ¼ cup water
- 2 tablespoons butter

INSTRUCTIONS:

1. In a large bowl, combine 3/4 cup flour, sugar, yeast and salt.
2. In a small saucepan, heat the milk, water and butter to 120°-130°F.
3. Add to dry ingredients; beat just until moistened. Stir in enough remaining flour to form a soft dough. Turn onto a floured surface; knead until smooth and elastic, about 6-8 minutes. Cover and let rest for 10 minutes.
4. Divide dough into 12 pieces; shape each piece into a roll. Arrange in a greased 9-in. round baking pan. Cover and let rise until doubled, about 35 minutes.
5. Bake at 375° for 20-25 minutes or until golden brown.
6. Remove from pan to a wire rack to cool.

Pumpkin Pie Crunch Cake
12-15 servings

INGREDIENTS

- 1 can (15.5 oz.) pure pumpkin puree
- 1 can (12 oz.) evaporated milk
- 3 large eggs
- 1 cup sugar
- 1 tsp. ground cinnamon
- 1 box spice cake mix
- 1 cup butter, melted
- ¾ cup chopped pecans (optional)
- whipped cream for garnish (optional)

INSTRUCTIONS:

1. Preheat oven to 350F degrees. Grease a 9x13-inch pan. Set aside.
2. In a large bowl, combine pumpkin puree, evaporated milk, eggs, sugar and cinnamon until well-combined.
3. Pour this pumpkin mixture into the prepared baking pan.
4. Dump dry cake mix over the pumpkin mixture and spread out. Sprinkle nuts on top.
5. Evenly drizzle butter the top of the cake mix. Bake for about 50-55 minutes.
6. Let it cool before slicing and serving.
7. Serve with a dollop of whipped cream.

Note: Some people like to use yellow cake mix, but I like the extra spice.

Letter of Thanks
Author unknown

On the first day of Christmas my true love gave to me,
A Partridge in a Pear Tree.

My Darling John:
   I answered the door today and to my delightful surprise the postman handed me a partridge in a pear tree. What a marvelous gift. I just couldn't have been more surprised and pleased.
   With deepest love and affection. Your only true love.
      Agnes

On the second day of Christmas my true love gave to me,
Two turtle doves ...

Dearest John:
   Again today the postman brought me a beautiful gift from you. Just imagine—two turtle doves. I'm so delighted. Your gift is so thoughtful. They're absolutely adorable.
   All my love,
      Agnes

On the third day of Christmas my true love gave to me,
Three French hens ...

My Dear, Dear John:
   Aren't you the extravagant one. Now I really must protest. I don't deserve such generosity. Three French Hens. They're darling. But I must insist, you've been far too kind.
   Lovingly,
      Agnes

On the fourth day of Christmas my true love gave to me.
Four calling birds ...

My Dear Sweetheart:
Today again the postman knocked on my door and this time he delivered four calling birds. Now really John. They're beautiful, but don't you think enough is enough? You're just being too romantic.
Affectionately,
Agnes

On the fifth day of Christmas my true love gave to me.
Five golden rings ...

My Dear Sweet John:
What an absolutely wonderful surprise. Today the postman brought me five golden rings. One for each finger. You're just impossible, but I love it. Frankly, all those birds are beginning to get on my nerves.
With love,
Agnes

On the sixth day of Christmas my true love gave to me.
Six geese a laying ...

Dear John:
When I opened the door this morning there were six geese a-laying on my front steps. So you're back to the birds again. John they're huge! Where in the world will I keep them, or what will I do with all those eggs they're a-laying? The neighbors are complaining about all the noise and the smell and I can't sleep a wink. Please, please stop.
Cordially,
Agnes

On the seventh day of Christmas my true love gave to me.
Seven swans a swimming ...

Dear John:

What's with you and all these blasted birds? Now it's seven swans a-swimming. What kind of lousy joke is this? Bird droppings all over the house. My fingers are raw to the bone from building all these bird cages. I can't sleep. It's not funny any longer so stop it immediately.

    Sincerely,
    Agnes

On the eighth day of Christmas my true love gave to me.
Eight maids a-milking...

OK, Buster.

What in the world is going on? What in Sam Hill am I going to do with eight maids a-milking? I prefer the birds. It's not enough with all those birds and maids, they had to bring all their cows with them. The lawn is a mess. You have to be careful where you step, and the house smells awful. I'm warning you— lay off.

    Most Sincerely,
    Agnes

On the ninth day of Christmas my true love gave to me.
Nine pipers piping ...

Hey Jerk,

What are you, some kind of weirdo? Today there's nine pipers piping. All they do is chase the maids. The cows are giving too much milk. The neighbors refuse to buy the milk. The birds are all screeching because of the playing pipers and the maids refuse to eat goose eggs. What am I supposed to do? The neighbors have started eviction proceedings against me. I'll get you.

    With lasting Hatred,
    Agnes

On the tenth day of Christmas my true love gave to me.
Ten ladies dancing ...

You rotten knucklehead.

Now there's ten ladies dancing. All they do is dance all night long. I don't have enough food storage to last very many more days. They're eating me out of house and home. All the cows are getting sick, all the milk is going sour, and the Board of Health is threatening to condemn the place. I've had it, you stupid blockhead. I'm siccing the police on you.

One who means it,
    Agnes

On the eleventh day of Christmas my true love gave to me.
Eleven Lords a-leaping ...

Listen you Goon.

What's with eleven Lords a-leaping? All those maids and ladies and pipers are driving me nuts. All twenty-three of the birds have been trampled to death. I hope you're satisfied.

Your sworn enemy,
    Agnes

On the twelfth day of Christmas my true love gave to me.
Twelve drummers drumming ...

Dear Sir:

This is to acknowledge your latest gift of twelve drummers drumming which you have seen fit to inflict upon my client. Miss McFurry's destruction was of course total, and she is now at Happydale Sanitarium where attendants have instructions to shoot you on sight.

Enclosed, please find a bill for all damages and a warrant for your arrest.

Yours truly,
    G.F. Bailey
    Attorney at Law

December 26

Thank-You Cards
Craft

MATERIALS

Wax paper
White tissue paper or Kleenex
Dried flowers
Paper cut-outs
Card stock
Ribbon
White glue

DIRECTIONS

1. Cut a piece of wax paper the same size as the front of your thank you card.
2. Arrange dried flowers or paper cut-outs on top of wax paper.
3. Mix together in a small bowl equal parts of water and glue.
4. Separate a tissue and lay a single sheet of it over your design.
5. With a paint brush paint glue mixture over the tissue. Be careful not to do it to hard or the tissue will tear. This is a little messy but the result are great. Let dry overnight or till completely dry.
6. When paper is completely dry. Iron design wax paper side on a low iron setting, I generally use a lightweight pressing cloth to do this so I don't get wax on my iron. This will make the design look more like parchment paper.
7. Now punch a couple of holes in the design and the card and attach your parchment to the card with a piece of ribbon. Write your thank you on the inside of the card. Everyone enjoys knowing what they gave you was appreciated.

Turkey Pot Pie
Serves 6

INGREDIENTS

1	recipe pastry for a (10 inch) double crust pie
4	tablespoons butter, divided
1	small onion, minced
2	stalks celery, chopped
2	carrots, diced
3	tablespoons dried parsley
1	teaspoon dried oregano
	salt and pepper to taste
2	cups chicken broth (or leftover turkey gravy)
3	potatoes, peeled and cubed
1½	cups cubed cooked turkey or chicken
3	tablespoons all-purpose flour
½	cup milk

INSTRUCTIONS

1. Preheat oven to 425° degrees F (220 degrees C). Roll out bottom pie crust, press into a 10 inch pie pan, and set aside.

2. Melt 2 tablespoons butter in a large skillet over medium heat; add the onion, celery, carrots, parsley, oregano, and salt and pepper. Cook and stir until the vegetables are soft. Stir in the bouillon and water. Bring mixture to a boil. Stir in the potatoes, and cook until tender but still firm.

3. In a medium saucepan, melt the remaining 2 tablespoons butter. Stir in the turkey and flour. Add the milk, and heat through. Stir the turkey mixture into the vegetable mixture, and cook until thickened. Cool slightly, then pour mixture into the unbaked pie shell. Roll out the top crust, and place on top of filling. Flute edges, and make 4 slits in the top crust to let out steam.

4. Bake in the preheated oven for 15 minutes. Reduce oven temperature to 350°F, and continue baking for 20 minutes, or until crust is golden brown.

December 27

The Christmas Cuckoo

by Frances Browne

Once upon a time there stood in the midst of a bleak moor, in the North Country, a certain village. All its inhabitants were poor, for their fields were barren, and they had little trade; but the poorest of them all were two brothers called Scrub and Spare, who followed the cobbler's craft. Their hut was built of clay and wattles. The door was low and always open, for there was no window. The roof did not entirely keep out the rain and the only thing comfortable was a wide fireplace, for which the brothers could never find wood enough to make sufficient fire. There they worked in most brotherly friendship, though with little encouragement.

On one unlucky day a new cobbler arrived in the village. He had lived in the capital city of the kingdom and, by his own account, cobbled for the queen and the princesses. His awls were sharp, his lasts were new; he set up his stall in a neat cottage with two windows. The villagers soon found out that one patch of his would outwear two of the brothers'. In short, all the mending left Scrub and Spare, and went to the new cobbler.

The season had been wet and cold, their barley did not ripen well, and the cabbages never half-closed in the garden. So the brothers were poor that winter, and when Christmas came they had nothing to feast on but a barley loaf and a piece of rusty bacon. Worse than that, the snow was very deep and they could get no firewood.

Their hut stood at the end of the village; beyond it spread the bleak moor, now all white and silent. But that moor had once been a forest; great roots of old trees were still to be found in it, loosened from the soil and laid bare by the winds and rains. One of these, a rough, gnarled log, lay hard by their door, the half of it above the snow, and Spare said to his brother: --

"Shall we sit here cold on Christmas while the great root lies yonder? Let us chop it up for firewood, the work will make us warm."

"No," said Scrub, "it's not right to chop wood on Christmas; besides, that root is too hard to be broken with any hatchet."

"Hard or not, we must have a fire," replied Spare. "Come, brother, help me in with it. Poor as we are there is nobody in the village will have such a yule log as ours."

Scrub liked a little grandeur, and, in hopes of having a fine yule log, both brothers strained and strove with all their might till, between pulling and pushing, the great old root was safe on the hearth, and beginning to crackle and blaze with the red embers.

Crazy About Christmas

In high glee the cobblers sat down to their bread and bacon. The door was shut, for there was nothing but cold moonlight and snow outside; but the hut, strewn with fir boughs and ornamented with holly, looked cheerful as the ruddy blaze flared up and rejoiced their hearts.

Then suddenly from out the blazing root they heard: "Cuckoo! cuckoo!" as plain as ever the spring-bird's voice came over the moor on a May morning.

"What is that?" said Scrub, terribly frightened; "it is something bad!"

"Maybe not," said Spare.

And out of the deep hole at the side of the root, which the fire had not reached, flew a large, gray cuckoo, and lit on the table before them. Much as the cobblers had been surprised, they were still more so when it said: --

"Good gentlemen, what season is this?"

"It's Christmas," said Spare.

"Then a merry Christmas to you!" said the cuckoo. "I went to sleep in the hollow of that old root one evening last summer, and never woke till the heat of your fire made me think it was summer again. But now since you have burned my lodging, let me stay in your hut till the spring comes round, -- I only want a hole to sleep in, and when I go on my travels next summer be assured I will bring you some present for your trouble."

"Stay and welcome," said Spare, while Scrub sat wondering if it were something bad or not.

"I'll make you a good warm hole in the thatch," said Spare. "But you must be hungry after that long sleep, -- here is a slice of barley bread. Come help us to keep Christmas!"

The cuckoo ate up the slice, drank water from a brown jug, and flew into a snug hole which Spare scooped for it in the thatch of the hut.

Scrub said he was afraid it wouldn't be lucky; but as it slept on and the days passed he forgot his fears.

So the snow melted, the heavy rains came, the cold grew less, the days lengthened, and one sunny morning the brothers were awakened by the cuckoo shouting its own cry to let them know the spring had come.

"Now I'm going on my travels," said the bird, "over the world to tell men of the spring. There is no country where trees bud, or flowers bloom, that I will not cry in before the year goes round. Give me another slice of barley bread to help me on my journey, and tell me what present I shall bring you at the twelve month's end."

Scrub would have been angry with his brother for cutting so large a slice, their store of barley being low, but his mind was occupied with what present it would be most prudent to ask for.

"There are two trees hard by the well that lies at the world's end," said the cuckoo; "one of them is called the golden tree, for its leaves are all of beaten gold. Every winter they

December 27

fall into the well with a sound like scattered coin, and I know not what becomes of them. As for the other, it is always green like a laurel. Some call it the wise, and some the merry, tree. Its leaves never fall, but they that get one of them keep a blithe heart in spite of all misfortunes, and can make themselves as merry in a hut as in a palace."

"Good master cuckoo, bring me a leaf off that tree!" cried Spare.

"Now, brother, don't be a fool!" said Scrub; "think of the leaves of beaten gold! Dear master cuckoo, bring me one of them!"

Before another word could be spoken the cuckoo had flown out of the open door, and was shouting its spring cry over moor and meadow.

The brothers were poorer than ever that year. Nobody would send them a single shoe to mend, and Scrub and Spare would have left the village but for their barley-field and their cabbage garden. They sowed their barley, planted their cabbage, and, now that their trade was gone, worked in the rich villagers' fields to make out a scanty living.

So the seasons came and passed; spring, summer, harvest, and winter followed each other as they have done from the beginning. At the end of the latter Scrub and Spare had grown so poor and ragged that their old neighbors forgot to invite them to wedding feasts or merrymakings, and the brothers thought the cuckoo had forgotten them, too, when at daybreak on the first of April they heard a hard beak knocking at their door, and a voice crying: --

"Cuckoo! cuckoo! Let me in with my presents!"

Spare ran to open the door, and in came the cuckoo, carrying on one side of its bill a golden leaf larger than that of any tree in the North Country; and in the other side of its bill, one like that of the common laurel, only it had a fresher green.

"Here," it said, giving the gold to Scrub and the green to Spare, "it is a long carriage from the world's end. Give me a slice of barley bread, for I must tell the North Country that the spring has come."

Scrub did not grudge the thickness of that slice, though it was cut from their last loaf. So much gold had never been in the cobbler's hands before, and he could not help exulting over his brother.

"See the wisdom of my choice," he said, holding up the large leaf of gold. "As for yours, as good might be plucked from any hedge, I wonder a sensible bird would carry the like so far."

"Good master cobbler," cried the cuckoo, finishing its slice, "your conclusions are more hasty than courteous. If your brother is disappointed this time, I go on the same journey every year, and for your hospitable entertainment will think it no trouble to bring each of you whichever leaf you desire."

"Darling cuckoo," cried Scrub, "bring me a golden one."

Crazy About Christmas

And Spare, looking up from the green leaf on which he gazed as though it were a crown-jewel, said, "Be sure to bring me one from the merry tree."

And away flew the cuckoo.

"This is the feast of All Fools, and it ought to be your birthday," said Scrub. "Did ever man fling away such an opportunity of getting rich? Much good your merry leaves will do in the midst of rags and poverty!"

But Spare laughed at him, and answered with quaint old proverbs concerning the cares that come with gold, till Scrub, at length getting angry, vowed his brother was not fit to live with a respectable man; and taking his lasts, his awls, and his golden leaf, he left the wattle hut, and went to tell the villagers.

They were astonished at the folly of Spare, and charmed with Scrub's good sense, particularly when he showed them the golden leaf, and told that the cuckoo would bring him one every spring.

The new cobbler immediately took him into partnership; the greatest people sent him their shoes to mend. Fairfeather, a beautiful village maiden, smiled graciously upon him; and in the course of that summer they were married, with a grand wedding feast, at which the whole village danced except Spare, who was not invited, because the bride could not bear his low-mindedness, and his brother thought him a disgrace to the family.

As for Scrub he established himself with Fairfeather in a cottage close by that of the new cobbler, and quite as fine. There he mended shoes to everybody's satisfaction, had a scarlet coat and a fat goose for dinner on holidays. Fairfeather, too, had a crimson gown, and fine blue ribbons; but neither she nor Scrub was content, for to buy this grandeur the golden leaf had to be broken and parted With piece by piece, so the last morsel was gone before the cuckoo came with another.

Spare lived on in the old hut, and worked in the cabbage garden. Scrub had got the barley-field because he was the elder. Every day his coat grew more ragged, and the hut more weather- beaten; but people remarked that he never looked sad or sour. And the wonder was that, from the time any one began to keep his company, he or she grew kinder, happier, and content.

Every first of April the cuckoo came tapping at their doors with the golden leaf for Scrub, and the green for Spare. Fairfeather would have entertained it nobly with wheaten bread and honey, for she had some notion of persuading it to bring two golden leaves instead of one; but the cuckoo flew away to eat barley bread with Spare, saying it was not fit company for fine people, and liked the old hut where it slept so snugly from Christmas till spring.

Scrub spent the golden leaves, and remained always discontented; and Spare kept the merry ones.

December 27

I do not know how many years passed in this manner, when a certain great lord, who owned that village, came to the neighborhood. His castle stood on the moor. It was ancient and strong, with high towers and a deep moat. All the country as far as one could see from the highest turret belonged to its lord; but he had not been there for twenty years, and would not have come then only he was melancholy. And there he lived in a very bad temper. The servants said nothing would please him, and the villagers put on their worst clothes lest he should raise their rents.

But one day in the harvest-time His Lordship chanced to meet Spare gathering watercresses at a meadow stream, and fell into talk with the cobbler. How it was nobody could tell, but from that hour the great lord cast away his melancholy. He forgot all his woes, and went about with a noble train, hunting, fishing, and making merry in his hall, where all travelers were entertained, and all the poor were welcome.

This strange story spread through the North Country, and great company came to the cobbler's hut, -- rich men who had lost their money, poor men who had lost their friends, beauties who had grown old, wits who had gone out of fashion, -- all came to talk with Spare, and, whatever their troubles had been, all went home merry.

The rich gave him presents, the poor gave him thanks. Spare's coat ceased to be ragged, he had bacon with his cabbage, and the villagers began to think there was some sense in him.

By this time his fame had reached the capital city, and even the court. There were a great many discontented people there; and the king had lately fallen into ill humor because a neighboring princess, with seven islands for her dowry, would not marry his eldest son.

So a royal messenger was sent to Spare, with a velvet mantle, a diamond ring, and a command that he should repair to court immediately.

"Tomorrow is the first of April," said Spare, "and I will go with you two hours after sunrise."

The messenger lodged all night at the castle, and the cuckoo came at sunrise with the merry leaf.

"Court is a fine place," it said, when the cobbler told it he was going, "but I cannot come there; they would lay snares and catch me; so be careful of the leaves I have brought you, and give me a farewell slice of barley bread."

Spare was sorry to part with the cuckoo, little as he had of its company, but he gave it a slice which would have broken Scrub's heart in former times, it was so thick and large. And having sewed up the leaves in the lining of his leather doublet, he set out with the messenger on his way to court.

His coming caused great surprise there. Everybody wondered what the king could see in such a common-looking man; but scarcely had His Majesty conversed with him half an

 Crazy About Christmas

hour, when the princess and her seven islands were forgotten and orders given that a feast for all comers should be spread in the banquet hall.

The princes of the blood, the great lords and ladies, the ministers of state, after that discoursed with Spare, and the more they talked the lighter grew their hearts, so that such changes had never been seen at court.

The lords forgot their spites and the ladies their envies, the princes and ministers made friends among themselves, and the judges showed no favor.

As for Spare, he had a chamber assigned him in the palace, and a seat at the king's table. One sent him rich robes, and another costly jewels; but in the midst of all his grandeur he still wore the leathern doublet, and continued to live at the king's court, happy and honored, and making all others merry and content.

Granny's Wonderful Chair and its Tales of Fairy Times ©1916

December 27

Embossed Foil Art
Craft/Decoration/Gift

MATERIALS

Cardboard or Foam Core Board
Craft Glue such as Aleene's Tacky Glue
Aluminum Foil
glue stick
cotton swabs
black shoe polish
'old rag or paper towels
pencil

DIRECTIONS

1. Select a piece of cardboard, like an old cereal box and cut to the size you want.
2. Select an image you want to create. I find coloring pages work great because they have easy lines to follow or freehand your own design. To transfer the image simply use the side of your pencil to rub graphite on backside of your image then turn it over and trace it onto your cardboard. Use a pencil to draw your image on the cardboard.
3. Use a good craft glue and not school glue as it tends to run or spread. Run a nice bead of glue on your pencil lines. Allow to dry completely.
4. Once the glue is completely dry cut a piece of foil a few inches larger than the cardboard so you can fold to the back later.
5. Using your glue stick cover the back of the foil with glue. Press the foil over your glue design using your finger to *gently* press the foil down so it adheres to the cardboard. Fold four edges of the foil to back. It is very important to do this gently so you don't tear the foil.
6. Use a cotton swab to gently press the foil around the glue lines so the shapes become visible.
7. Draw patterns in all of the spaces with a dull pencil, they can be lines, circles, squiggles, etc. use your imagination.
8. Once all the spaces are filled, rub over the whole thing with black shoe polish (I like the bottles with the sponge applicator), wait a few seconds then wipe off with soft rag. The shoe polish enhances the design. The final result will look like pewter.

Barley Cream with Fruit
A Scandinavian Christmas Dessert

INGREDIENTS
- 1 cup pearl barley
- 4 cups of almond or regular milk
- 1 vanilla pod or 2 Tbsp vanilla extract
- 1 cup heavy whipping cream
- 2 tablespoons sugar
- ½ cup lignon berry jam or strawberry jam
- ¼ cup powdered sugar
- ½ cup water

INSTRUCTIONS
1. Place pearl barley in a medium sized pan and add milk and vanilla.
2. Let simmer for one hour. Barley will absorb the milk so watch so it does not burn. Strain the barley if necessary.
3. Let cool.
4. Mix the jam, powdered sugar, and water in a saucepan let simmer.
5. Whip cream and sugar and fold the cream into the cooled barley. Serve the barley cream with the red sauce.

December 28

Offero, The Legend of St. Christopher
Adapted from Golden Legend

There was a mighty man of old who dwelt in the land of Canaan. Large was he and tall of stature and stronger than any man whom the world had ever seen. Therefore was he called Offero, or, "The Bearer." Now he served the king of Canaan, but he was proud of his great strength and upon a time it came in his mind that he would seek the greatest king who then reigned and him only would he serve and obey.

So he traveled from one country to another until at length he came to one where ruled a powerful king whose fame was great in all the land.

"Thou art the conqueror of nations?" asked Offero.

"I am," replied the king.

"Then take me into your service, for I will serve none but the mightiest of earth."

"That then am I," returned the king, "for truly I fear none."

So the king received Offero into his service and made him to dwell in his court.

But once at eventide a minstrel sang before the king a merry song in which he named oft the evil one. And every time that the king heard the name of Satan he grew pale and hastily made the sign of the cross upon his forehead. Offero marveled thereat and demanded of the king the meaning of the sign and wherefore he thus crossed himself. And because the king would not tell him Offero said, "If thou tell me not, I shall no longer dwell with thee." Then the king answered, saying, "Always when I hear Satan named, I fear that he may have power over me and therefore I make this sign that he harm me not."

"Who is Satan?" asked Offero.

"He is a wicked monarch," replied the king, "wicked but powerful."

"More powerful than thou art?"

"Aye, verily."

"And fearest thou that he hurt thee?"

"That do I, and so do all."

"Then," cried Offero, "is he more mighty and greater than thou art. I will go seek him. Henceforth he shall be my master for I would fain serve the mightiest and the greatest lord of all the world."

So Offero departed from the king and sought Satan. Everywhere he met people who had given themselves over to his rule and at last one day as he was crossing a wide desert he saw a great company of knights approaching. One of them, mounted upon a great black horse, came to him and demanded whither he went, and Offero made answer, "I seek Satan, for he is mighty, and I would fain serve him."

Crazy About Christmas

Then returned the knight, "I am he whom thou seekest."

When Offero heard these words he was right glad and took Satan to be his lord and master.

This king was indeed powerful and a long time did Offero serve him, but it chanced one day as they were journeying together they came to a place where four roads met and in the midst of the space stood a little cross. As soon as Satan saw the cross he was afraid and turned quickly aside and fled toward the desert. Offero followed him marveling much at the sight. And after, when they had come back to the highway they had left, he inquired of Satan why he was thus troubled and had gone so far out of his way to avoid the cross. But Satan answered him not a word.

Then Offero said to him, "If thou wilt not tell me, I shall depart from thee straightway and shall serve thee no more."

"Know then," said Satan, "there was a man called Christ who suffered on the cross and whenever I see his sign I am sore afraid and flee from it, lest he destroy me."

"If then thou art afraid of his sign," cried Offero, "he is greater and more mighty than thou, and I see well that I have labored in vain, for I have not found the greatest lord of the world. I will serve thee no longer. Go thy way alone, for I will go to seek Christ."

And when he had long sought and demanded where he should find Him, he came at length into a great desert where dwelt a hermit, a servant of the Christ. The hermit told him of the Master whom he was seeking and said to him, "This king whom thou dost wish to serve is not an earthly ruler and he requireth that thou oft fast and make many prayers."

But Offero understood not the meaning of worship and prayer and he answered, "Require of me some other thing and I shall do it, but I know naught of this which thou requirest."

Then the hermit said to him, "Knowest thou the river, a day's journey from here, where there is neither ford nor bridge and many perish and are lost? Thou art large and strong. Therefore go thou and dwell by this river and bear over all who desire to cross its waters. That is a service which will be well pleasing to the Christ whom thou desirest to serve, and sometime, if I mistake not, he whom thou seekest will come to thee."

Offero was right joyful at these words and answered, "This service may I well do."

So he hastened to the river and upon its banks he built himself a little hut of reeds. He bare a great pole in his hand to sustain him in the water and many weary wayfarers did he help to cross the turbulent stream. So he lived a long time, bearing over all manner of people without ceasing, and still he saw nothing of the Christ.

Now it happened one night that a storm was raging and the river was very high. Tired with his labors, Offero had just flung himself down on his rude bed to sleep when he heard the voice of a child which called him and said, "Offero, Offero, come out and bear me over."

Offero arose and went out from his cabin, but in the darkness he could see no one. And when he was again in the house, he heard the same voice and he ran out again and found

December 28

no one. A third time he heard the call and going out once more into the storm, there upon the river bank he found a fair young child who besought him in pleading tones, "Wilt thou not carry me over the river this night, Offero?"

The strong man gently lifted the child on his shoulders, took his staff and stepped into the stream. And the water of the river arose and swelled more and more and the child was heavy as lead. And alway as he went farther, higher and higher swelled the waters and the child more and more waxed heavy, insomuch that he feared that they would both be drowned. Already his strength was nearly gone, but he thought of his Master whom he had not yet seen, and staying his footsteps with his palm staff struggled with all his might to reach the opposite shore. As at last he climbed the steep bank, suddenly the storm ceased and the waters calmed.

He set the child down upon the shore, saying, "Child, thou hast put me in great peril. Had I carried the whole world on my shoulders, the weight had not been greater. I might bear no greater burden."

"Offero," answered the child, "Marvel not, but rejoice; for thou hast borne not only all the world upon thee, but thou hast borne him that created and made all the world upon thy shoulders. I am Christ the king whom thou servest in this work. And for a token, that thou mayst know what I say to be the truth, set thy staff in the earth by thy house and thou shalt see in the morning that it shall bear flowers and fruit." With these words the child vanished from Offero's sight.

But Offero did even as he was bidden and set his staff in the earth and when he arose on the morrow, he found it like a palm-tree bearing flowers and leaves and clusters of dates. Then he knew that it was indeed Christ whom he had borne through the waters and he rejoiced that he had found his Master. From that day he served Christ faithfully and was no more called Offero, but Christopher, the Christ bearer.

Crazy About Christmas

The Quest for Stories
Story Improvisation
Craft/Activity

MATERIALS

3/4 inch unfinished wood blocks
Mod Podge®
Paint brush
72 3/4" or less images

DIRECTIONS

1. Most bags of blocks have 24, we only need 12 to start with, or you can make two sets and give one away. I have provide a baker's dozen of images so you can pick and choose.
2. Print out the images provided (page 236) on a piece of paper or on to a full blank sheet of label paper. Do not print these images out with an ink jet printer as the ink will smear since it is not waterproof.
3. The images provided are a little bit smaller than the blocks so when you seal them onto the blocks the edges don't get caught. Cut all the squares out. Decide which images you want on each block. You will need six images for each block.
4. Line the blocks up so you can do several of them at a time. Brush a layer of Mod Podge® on the block and then place the image on the block. Place all twelve images on the one side before you go back and put on a second coat of Mod Podge®. If you are using sticker paper or label paper you can go ahead and put on all the images and then just seal them with some kind of lacquer.
5. Repeat the process until all six sides are done, allowing for drying time. Please note that you can do more than one side at a time as long as the bottom is dry. Give it a second coat if you want to.

Note: You can buy your wooden blocks/cubes at most craft stores or even online.

Variation: If you want to make more blocks either use a permanent marker or look for images online or cut them out of magazines. Just remember they should be the same size as the ones I provided. You can even use pictures of family and friends on these blocks to add to the fun of telling the stories.

December 28

THE QUEST FOR STORIES is an improvisational storytelling activity. In this game, you create stories based on the roll of the cubes you have. If you are a writer, it can help you create original stories prompted by the roll of the cubes. It is also a great party game to play with a whole room of people who can come up with some of the most amazing stories. Each person playing will have the opportunity to select a dice and add to the story. The rules are simple.

GAME RULES

You can use from 6-12 dice for each story. I recommend using six dice if you are playing with under three people. If you have more than three, I suggest letting each person draw a cube from the bag and place it on the table. If you are feeling adventurous, use all 12 cubes. Have one person roll the cubes. Place the rolled cubes on a tray or in the center of the table. I like a small tray that lets the cubes be passed around the room.

To begin the play, the first person selects a cube from those rolled, places it down, and begins the story based on how they see or understand the cube. For instance, I might pick up a cube with a map on it and start my story with, "It was dark outside, and they could no longer see the map that they had brought with them, so they decided to find a safe place to camp for the night.' How long their part of the story is up to them; just remember to be courteous to everyone and don't make it too long. When they are done, pass the tray to the next person, let them select a cube, place it next to the first cube and add to the existing storyline.

Let's say they pick up a cube with a candle on it; this could be interpreted in many ways. Someone might see it simply as a candle, while someone else might just see it as light—there is no one correct answer. So the next person might continue the story by saying, "It was so dark they were stumbling over tree roots and other brush, they could see nothing until in the distance they saw a glow of light and decided to walk that way for a closer look. Maybe they would find someone to help them."

Play continues until you run out of cubes. The person who draws the last cube must finish the story, bring it to its end. Something to note is that each cube can only be drawn once, but you can and should refer back to it as you continue the story if it helps with the storyline.

Have fun, be inventive, and enjoy creating lots of new stories.

 Crazy About Christmas

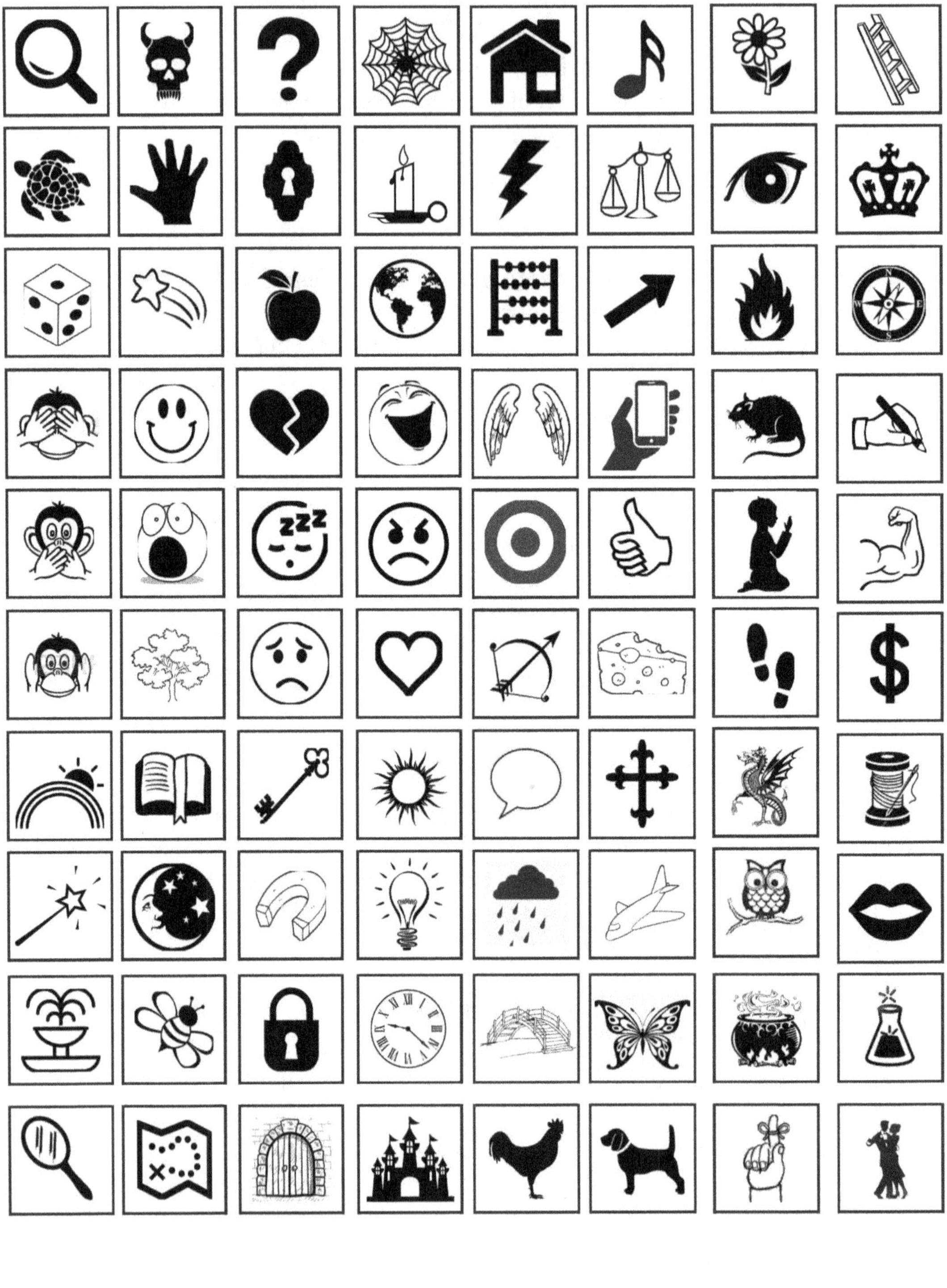

December 28

Humble Pie
Serves 8-10

INGREDIENTS

1	pound lean ground beef or ground turkey
1	onion, diced
1	stalk celery, diced
1	tablespoon Worcestershire sauce
1	tablespoon minced garlic
1	can Cream of Mushroom Soup
1½	cups milk
10	large potatoes, diced
	salt and pepper to taste
¼	cup butter
½	cup shredded cheddar cheese

This meat and potato pie is a family favorite all year long.

INSTRUCTIONS

1. Preheat oven to 350°.
2. Fill a large pot with water and heat to boiling.
3. Meanwhile scrub and dice (I leave the skins on unless they are tough) the potatoes. Drop into boiling water and cook about 10 minutes or until soft. Drain water from potatoes.
4. Add 1-cup milk, butter, salt and pepper to potatoes and whip until smooth, they will be softer than usual. Adjust seasoning to taste and set aside.
5. Brown ground beef with onion and celery. Crumble meat. After meat is browned add can of cream of mushroom soup, 1/2 cup milk, Worcestershire sauce, minced garlic and mix until you have a smooth gravy. Remove from the heat.
6. In a large baking bowl, spray cooking oil on the inside, then cover the bottom and sides of bowl with a layer of mashed potatoes, then a layer of meat, then a layer of potatoes, ending with a layer of potatoes. Depending on the size of the bowl you will have 2-3 layers of meat sandwiched between layers of mashed potatoes.
7. Bake for about 20 minutes or until heated all the way through.
8. Sprinkle the top with grated cheese 5 minutes before serving.

Kindness is like snow. It beautifies everything it covers.

Kahlil Gibran

December 29

The Legend of the Snow Maiden
*An old Russian Folk Tale
as told by MyLinda Butterworth*

A very long time ago, in the forests of Russia, there lived a peasant named Ivan and his wife, Maria. Although they had many friends and loved each other very much, they were saddened because they had no children of their own. More than anything in the world, they wanted a son or a daughter to share their love with, to laugh and play with. One winter day, they stood watching some children in the forest having a wonderful time romping and playing in the snow. They watched as they built snowmen and as they made and threw snowballs at one another. Suddenly Ivan turned to his wife and said, "Maria, the children look like they are having such fun making a snowman, why don't we make one of our own?" So Ivan and Maria went out into the forest and began making a person out of snow.

Maria then said, "Ivan, since we have no children of our own, let us make a snow girl." Ivan agreed, and they proceeded to craft a pretty little maiden out of snow. They rolled and patted the snow into dainty little hands and feet, then they gave their little snow maiden braids and little eyes and a petite nose and mouth. When they were finished, they thought that she was the prettiest little girl that they had ever seen. Overcome by their creation. Ivan said, "Little snow maiden, speak to me," and Maria chimed in, "Yes, won't you please come to life so you can play with the other children!" As they gazed at their little snow girl they noticed that her eyes began to flutter and her cheeks began to glow a rosy color. At first they thought they were imagining things and Maria rubbed her eyes and looked again to behold charming little girl standing before them, where only a few moments ago their snow maiden had stood. In amazement Ivan finally said, "Where do you come from child? Who are you?"

"I have come from the land of winter. From the land of snow and ice and cold," the child replied. "I am come to be your daughter, your own little girl." With that the little girl ran and threw her arms around the couple and hugged them, and all three of them wept for joy. When the tears ended, they all began to talk at once and laughter followed their excitement, for this was the happiest day of their lives. They called to all of their neighbors in the nearby huts and introduce them to their beautiful little girl. Everyone stayed up late that night, marveling over the miracle that had happened. There was much singing, dancing and celebrating.

All during the long winter the little snow maiden played with the other children, and her parents beamed as they beheld their little girl and thought she was the prettiest of all. Everyone loved the little snow maiden, as she was a well mannered, happy child. She would run and play with the other children all day. Ivan and Maria were very happy.

When the first signs of spring appeared, the air grew warmer, the snow started to melt, and their little snow maiden seemed to grow more tired each day. She was no longer lively and actually appeared to be unhappy.

One day she came to her parents, her eyes filled with tears and sang a little song:

"The time has come for me to go. Away up North to the land of snow."

Her mother and father begged her to stay, saying they would not allow her to leave. They became so sad they began to cry. Ivan jumped up and stood in front of the door to stop the little snow maiden from leaving while Maria grabbed her and hugged her tightly. But as Maria held her little girl, the child began to melt. Soon there was nothing left of the Snow Maiden except her white fur cap and white fur coat. There where the snow maiden once stood was only a puddle of water. Maria sank to the floor and wept, while Ivan tried to console her, but he too had tears in his eyes.

As Maria and Ivan talked about their daughter, they wondered if perhaps someday their little snow maiden might return. All summer long they were lonely. It was difficult for them to hear the children laughing for it reminded them of their little girl. Summer turned to fall and fall into winter, and once again the snow began to fall and the weather was cold and icy outside. One night as Ivan and Maria watched the snow falling gently outside their window there came a knock on the door. They wondered who could be calling at this late hour, but then they heard a familiar voice singing a song:

"Mother! Father! Open the door! The snow has brought me back once more!"

Ivan ran to the door and threw it open. There was their little snow maiden. Maria ran to her daughter and the three of them hugged and kissed, laughed and cried. All that winter she lived with them and played with the other village children. But with each spring thaw, she returned to the land of winter from whence she came, where it was always cold with ice and snow. Ivan and Maria no longer wept for their daughter for they knew that when the weather turned cold and the snow began to blanket the land that their little snow maiden would return. And so it was for the rest of their lives, that every winter the little snow maiden would return to the couple and every spring she bid them farewell.

December 29

Snowflake
Paper Craft/Decoration

MATERIALS

paper (copy paper or tissue paper)
scissors
pattern

DIRECTIONS

This is the true pattern for cutting snowflakes. Once you learn how to fold your paper correctly your only limit on the designs is your own imagination. Decorate and transform any area into a whimsical fantasy.

1. Begin by cutting your 8½ x 11-inch paper into a square 8½ x 8½-inch. Make a larger square if you want to cut a larger image (Figure A).

2. Fold corner A down to corner D to form a triangle (Figure B). Cut the strip at the bottom of the triangle off. Remember you can enlarge the pattern you want to use.

3. Fold corner B down to corner C to form a smaller triangle (Figure C).

4. Your triangle should look like Figure D.

Figure A

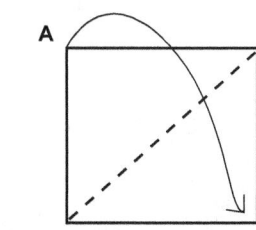
Figure B

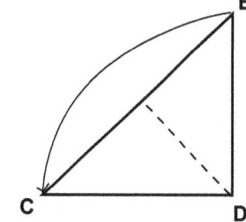
Figure C

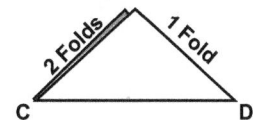
Figure D

Crazy About Christmas

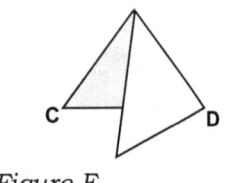

Figure E

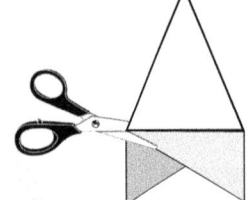

Figure F

Figure G

Figure H

5. Now the tricky part is to fold this triangle into three equal parts. Begin by folding the right corner over to the left but do not make a crease yet. Corner D will be below the edge (Figure E).

6. Fold the left corner gently to the right. When you have formed three equal parts, crease the folds firmly. Turn your triangle over and see that you have two little triangles at the bottom of your fold. Trim off the two little triangles (Figure F).

7. Put a small amount of tape on the sides of your folded paper that will be cut away. Tape your cutout pattern in place or pencil in the pattern on your folded triangle. This **true pattern for snowflakes** is now ready to cut (Figure G).

8. Start with the point of your triangle facing down and with the three folds in your left hand. Cut away the smaller parts of your pattern first, working your way up to the larger cuts. The lighter weight the paper the easier it is to cut. Use your imagination and creativity (Figure H).

9. If you want to flatten your snowflakes and remove most of the creases simply iron them on low.

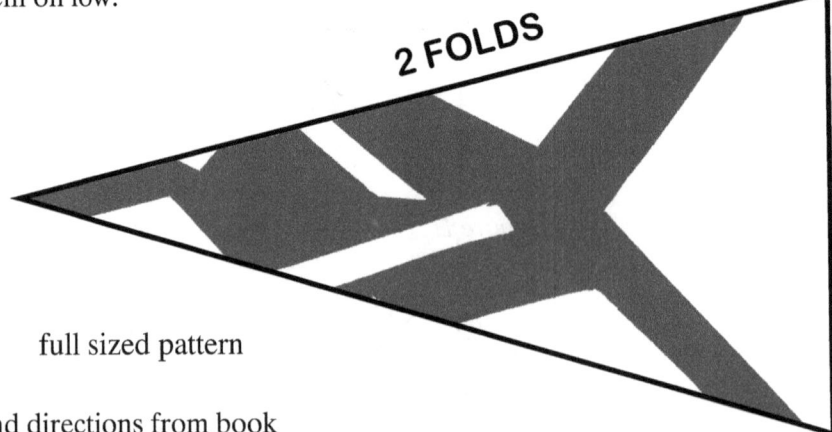

full sized pattern

Pattern and directions from book
Winter Fun with Magic Scissors by Linda S. Day & MyLinda Butterworth

December 29

Homemade Marshmallows
40 large marshmallow

INGREDIENTS

¾-oz unflavored gelatin (3 envelopes of Knox gelatin)
½ cup cold water
2 cups granulated sugar
⅔ cups light corn syrup
¼ cup water
¼ teaspoon salt
1 tablespoon vanilla extract

INSTRUCTIONS

1. Line 9 x 9-inch pan with plastic wrap and lightly oil it. Set aside.
2. In the bowl of an electric mixer, sprinkle gelatin over 1/2 cup cold water. Soak for about 10 minutes.
3. Meanwhile, combine sugar, corn syrup and 1/4 cup water in a small saucepan. Bring the mixture to a rapid boil and boil hard for 1 minute.
4. Pour the boiling syrup into soaked gelatin and turn on the mixer, using the whisk attachment, to high speed. Add the salt and beat for 12 minutes. After 12 minutes, add in the vanilla extract beat to incorporate.
5. Scrape marshmallow into the prepared pan and spread evenly (Lightly greasing your hands and the spatula helps a lot here). Take another piece of lightly oiled plastic wrap and press lightly on top of the marshmallow, creating a seal. Let mixture sit for a few hours, or overnight, until cooled and firmly set.
6. In a shallow dish, combine equal parts cornstarch and confectioners' sugar. Remove marshmallow from pan and cut into equal pieces with scissors (the best tool for the job) or a chef's knife (for fun try a cookie cutter). Dredge each piece of marshmallow in confectioners' sugar mixture.
7. Store in an airtight container.

NOTE: You can use any flavoring you want and use a couple drops of food coloring to change the color.

Let your dreams be bigger than your fears and your actions be louder than your words

M. Scott Peck

December 30

The White Dwarf
Author unknown

What a nuisance the wise men were! They had no idea how to get to Bethlehem, or even that Bethlehem was their destination. The North Star, who as you know is chief navigator in the night sky, called together volunteers from the galaxy. Stars and planets, meteors and asteroids, and even a few black holes from the outer reaches all waited for his directions. "Where are the wise men now?" the North Star asked the sun in our solar system, who is a kind of clerical worker in the galaxy, filing reports on the doings of humans, who are quite unique.

The Sun looked down at earth, and saw the wise men starting off towards the west. "Off to Brazil!" he reported.

"Well, you see the problem," the North Star explained to the galactic gathering. "They haven't the foggiest idea where they're supposed to be going. Any ideas?"

A school of asteroids flew past, bumping into each other and shouting. "We'll fall in a path towards Bethlehem," they said, "and show the way!"

And the asteroids zoomed towards earth to make a road, but by the time they'd passed through the earth's atmosphere, they were nothing but dust whirled round the world.

A gang of meteors flashed up, tough ones as big as small moons, and hailed the North Star. "Here's the deal," said the lead meteor. "We zoom in, make it past the atmosphere, and crash land all around Bethlehem and the wise men. No way they're going to miss that."

The North Star considered his options. "If we could guide them without blowing up half the planet," he said, "it would be better in the long run."

The meteors shrugged. "You snooze, you lose," said the leader, and they all left for the rough side of the galaxy.

"Where are the wise men now?" the North Star asked the Sun, who peered down on earth.

"Heading north," said the Sun. "Off to the French Riviera."

Off to one side, a very faint star - what we call a white dwarf, for it had become smaller with time, and denser with matter, and less bright - spoke up to the North Star. "I'm right over Bethlehem," he said, "from where the wise men are now. They can see me in the east."

The North Star peered through the endless eons of space. "I can hardly see you from here," he said. "How will they see you through all the air around the earth?"

"I think," said the little white dwarf star, "that if I try very hard - and I have been practicing, every day - I can go nova." Now, when a star goes nova, it explodes all the gases off its surface. For a few weeks, it will burn 100,000 times more brightly, and ordinary people who never saw the faint star before, will suddenly see it as if it were a brand new star, brighter than any other in the sky.

All the stars laughed at the white dwarf. "Anyone else got any ideas?" growled the North Star, and they quieted down. "Okay," the North Star told the white dwarf, "Give it your best shot."

Now, what the other stars didn't know, was that the white dwarf was part of a pair of stars, and his silent partner was a much bigger star, called a red giant. And the red giant had shared a great deal of his explosive gases with his small friend the white dwarf, so the white dwarf really was ready to go nova. "Countdown!" the white dwarf shouted. And the two of them were off: "3...2...1...nova!"

No explosion, no big bang - not a fizzle. Watching from nearby, several solar systems sneered. "We can do this," said the red giant star, and the white dwarf star got even hotter and hotter, and tried again.

Nothing happened. Not a pop. The North Star himself sighed from across the cosmos, twinkling in embarrassment. "Don't give up!" shouted the red giant, "Third time lucky - a universal principle." In one last effort, the white dwarf put his very last photon of energy into exploding himself to bits.

And then suddenly, with a great whoosh, all his gases all caught fire in a glorious flash and he exploded hugely into space. A cheer rang out across the galaxies, to the farthest, oldest edge of the swelling cosmos. Even the black holes shivered with silent applause from deep in their cavernous hearts.

The wise men, which had been absent-mindedly wandering northward, saw a new star suddenly appear in the east. "Finally, a sign," they told each other, and with certainty in their footsteps, they changed their course. The North Star, that old navigator, looked on, and welcomed the white dwarf to the ranks of stars that guide humans' lives.

December 30

Cascading Star Mobile
Craft/Decoration

MATERIALS

Assorted scrapbook paper or copy paper
Pattern
Scissors
10-12-inch embroidery hoop
1/8" ribbon or yarn in white or silver
2 yards 1-inch ribbon
Tape
Glue

DIRECTIONS

1. Cut out about 140 stars in different sizes and patterns. You can do them by hand or using a paper punch or cutting machine.
2. Cut 10-12 strands of ribbon 24-inches long
3. Take first star and tape to ribbon 4-inches from one end. This gives you enough to attach the ribbon to the embroidery hoop later.
4. Glue a matching sized star to the other side. Continue to tape and glue stars to each ribbon until you use up all the stars Make sure that one set of stars covers the end of the ribbon. Note I have seen this project done without the matching star on the back, but I prefer the finished look, it also gives it more weight.
5. Open up your embroidery hoop and lay in the center of the table, setting the inside hoop aside. Now take your star strands and space them out around the hoop draping the loose ribbon over the embroidery hoop.
6. Mark with a pencil where each ribbon should hang on the hoop. Then take the first ribbon and drape over the top and tape down to the inside leaving a 3-inch tail which you will then continue to wrap around the hoop till there is not more ribbon. Tape the tail end to the inside of the hoop. Do this for every ribbon strand.
7. When all strands are finished place the inner hoop inside and tighten.
8. Take the wider ribbon and cut in half. Fold in half and tie together leaving a loop at the center to hang it up. Separate the four ends and loop ribbon around hoop at equal spacing and tie or stitch around the hoop. Hang from ceiling.

Snowdrop Pecan Pie
Serves 10

Ingredients

1 (9 inch) frozen pie crust, thawed
2 eggs, beaten
1 can (14 ounce) sweetened condensed milk
⅓ cup light corn syrup
4 ounces white chocolate, melted
⅓ cup melted butter
2 teaspoons vanilla extract
3 tablespoons milk
2 cups chopped pecans
10 pecan halves

Instructions

1. Preheat the oven to 425°F.
2. In a small bowl place white chocolate. Place in microwave for 1 minute. Remove and mix until completely melted. Be careful not to overcook or it will burn.
3. Combine eggs, condensed milk, corn syrup, white chocolate, butter, vanilla and milk in a bowl, mix well.
4. Stir in the chopped pecans. Pour into pie shell and garnish with pecan halves.
5. Bake for 12 minutes. Reduce the oven temperature to 350° and continue to bake for 30 minutes or until set.

December 31

A HAPPY NEW YEAR
Francis Forrester

A Happy New Year to you, my children! May blessings rich as love can give, numerous as snowflakes, and enduring as the everlasting hills, descend gently on your unwrinkled brows, and fill your youthful hearts! May no sorrows poison the stream of your young lives, no misfortunes freeze your flowing spirits, no vices mar the beauty of your characters; but may innocent mirth well up within you, like the crystal waters from a fairy's fountain,--jocund laughter dance merrily upon your lips, sunshine flash from your eyes, and goodness adorn your conduct forever! Such is my meaning, my children, when I wish you a Happy New Year. Huzza, then, for the glad, gleesome Happy New Year!

The New Year! Who doesn't love the New Year? True, Mr. JANUARY is a frisky youth, pouring mighty gusts of wind from his puffy cheeks into people's faces, and bringing down clouds of snow-flakes from the sky with his mysterious wand, as if he wanted to be thought a great magician. Then he has icicles for eyelashes, and he wears a snow-wreath for a cap. Wherever he goes, the brooks and rivers do him homage. They cease to flow in his presence. They transform themselves into solid paths, along which he may march like a monarch enjoying a triumph. Besides all this, the young fellow acts the part of chief of police. He keeps everybody moving on the state highway. "Move along!--move along! Quick!--stir yourselves!" he cries to every creature he meets: and he is so testy that, if he is not obeyed, he will sting the toes, bite the fingers, tingle the cheeks, and hang icicles on the noses of the disobedient. He means all this for frolic and fun; and so it is, if not carried too far, as it is sure to be if he is not obeyed.

But, notwithstanding all these odd tricks, who doesn't love young January? I would like to see the boy or girl who does not. He would be a curiosity; and I should be tempted to send him to some old curiosity-shop for exhibition. Why, you know that Mr. January has an old friend of children, named Santa Claus, or St. Nicholas, who always comes with him, crouching down, like an over-loaded donkey, beneath a load of pleasant nick-nacks for the boys and girls. Young January carries his friend all over the land, and sends him, by the way of chimneys, windows, or doors, into almost every house, with orders to leave some of his wonderful toys in every pair of stockings he may find on the chimney-piece. Then what fun there is every New Year's morning, when the boys and girls peep into their stockings, to find out what the venerable and jocose St. Nicholas has been pleased to put there! And how many young hearts are made glad by these New Year's Gifts! I love rollicking young January for this. Huzza, again, then, I say!--huzza for the glad New Year!

And old Sol, the monarch of the skies, loves him, too. That good old sky-king gets up earlier, and goes to bed later, every day, from the time young January first shows his little puffy face until he retires to his summer residence. Why he should do this, if he doesn't love him, it would puzzle a Philadelphia lawyer to tell. And I think I know why the sky-king loves him. Wouldn't you like to know, too, Miss Laughinglips?

Listen! Put your ear close to my lips, and I will tell you! Young January brings a little bird with him, a beautiful little bird, prettier than humming-bird or bird of Paradise. This bird sings such a love of a song, in such a bewitching voice, that whoever hears it is charmed by it. As the charm works, the listener forgets his past sorrows, dries up his tears, sees beautiful visions of lovely landscapes and golden skies, grows young in heart and strong in purpose again, and is made very happy. Now, this little warbler young January sends into a hundred thousand homes, and bids him sing his song by a hundred thousand hearthsides. Would you like to know the name of this dear little bird? It is Hope! Everybody hopes in January, you know; and that is why the New Year brings with it so much of life, pleasure, and joy.

Well, I hear the little birdling's song today, and I hope. I hope that you, my dear children, may all live innocently and happily through the year. I hope you will all grow wiser, better, more useful, more fit for heaven. I hope our magazine will be better, more beautiful, more amusing, more instructive than ever; and I hope that you will all continue to read its pages until you cease to be children. Once more, then, I wish you a Happy New Year! Once more let us say, Huzza for the glad New Year!

F. F.

from Woodworth's Youth's Cabinet, January 1856, pp. 1-3

Personalized Calendar
Craft/Gift

MATERIALS

13   sheets card stock
        crayons, markers
        Photos, comic strips, magazine clippings,
          coloring pages, etc.
        Stickers

Directions
1. Decide if you want a theme, like landscapes, comics, recipes, science projects, animals, quotes with a picture, etc. It is not necessary to have a theme but some people like to have one.
2. If the whole family is involved let each person pick out a single month they want to design.
3. Go to an online site do a search for printable calendar, there are a lot to choose from. Pick one that you like the layout for, some of them are templates that you can customize for your word processor or spreadsheet. Once you have the one you want print out one sheet for each month of the year on card stock.
4. The blank sheet of paper represents the cover and the image for January. The calendar sheet for January will have the image for February on the back. To make sure you put your images in the right direction stack the months in front of you, turn January over and put a penciled 'X' on the upper right hand corner, then turn over February and do the same thing. Continue flipping each month over until you get to December. By doing this you will avoid having spent the time to create a great page and it being upside down.
5. Decorate your page however you want. Draw a picture, cut out and glue images from magazines, comic books, make a scrapbook photo page, write your favorite recipe, print coloring book images from the computer on one side and let your child color it, you are only limited by your imagination.
6. Take your calendar to local office store and ask them to put either a coil or comb binding on your calendar. You can then either punch holes in the center of each page or use a binder clip in the center and hang on a push pin (my favorite way).
7. To finalize your calendar you can put stickers on special days, like birthdays or holidays.

Party Chow Snack Mix

INGREDIENTS

- 9 cups Chex (any type)
- 1 cup semi-sweet chocolate chips
- 2 cup peanut butter
- 4 cup butter
- 1 teaspoon vanilla
- 1 2 cup powdered sugar

INSTRUCTIONS

1. Melt chocolate chips, peanut butter in microwave.
2. Stir until smooth
3. Add vanilla and stir.
4. Put Chex in a large bowl and pour sauce over cereal. Mix until coated.
5. Put into a large plastic bag with powdered sugar and shake well to coat.
6. Spread mixture evenly on wax paper and allow to cool.
7. Can be stored in an air-tight container, shake before eating..

Variation: You can add peanuts to the sauce just before you mix it with the Chex.

Variation 2: Mix in a small bag of Peanut Butter M&Ms after dusting with powdered sugar.

Variation 3: Make it Smores Party Chow Mix add 1 1/2 cups Mallow Bits and swap out 4 cups of the Chex cereal for Golden Graham® cereal. Add 1 cup of plain Golden Graham cereal when you add the marshmallows. Mix well.

Note: This is frequently referred to as Muddy Buddies.

Happy New Year —January 1

The Fairy's New Year Gift
by Emilie Poulsson

Two little boys were at play one day when a Fairy suddenly appeared before them and said, "I have been sent to give you New Year presents."

She handed to each child a package, and in an instant was gone.

Carl and Philip opened the packages and found in them two beautiful books, with pages as pure and white as the snow when it first falls.

Many months passed and the Fairy came again to the boys. "I have brought you each another book?" said she, "and will take the first ones back to Father Time who sent them to you."

"May I not keep mine a little longer?" asked Philip. "I have hardly thought about it lately. I'd like to paint something on the last leaf that lies open."

"No," said the Fairy; "I must take it just as it is."

"I wish that I could look through mine just once," said Carl; "I have only seen one page at a time, for when the leaf turns over it sticks fast, and I can never open the book at more than one place each day."

"You shall look at your book," said the Fairy, "and Philip, at his." And she lit for them two little silver lamps, by the light of which they saw the pages as she turned them.

The boys looked in wonder. Could it be that these were the same fair books she had given them a year ago? Where were the clean, white pages, as pure and beautiful as the snow when it first falls? Here was a page with ugly, black spots and scratches upon it; while the very next page showed a lovely little picture. Some pages were decorated with gold and silver and gorgeous colors, others with beautiful flowers, and still others with a rainbow of softest, most delicate brightness. Yet even on the most beautiful of the pages there were ugly blots and scratches.

Carl and Philip looked up at the Fairy at last.

"Who did this?" they asked. "Every page was white and fair as we opened to it; yet now there is not a single blank place in the whole book!"

"Shall I explain some of the pictures to you?" said the Fairy, smiling at the two little boys.

"See, Philip, the spray of roses blossomed on this page when you let the baby have your playthings; and this pretty bird, that looks as if it were singing with all its might, would never have been on this page if you had not tried to be kind and pleasant the other day, instead of quarreling."

"But what makes this blot?" asked Philip.

"That," said the Fairy sadly; "that came when you told an untruth one day, and this when you did not mind mamma. All these blots and scratches that look so ugly, both in your book and in Carl's, were made when you were naughty. Each pretty thing in your books came on its page when you were good."

"Oh, if we could only have the books again!" said Carl and Philip.

"That cannot be," said the Fairy. "See! they are dated for this year, and they must now go back into Father Time's bookcase, but I have brought you each a new one. Perhaps you can make these more beautiful than the others."

So saying, she vanished, and the boys were left alone, but each held in his hand a new book open at the first page.

And on the back of this book was written in letters of gold, "For the New Year."

from *Good Stories for Great Holidays* ©1914

Happy New Year —January 1

Personalized Journal
Craft

MATERIALS
Composition Book or blank art book
Scrapbook Paper or Wrapping Paper
Rubber Cement or Glue Sticks
Duct Tape

DIRECTIONS
1. Select the paper you want to cover the outside of your journal. Most composition books will need two 8 1/2" x 11" for the outside and 2 additional sheets for the inside. If you are going to use 12 x 12-inch sheets of scrapbook paper or wrapping paper you will need to lay your composition book flat and trace the size, then add 1 inch all the way around.
2. Open your composition book and lay with pages down flat on a table.

3. Start with the front and cover the top of book with rubber cement or a glue stick. If use a glue stick make sure you cover the surface well.
4. Place paper over the front cover from the center out leaving enough paper extending the edge of the book to fold to the inside. Then smooth the paper out so that you do not have any bubbles and that the paper is glued on securely. Sometimes you can use an old credit card to rub it down and remove bubbles.
5. Do the same thing on the back of the book.
6. Leave open flat until paper completely dries.

7. Once dry turn the book over. Cut the paper at the corners of the book on a diagonal leaving just a enough to fold over the corner, as most composition books have rounded corners.

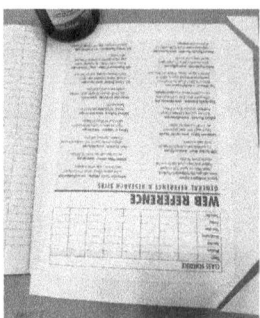

8. Fold over the corner. While it is folded over clip on either side to cover the corner. Glue down.

9. Rubber Cement or glue down the remaining flaps to the inside of the book and let dry. Follow the directions above to finish the back of the book.

Happy New Year —January 1

10. Cut two sheets of paper a quarter of an inch smaller than the inside cover. Cover the paper in rubber cement or glue, lay paper at the inside edge and then smooth from the inside to the outside pressing out all the air bubbles.

11. Cut a piece of duct tape a little longer than the center of the book. Open up book and place over the spine. Press down duct tape on the right of the spine, then stand the book on it's nose and smooth duct tape over spine of the book and onto the back. This will give the spine the stretch it needs Then trim off the excess duct tape from the top and bottom of the book.

12. At this point you can create a bookplate for the front or the inside of your journal to personalize it. (*see* image for instruction 10 for bookplate idea)

VARIATION: *Use different paper for the front and back.*
* *Draw your own images and attach to the journal or print out a photograph on heavy paper.*
* *You can cover the entire journal with clear contact paper for extra protection.*
* *Glue a piece of ribbon to the front and back edge before you do task 10 so that you can tie your journal closed.*
* *Add your favorite sayings to the top some pages or stickers.*

NOTE: *I do not recommend using card stock scrapbook paper unless you are going to use spray adhesive or rubber cement, it is hard to fold and adhere, but you can do it and they are beautiful. The small journal I did in card stock, but you need to use something to help really crease the edges well before gluing them down.*

Lentil, Kielbasa, and Garlic Stew
Serves 10

INGREDIENTS

- 2 tablespoons. olive oil
- 2 pounds. kielbasa, cut into thick pieces
- 1 large onion, diced
- 1 pound. carrots, cut into pieces
- 4 medium stalks celery, diced
- 5 clove garlic, chopped
- 6 cups water
- 2 cans chicken broth
- 2 cans diced tomatoes
- 1½ bag lentils

INSTRUCTIONS

1. In a large skillet, heat a tablespoon of oil on medium until hot. Add cut kielbasa and cook 4 to 5 minutes or until browned. Set aside
2. In same large pot, heat remaining oil on medium. Add onion, carrots, and celery; cook 15 minutes or until vegetables are golden, stirring often. Stir in garlic; cook 1 minute.
3. Rinse lentils and remove any stones.
4. Add water, broth, tomatoes, and lentils to pot; heat to boiling on high. Reduce heat to medium-low; simmer, uncovered, 40 minutes or until lentils are tender. Stir in kielbasa; heat through.
5. Serve in bowls with crusty bread.

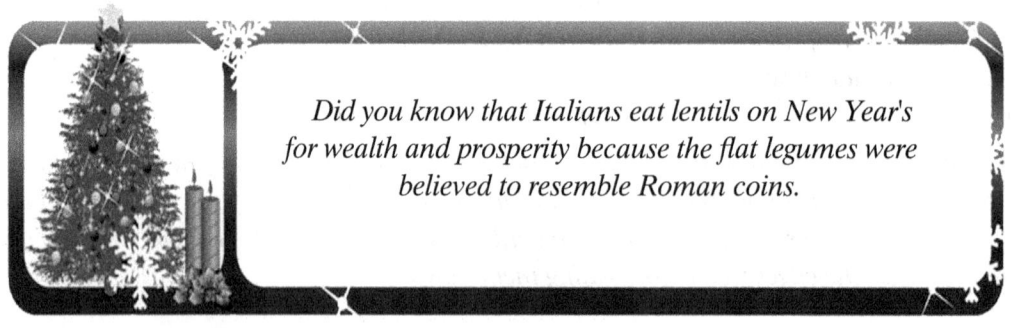

Did you know that Italians eat lentils on New Year's for wealth and prosperity because the flat legumes were believed to resemble Roman coins.

Where Love Is, There God Is Also
Count Lev Nikolaevich Tolstoy (also known as Leo Tolstoy)

In a certain town there lived a cobbler, Martin Avdéitch by name. He had a tiny room in a basement, the one window of which looked out on to the street. Through it one could only see the feet of those who passed by, but Martin recognized the people by their boots. He had lived long in the place and had many acquaintances. There was hardly a pair of boots in the neighborhood that had not been once or twice through his hands, so he often saw his own handiwork through the window. Some he had re-soled, some patched, some stitched up, and to some he had even put fresh uppers. He had plenty to do, for he worked well, used good material, did not charge too much, and could be relied on. If he could do a job by the day required, he undertook it; if not, he told the truth and gave no false promises; so he was well known and never short of work.

Martin had always been a good man; but in his old age he began to think more about his soul and to draw nearer to God. While he still worked for a master, before he set up on his own account, his wife had died, leaving him with a three-year old son. None of his elder children had lived, they had all died in infancy. At first Martin thought of sending his little son to his sister's in the country, but then he felt sorry to part with the boy, thinking: "It would be hard for my little Kapitón to have to grow up in a strange family; I will keep him with me."

Martin left his master and went into lodgings with his little son. But he had no luck with his children. No sooner had the boy reached an age when he could help his father and be a support as well as a joy to him, than he fell ill and, after being laid up for a week with a burning fever, died. Martin buried his son, and gave way to despair so great and overwhelming that he murmured against God. In his sorrow he prayed again and again that he too might die, reproaching God for having taken the son he loved, his only son while he, old as he was, remained alive. After that Martin left off going to church.

One day an old man from Martin's native village who had been a pilgrim for the last eight years, called in on his way from Tróitsa Monastery. Martin opened his heart to him, and told him of his sorrow.

"I no longer even wish to live, holy man," he said. "All I ask of God is that I soon may die. I am now quite without hope in the world."

The old man replied: "You have no right to say such things, Martin. We cannot judge God's ways. Not our reasoning, but God's will, decides. If God willed that your son should die and you should live, it must be best so. As to your despair ? that comes because you wish to live for your own happiness."

"What else should one live for?" asked Martin.

"For God, Martin," said the old man. "He gives you life, and you must live for Him. When you have learnt to live for Him, you will grieve no more, and all will seem easy to you."

Martin was silent awhile, and then asked: "But how is one to live for God?"

The old man answered: "How one may live for God has been shown us by Christ. Can you read? Then buy the Gospels, and read them: there you will see how God would have you live. You have it all there."

These words sank deep into Martin's heart, and that same day he went and bought himself a Testament in large print, and began to read.

At first he meant only to read on holidays, but having once begun he found it made his heart so light that he read every day. Sometimes he was so absorbed in his reading that the oil in his lamp burnt out before he could tear himself away from the book. He continued to read every night, and the more he read the more clearly he understood what God required of him, and how he might live for God. And his heart grew lighter and lighter. Before, when he went to bed he used to lie with a heavy heart, moaning as he thought of his little Kapitón; but now he only repeated again and again: "Glory to Thee, glory to Thee, O Lord! Thy will be done!"

From that time Martin's whole life changed. Formerly, on holidays he used to go and have tea at the public house, and did not even refuse a glass or two of vódka. Sometimes, after having had a drop with a friend, he left the public house not drunk, but rather merry, and would say foolish things: shout at a man, or abuse him. Now, all that sort of thing passed away from him. His life became peaceful and joyful. He sat down to his work in the morning, and when he had finished his day's work he took the lamp down from the wall, stood it on the table, fetched his book from the shelf, opened it, and sat down to read. The more he read the better he understood, and the clearer and happier he felt in his mind.

It happened once that Martin sat up late, absorbed in his book. He was reading Luke's Gospel; and in the sixth chapter he came upon the verses:

"To him that smiteth thee on the one cheek offer also the other; and from him that taketh away thy cloak withhold not thy coat also. Give to every man that asketh thee; and of him that taketh away thy goods ask them not again. And as ye would that men should do to you, do ye also to them likewise."

He also read the verses where our Lord says:

January 2

"And why call ye me, Lord, Lord, and do not the things which I say? Whosoever cometh to me, and heareth my sayings, and doeth them, I will shew you to whom he is like: He is like a man which built an house, and digged deep, and laid the foundation on a rock: and when the flood arose, the stream beat vehemently upon that house, and could not shake it: for it was founded upon a rock. But he that heareth and doeth not, is like a man that without a foundation built an house upon the earth, against which the stream did beat vehemently, and immediately it fell; and the ruin of that house was great."

When Martin read these words his soul was glad within him. He took off his spectacles and laid them on the book, and leaning his elbows on the table pondered over what he had read. He tried his own life by the standard of those words, asking himself:

"Is my house built on the rock, or on sand? If it stands on the rock, it is well. It seems easy enough while one sits here alone, and one thinks one has done all that God commands; but as soon as I cease to be on my guard, I sin again. Still I will persevere. It brings such joy. Help me, O Lord!"

He thought all this, and was about to go to bed, but was loth to leave his book. So he went on reading the seventh chapter ? about the centurion, the widow's son, and the answer to John's disciples ? and he came to the part where a rich Pharisee invited the Lord to his house; and he read how the woman who was a sinner, anointed his feet and washed them with her tears, and how he justified her. Coming to the forty-fourth verse, he read:

"And turning to the woman, he said unto Simon, Seest thou this woman? I entered into thine house, thou gavest me no water for my feet: but she hath wetted my feet with her tears, and wiped them with her hair. Thou gavest me no kiss; but she, since the time I came in, hath not ceased to kiss my feet. My head with oil thou didst not anoint: but she hath anointed my feet with ointment."

He read these verses and thought: "He gave no water for his feet, gave no kiss, his head with oil he did not anoint?" And Martin took off his spectacles once more, laid them on his book, and pondered.

"He must have been like me, that Pharisee. He too thought only of himself ? how to get a cup of tea, how to keep warm and comfortable; never a thought of his guest. He took care of himself, but for his guest he cared nothing at all. Yet who was the guest? The Lord himself! If he came to me, should I behave like that?"

Then Martin laid his head upon both his arms and, before he was aware of it, he fell asleep.

"Martin!" he suddenly heard a voice, as if some one had breathed the word above his ear. He started from his sleep. "Who's there?" he asked.

He turned round and looked at the door; no one was there. He called again. Then he heard quite distinctly: "Martin, Martin! Look out into the street to-morrow, for I shall come."

Crazy About Christmas

Martin roused himself, rose from his chair and rubbed his eyes, but did not know whether he had heard these words in a dream or awake. He put out the lamp and lay down to sleep.

Next morning he rose before daylight, and after saying his prayers he lit the fire and prepared his cabbage soup and buckwheat porridge. Then he lit the samovár, put on his apron, and sat down by the window to his work. As he sat working Martin thought over what had happened the night before. At times it seemed to him like a dream, and at times he thought that he had really heard the voice. "Such things have happened before now," thought he.

So he sat by the window, looking out into the street more than he worked, and whenever any one passed in unfamiliar boots he would stoop and look up, so as to see not the feet only but the face of the passer-by as well. A house-porter passed in new felt boots; then a water-carrier. Presently an old soldier of Nicholas' reign came near the window, spade in hand. Martin knew him by his boots, which were shabby old felt ones, galoshed with leather. The old man was called Stepánitch: a neighboring tradesman kept him in his house for charity, and his duty was to help the house-porter. He began to clear away the snow before Martin's window. Martin glanced at him and then went on with his work.

"I must be growing crazy with age," said Martin, laughing at his fancy. "Stepánitch comes to clear away the snow, and I must needs imagine it's Christ coming to visit me. Old dotard that I am!"

Yet after he had made a dozen stitches he felt drawn to look out of the window again. He saw that Stepánitch had leaned his spade against the wall, and was either resting himself or trying to get warm. The man was old and broken down, and had evidently not enough strength even to clear away the snow.

"What if I called him in and gave him some tea?" thought Martin. "The samovár is just on the boil."

He stuck his awl in its place, and rose; and putting the samovár on the table, made tea. Then he tapped the window with his fingers. Stepánitch turned and came to the window. Martin beckoned to him to come in, and went himself to open the door.

"Come in," he said, "and warm yourself a bit. I'm sure you must be cold."

"May God bless you!" Stepánitch answered. "My bones do ache to be sure." He came in, first shaking off the snow, and lest he should leave marks on the floor he began wiping his feet; but as he did so he tottered and nearly fell.

"Don't trouble to wipe your feet," said Martin "I'll wipe up the floor ? it's all in the day's work. Come, friend, sit down and have some tea."

Filling two tumblers, he passed one to his visitor, and pouring his own out into the saucer, began to blow on it.

January 2

Stepánitch emptied his glass, and, turning it upside down, put the remains of his piece of sugar on the top. He began to express his thanks, but it was plain that he would be glad of some more.

"Have another glass," said Martin, refilling the visitor's tumbler and his own. But while he drank his tea Martin kept looking out into the street.

"Are you expecting any one?" asked the visitor.

"Am I expecting any one? Well, now, I'm ashamed to tell you. It isn't that I really expect any one; but I heard something last night which I can't get out of my mind. Whether it was a vision, or only a fancy, I can't tell. You see, friend, last night I was reading the Gospel, about Christ the Lord, how he suffered, and how he walked on earth. You have heard tell of it, I dare say."

"I have heard tell of it," answered Stepánitch; "but I'm an ignorant man and not able to read."

"Well, you see, I was reading of how he walked on earth. I came to that part, you know, where he went to a Pharisee who did not receive him well. Well, friend, as I read about it, I thought now that man did not receive Christ the Lord with proper honor. Suppose such a thing could happen to such a man as myself, I thought, what would I not do to receive him! But that man gave him no reception at all. Well, friend, as I was thinking of this, I began to doze, and as I dozed I heard some one call me by name. I got up, and thought I heard someone whispering, ?Expect me; I will come to-morrow.' This happened twice over. And to tell you the truth, it sank so into my mind that, though I am ashamed of it myself, I keep on expecting him, the dear Lord!"

Stepánitch shook his head in silence, finished his tumbler and laid it on its side; but Martin stood it up again and refilled it for him.

"Here drink another glass, bless you! And I was thinking too, how he walked on earth and despised no one, but went mostly among common folk. He went with plain people, and chose his disciples from among the likes of us, from workmen like us, sinners that we are. ?He who raises himself,' he said, ?shall be humbled and he who humbles himself shall be raised.' ?You call me Lord,' he said, ?and I will wash your feet.' ?He who would be first,' he said, ?let him be the servant of all; because,' he said, ?blessed are the poor, the humble, the meek, and the merciful.'"

Stepánitch forgot his tea. He was an old man easily moved to tears, and as he sat and listened the tears ran down his cheeks.

"Come, drink some more," said Martin. But Stepánitch crossed himself, thanked him, moved away his tumbler, and rose.

"Thank you, Martin Avdéitch," he said, "you have given me food and comfort both for soul and body."

Crazy About Christmas

"You're very welcome. Come again another time. I am glad to have a guest," said Martin.

Stepánitch went away; and Martin poured out the last of the tea and drank it up. Then he put away the tea things and sat down to his work, stitching the back seam of a boot. And as he stitched he kept looking out of the window, waiting for Christ, and thinking about him and his doings. And his head was full of Christ's sayings.

Two soldiers went by: one in government boots, and the other in boots of his own; then the master of a neighboring house, in shining galoshes; then a baker carrying a basket. All these passed on. Then a woman came up in worsted stockings and peasant-made shoes. She passed the window, but stopped by the wall. Martin glanced up at her through the window, and saw that she was a stranger, poorly dressed, and with a baby in her arms. She stopped by the wall with her back to the wind, trying to wrap the baby up, though she had hardly anything to wrap it in. The woman had only summer clothes on, and even they were shabby and worn. Through the window Martin heard the baby crying, and the woman trying to soothe it, but unable to do so. Martin rose and going out of the door and up the steps he called to her.

"My dear, I say, my dear!"

The woman heard, and turned round.

"Why do you stand out there with the baby in the cold? Come inside. You can wrap him up better in a warm place. Come this way!"

The woman was surprised to see an old man in an apron, with spectacles on his nose, calling to her, but she followed him in.

They went down the steps, entered the little room, and the old man led her to the bed.

"There, sit down, my dear, near the stove. Warm yourself, and feed the baby."

"Oh, I haven't got any milk. I have eaten nothing myself since early morning," said the woman, but still she took the baby to her breast.

Martin shook his head. He brought out a basin and some bread. Then he opened the oven door and poured some cabbage soup into the basin. He took out the porridge pot also but the porridge was not yet ready, so he spread a cloth on the table and served only the soup and bread.

"Sit down and eat, my dear, and I'll mind the baby. Why, bless me, I've had children of my own; I know how to manage them."

The woman crossed herself, and sitting down at the table began to eat, while Martin put the baby on the bed and sat down by it. He chucked and chucked, but having no teeth he could not do it well and the baby continued to cry. Then Martin tried poking at him with his finger; he drove his finger straight at the baby's mouth and then quickly drew it back, and did this again and again. He did not let the baby take his finger in its mouth, because

January 2

it was all black with cobbler's wax. But the baby first grew quiet watching the finger, and then began to laugh. And Martin felt quite pleased.

The woman sat eating and talking, and told him who she was, and where she had been.

"I'm a soldier's wife," said she. "They sent my husband somewhere, far away, eight months ago, and I have heard nothing of him since. I had a place as cook till my baby was born, but then they would not keep me with a child. For three months now I have been struggling, unable to find a place, and I've had to sell all I had for food. I tried to go as a wet-nurse, but no one would have me; they said I was too starved-looking and thin. Now I have just been to see a tradesman's wife (a woman from our village is in service with her) and she has promised to take me. I thought it was all settled at last, but she tells me not to come till next week. It is far to her place, and I am fagged out, and baby is quite starved, poor mite. Fortunately our landlady has pity on us, and lets us lodge free, else I don't know what we should do."

Martin sighed. "Haven't you any warmer clothing?" he asked.

"How could I get warm clothing?" said she. "Why I pawned my last shawl for sixpence yesterday."

Then the woman came and took the child, and Martin got up. He went and looked among some things that were hanging on the wall, and brought back an old cloak.

"Here," he said, "though it's a worn-out old thing, it will do to wrap him up in."

The woman looked at the cloak, then at the old man, and taking it, burst into tears. Martin turned away, and groping under the bed brought out a small trunk. He fumbled about in it, and again sat down opposite the woman. And the woman said:

"The Lord bless you, friend. Surely Christ must have sent me to your window, else the child would have frozen. It was mild when I started, but now see how cold it has turned. Surely it must have been Christ who made you look out of your window and take pity on me, poor wretch!"

Martin smiled and said, "It is quite true; it was he made me do it. It was no mere chance made me look out."

And he told the woman his dream, and how he had heard the Lord's voice promising to visit him that day.

"Who knows? All things are possible," said the woman. And she got up and threw the cloak over her shoulders, wrapping it round herself and round the baby. Then she bowed, and thanked Martin once more.

"Take this for Christ's sake," said Martin, and gave her sixpence to get her shawl out of pawn. The woman crossed herself, and Martin did the same, and then he saw her out.

After the woman had gone, Martin ate some cabbage soup, cleared the things away, and sat down to work again. He sat and worked, but did not forget the window, and every time a shadow fell on it he looked up at once to see who was passing. People he knew and strangers passed by, but no one remarkable.

After a while Martin saw an apple-woman stop just in front of his window. She had a large basket, but there did not seem to be many apples left in it; she had evidently sold most of her stock. On her back she had a sack full of wood chips, which she was taking home. No doubt she had gathered them at some place where building was going on. The sack evidently hurt her, and she wanted to shift it from one shoulder to the other, so she put it down on the footpath and, placing her basket on a post, began to shake down the chips in the sack. While she was doing this a boy in a tattered cap ran up, snatched an apple out of the basket, and tried to slip away; but the old woman noticed it, and turning, caught the boy by his sleeve. He began to struggle, trying to free himself, but the old woman held on with both hands, knocked his cap off his head, and seized hold of his hair. The boy squawked and the old woman scolded him. Martin dropped his awl, not waiting to stick it in its place, and rushed out of the door. Stumbling up the steps, and dropping his spectacles in his hurry, he ran out into the street. The old woman was pulling the boy's hair and scolding him, and threatening to take him to the police. The lad was struggling and protesting, saying, "I did not take it. What are you beating me for? Let me go!"

Martin separated them. He took the boy by the hand and said, "Let him go, Granny. Forgive him for Christ's sake."

"I'll pay him out, so that he won't forget it for a year! I'll take the rascal to the police!"

Martin began entreating the old woman.

"Let him go, Granny. He won't do it again. Let him go for Christ's sake!"

The old woman let go, and the boy wished to run away, but Martin stopped him.

"Ask the Granny's forgiveness!" said he. "And don't do it another time. I saw you take the apple."

The boy began to cry and to beg pardon.

"That's right. And now here's an apple for you," and Martin took an apple from the basket and gave it to the boy, saying, "I will pay you, Granny."

"You will spoil them that way, the young rascals," said the old woman. "He ought to be whipped so that he should remember it for a week."

"Oh, Granny, Granny," said Martin, "that's our way? but it's not God's way. If he should be whipped for stealing an apple, what should be done to us for our sins?"

The old woman was silent.

And Martin told her the parable of the lord who forgave his servant a large debt, and how the servant went out and seized his debtor by the throat. The old woman listened to it all, and the boy, too, stood by and listened.

January 2

"God bids us forgive," said Martin, "or else we shall not be forgiven. Forgive every one; and a thoughtless youngster most of all."

The old woman wagged her head and sighed.

"It's true enough," said she, "but they are getting terribly spoilt."

"Then we old ones must show them better ways," Martin replied.

"That's just what I say," said the old woman. "I have had seven of them myself, and only one daughter is left." And the old woman began to tell how and where she was living with her daughter, and how many grandchildren she had. "There now," she said, "I have but little strength left, yet I work hard for the sake of my grandchildren; and nice children they are, too. No one comes out to meet me but the children. Little Annie, now, won't leave me for any one. ?It's grandmother, dear grandmother, darling grandmother.'" And the old woman completely softened at the thought.

"Of course, it was only his childishness, God help him," said she, referring to the boy.

As the old woman was about to hoist her sack on her back, the lad sprang forward to her, saying, "Let me carry it for you, Granny. I'm going that way."

The old woman nodded her head, and put the sack on the boy's back, and they went down the street together, the old woman quite forgetting to ask Martin to pay for the apple. Martin stood and watched them as they went along talking to each other.

When they were out of sight Martin went back to the house. Having found his spectacles unbroken on the steps, he picked up his awl and sat down again to work. He worked a little, but could soon not see to pass the bristle through the holes in the leather; and presently he noticed the lamplighter passing on his way to light the street lamps.

"Seems it's time to light up," thought he. So he trimmed his lamp, hung it up, and sat down again to work. He finished off one boot and, turning it about, examined it. It was all right. Then he gathered his tools together, swept up the cuttings, put away the bristles and the thread and the awls, and, taking down the lamp, placed it on the table. Then he took the Gospels from the shelf. He meant to open them at the place he had marked the day before with a bit of morocco, but the book opened at another place. As Martin opened it, his yesterday's dream came back to his mind, and no sooner had he thought of it than he seemed to hear footsteps, as though some one were moving behind him. Martin turned round, and it seemed to him as if people were standing in the dark corner, but he could not make out who they were. And a voice whispered in his ear: "Martin, Martin, don't you know me?"

"Who is it?" muttered Martin.

"It is I," said the voice. And out of the dark corner stepped Stepánitch, who smiled and vanishing like a cloud was seen no more.

"It is I," said the voice again. And out of the darkness stepped the woman with the baby in her arms and the woman smiled and the baby laughed, and they too vanished.

"It is I," said the voice once more. And the old woman and the boy with the apple stepped out and both smiled, and then they too vanished.

And Martin's soul grew glad. He crossed himself put on his spectacles, and began reading the Gospel just where it had opened; and at the top of the page he read

"I was a hungered, and ye gave me meat: I was thirsty, and ye gave me drink: I was a stranger, and ye took me in."

And at the bottom of the page he read:

"Inasmuch as ye did it unto one of these my brethren even these least, ye did it unto me." And Martin understood that his dream had come true; and that the Savior had really come to him that day, and he had welcomed him.

Crowell Company's "Worth While Booklet" Series. 1885.

January 2

Ojo de Dios or God's Eye
Craft/Decoration

Materials

Craft sticks, twig, dowels
Yarn in several bright colors
Glue or hot glue

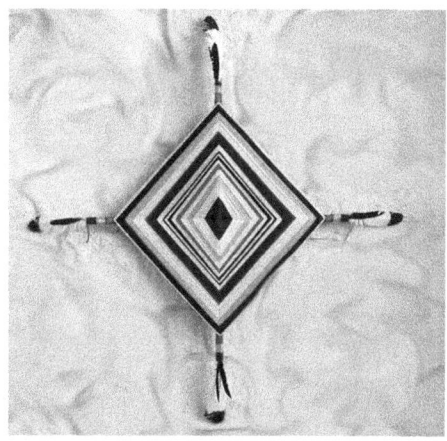

Directions

1. If you are using twigs, they will need a little preparation. Use small twigs that are about ¼" in diameter. Remove any loose bark from the twigs and make sure they have no weak spots that might break. Cut the twigs to 6"-8" lengths.

2. Glue two craft sticks or twigs together in a cross. Use a strong white glue like Tacky Glue or hot glue. Let glue dry. This may take several minutes.

3. Take one piece of yarn and wrap two to three times around center of sticks, then do the same thing in the other direction so you end up with a nice 'X' in the center. Giver your sticks a quarter turn and do it again. Give sticks one last turn and wrap once again. The center of your stick should be fully covered.

4. You are now ready to weave. You are going to take your yarn and go over, under and around the stick, then make a quarter turn and go over, under and around the stick (see image to your right). Another way to look at it is to take your yarn over the top of the stick and wrap it all the way around then turn it a quarter and do the whole process again. Every time you will need to turn it just a quarter of a turn making sure that you are always wrapping in the same direction and always taking yarn to the outside of the piece of yarn that is already there. Soon you will get into a rhythm...over, under, around, over, under, around.

5. Make sure you are pushing the yarn snugly toward the center as you work.

6. To change colors tie a length of another color of yarn onto the first one with a tight

Crazy About Christmas

knot or square, cut off excess yarn, then continue as before. Repeat for each additional color until finished.

7. Glue the final yarn end to the back of the cross to hold it in place. Make a hanger for the God's Eye with a length of yarn glued or tied to the sticks.

8. You might also add some decorations—tie on some feathers, add a tassel made from yarn, or attach a string of beads. Use your imagination! When you get good at this try adding another stick, the process is still the same just more of over, under, and around.

The Ojo de Dios, or God's Eye, is a simple weaving made across two sticks and is thought to have originated with the Huichol Indians of Jalisco, Mexico. The Huichol call their God's eyes Sikuli, which means "the power to see and understand things unknown." When a child is born, the central eye is woven by the father, then one eye is added for every year of the child's life until the child reaches the age of five. In other cultures this design is considered a good luck charm.

January 2

Soft Pretzels
makes 12 large pretzels

INGREDIENTS

1   package dry yeast (2¼ teaspoons)
1½ cups warm water
¼   cup brown sugar
1   tablespoon melted butter
4   cups unsifted flour
1   teaspoon salt

Baking Soda Bath
9   cups water
½   cup baking soda

    Coarse sea salt or pretzel salt
    Dipping sauces (optional)

INSTRUCTIONS

1. Whisk the yeast into warm water. Allow to sit for 1 minute.

2. Whisk in salt, brown sugar, and melted butter. Slowly add 3 cups of flour, 1 cup at a time. Mix with a wooden spoon (or dough hook attached to stand mixer) until dough is thick. Add 3/4 cup more flour until the dough is no longer sticky. If it is still sticky, add 1/4 - 1/2 cup more, as needed. Poke the dough with your finger - if it bounces back, it is ready to knead.

3. Turn the dough out onto a floured surface. Knead the dough for 3 minutes and shape into a ball. Cover lightly with a towel and allow to rest for 10 minutes.

4. Preheat oven to 400°. Line 2 baking sheets with parchment or silicone baking mats. Set aside.

5. With a sharp knife divide dough into 4 sections, then each section into 3, making a total of 12 sections.

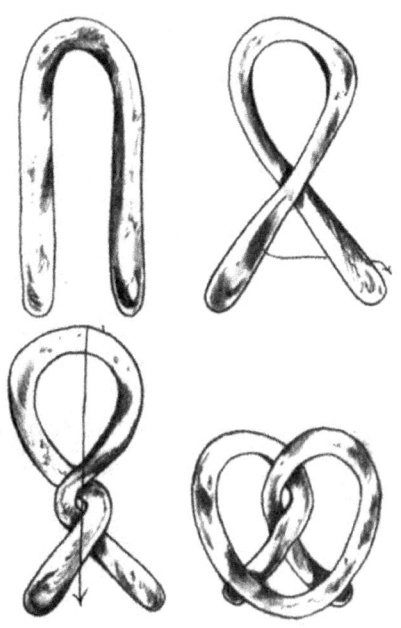

Roll dough into 12-14 inch rope. Form your rope into an upside down 'U'. Take the two ends of the U and make a full twist leaving tails. Now take the center of the 'O' and drop over the tails and you now have a perfectly twisted pretzel.

6. Pour 9 cups of water into a large pot, add baking soda and bring to a boil.
7. Drop 1-2 pretzels into the boiling water for 20-30 seconds. Any more than that and your pretzels will have a metallic taste. Using a slotted spatula, lift the pretzel out of the water and allow as much of the excess water to drip off. Place pretzel onto prepared baking sheet. Sprinkle each with coarse sea salt. Repeat with remaining pretzels.
8. Bake for 12-15 minutes or until golden brown.
9. Remove from the oven and serve warm. Eat them plain or have a variety of dipping sauces, mustard, honey or even dust them in cinnamon sugar.
10. Pretzels may be stored in an airtight container or zipped top bag for up to 3 days (they lose a little softness).

Tip: Pretzels freeze well, up to 2 months. To reheat, bake frozen pretzels at 350°F for 20 minutes or until warmed through or microwave until warm.

Variation: You can make pretzels into any shape you want. You can tie them in knots, shape them into hearts with a twist, letters, you get the idea.

Though the exact origins of the pretzel remain mysterious, legend has it that the story began around A.D. 610, when Italian monks presented their young students with treats of baked dough twisted in the shape of crossed arms. At the time, crossing one's arms was the traditional posture for prayer. As the custom spread through medieval Europe, the pretzel's three holes came to represent the Holy Trinity—Father, Son and Holy Spirit—and the twisty baked good became associated with good luck, long life and prosperity.

January 3

The Elves and the Shoemaker
A German folk tale
as told by MyLinda Butterworth

Once there was a shoemaker who worked hard and was very honest. Even so, he was as poor as a church mouse and could not earn enough to support himself and his wife. At last there came a time when all he had left was one piece of leather—just large enough to be made into one pair of shoes. The shoemaker cut the leather into pieces ready to stitch and make into shoes the next day. He left them on his work bench, intending to get up with the sun and start to work. The shoemaker was a good man, so his heart was light despite all his troubles. He went to bed peacefully, trusting that he would be able to finish the shoes the next day and sell them. Leaving all his cares to heaven, he settled his head on his pillow and fell asleep.

Bright and early the next morning the shoemaker rose and went to his work bench. To his amazement, there on the table were two shoes, already finished. They were beautifully made, neat and true, and with not a stitch out of place. But there was no sign that anyone had been in the house. The good man and his wife could not imagine how the shoes could have been made while they slept.

The first customer who came in the morning was so pleased with the shoes that he bought them immediately. The price he paid was enough that the shoemaker was now able to buy enough leather to make two more pairs of shoes.

The next evening the shoemaker cut out two pairs of shoes and went to bed early, as before. When he got up in the morning, there were the shoes on his bench, all finished and perfectly made just as before. Once again there was no sign that anyone had been in the house.

That day customers came in who paid the shoemaker handsomely for his goods, so he was able to buy leather for four pairs of shoes. Once again he cut out the shoes and left the pieces on the bench. Once again he found in the morning that all four pairs of shoes were made.

For some time the same thing happened, until the good man and his wife were thriving and prosperous. But they were not satisfied to have so much done for them and not know to whom they should be grateful. One evening about Christmas time, as they were sitting near the fire and chatting together, the shoemaker said to his wife, "I would like to stay up tonight so that we might see who it is who comes in during the night and makes the beautiful shoes we find each morning."

The wife agreed, so they hid themselves behind a curtain and waited to see what would happen. Just as the clock struck twelve, two tiny elves came dancing into the room. They hopped upon the bench, took up the work that was cut out, and began with their tiny little fingers to stitch, sew, and hammer so neatly and quickly that the shoemaker could not believe his eyes. These little elves wore nothing. They worked with tiny scissors and hammers and thread, and as they worked they sang this song:

We stitch and clip and hammer,
These shoes we'll make for you,
We're happy when we do good deeds,
Then we're quickly out of view!

No one ever worked so fast, as those two little elves did. They worked on until the job was quite finished and the shoes stood ready for use upon the table. Then they took hold of each other's hands and ran swiftly away, leaving the room as it was before.

"These little elves have made us rich and happy," said the shoemaker to his wife. "How can we thank them and do them a good service in return?"

"They were running around with nothing on, and must be frozen with the cold. I will make them tiny coats, pants and a cap," said the wife.

"And I will make them each a little pair of shoes," said her husband.

That very day they went about their tasks. The wife cut out two tiny pairs of yellow trousers; two teeny, weeny blue coats; and two bits of caps, bright orange, because she thought the elves would like bright colors; and her husband made two little pairs of shoes with long, pointed toes. They made the wee clothes as dainty as could be, with nice little stitches and pretty buttons, and by Christmas time they were finished.

On Christmas Eve the shoemaker cleaned his bench, and on it, instead of leather, he laid the two sets of clothing and the tiny shoes. Then he and his wife hid away as before to see what the elves would do.

Promptly at midnight, they came skipping in and were about to set to work. But instead of the leather cut and ready to assemble they found the charming little clothes and shoe. At first they were surprised, then excessively delighted. In the twinkling of an eye they put on and smoothed down the pretty clothes. Then they began to dance and sing in a circle:

"Now we're boys so fine and neat,
Why cobble more for other's feet?"

When the sun rose, they danced out of the window, over the green, and out of sight. The shoemaker and his wife never saw them again, but continued to do well, and had good luck for the rest of their lives.

January 3

Pine Cone Elves
Craft/Decoration

MATERIALS

Pine cones
Wooden ball for head
Wooden heart for feet
Felt
Bells, small
Paint for eyes & feet
assorted tiny toys, etc (optional)
Hot glue & white glue

DIRECTIONS:

1. Select pine cones based on the size you want your elves. Follow directions on page 40 for preparing them if you collected them yourself.
2. Cut out circle of felt for hat, then cut it in quarters. Cut it out of paper first to make sure the hat will fit the wooden ball. When you have it right cut it out of felt.
3. Cut out a long piece of felt for scarf, making it wide enough to cover their chin and neck.
4. Glue the two long edges of felt triangle to make hat. Glue bell onto the point of the hat.
5. Paint heart if you want the feet to be a color to match hat. Glue pine cone to heart to make the elves feet. Use enough glue here to make the pine cone stand up.
6. Glue wooden bead to top of pine cone. You might need to remove a couple of pieces of the pine cone to make a space to glue the ball on.
7. Glue hat onto head with white glue.
8. Wrap scarf around neck and loosely tie. Fringe the ends of scarf. To secure scarf you can place a drop of glue at the center back of the scarf.
9. Paint two dots for eyes.
10. Glue on tiny packages, trees, etc to finish the look.

Note: I do not tell you the sizes of the wooden ball or heart, because pine cones are different sizes. Select those items to match size of pine cone or vice versa.

Variation 1: If you intend to use these as ornaments you can make the feet out of felt instead of wood and attach a twine loop to hang them up.

Variation 2: You can add tiny pompoms or bells to end of shoes to up his fashion style. You can also cut out tiny felt mittens instead of packages to glue to either side.

Bacon Cheddar Potato Pancakes
4 Servings

INGREDIENTS

3 slices bacon
4 cups cold leftover mashed potatoes
2 eggs
1 teaspoon onion powder
1/2 teaspoon salt
1/2 teaspoon ground black pepper

INSTRUCTIONS

1. Place the bacon in a large, deep skillet, and cook over medium-high heat, turning occasionally, until evenly browned and crisp, about 10 minutes. Remove the bacon slices, crumble, and set aside. Leave the bacon drippings in the skillet.
2. Mix the mashed potatoes, eggs, onion powder, salt, and black pepper together in a bowl; stir in the crumbled bacon and Cheddar cheese.
3. Form the mixture into 8 patties. Heat the bacon drippings over medium heat, and pan-fry the patties in the drippings until crisp on each side, about 4 minutes per side.

January 4

Three Trees
Author Unknown

There were three small trees living near each other on a mountainside. The first little tree looked up at the stars and said: "I want to hold treasure. I want to be covered with gold and filled with precious stones. I'll be the most beautiful treasure chest in the world!"

The second little tree looked out at the small stream trickling by on its way to the ocean. "I want to be traveling mighty waters and carrying powerful kings. I'll be the strongest ship in the world!"

The third little tree looked down into the valley below where busy men and women worked in a busy town. "I don't want to leave the mountain top at all. I want to grow so tall that when people stop to look at me, they'll raise their eyes to heaven and think of God. I will be the tallest tree in the world."

Years passed. The rain came, the sun shone, and the little trees grew tall.

One day three woodcutters climbed the mountain. The first woodcutter looked at the first tree and said, "This tree is beautiful. It is perfect for me." With a swoop of his shining axe, the first tree fell. "Now I shall be made into a beautiful chest, I shall hold wonderful treasure!" The first tree said.

The second woodcutter looked at the second tree and said, "This tree is strong. It is perfect for me." With a swoop of his shining axe, the second tree fell. "Now I shall sail mighty waters!" thought the second tree. "I shall be a strong ship for mighty kings!"

The third tree felt her heart sink when the last woodcutter looked her way. She stood straight and tall and pointed bravely to heaven. But the woodcutter never even looked up. "Any kind of tree will do for me." He muttered. With a swoop of his shining axe, the third tree fell.

The first tree rejoiced when the woodcutter brought her to a carpenter's shop. But the carpenter fashioned the tree into feedbox for animals. The once-beautiful tree was not covered with gold, nor with treasure. She was coated with sawdust and filled with hay for hungry farm animals.

The second tree smiled when the woodcutter took her to a shipyard, but no mighty sailing ship was made that day. Instead the once-strong tree was hammered and sawed into a simple fishing boat. She was too small and too weak to sail to an ocean, or even a river; instead she was taken to a little lake.

The third tree was confused when the woodcutter cut her into strong beams and left her in a lumberyard. "What happened?" the once-tall tree wondered. "All I ever wanted was to stay on the mountain top and point to God..."

Many many days and night passed. The three trees nearly forgot their dreams. But one night, golden starlight poured over the first tree as a young woman placed her newborn baby in the feed box. "I wish I could make a cradle for him," her husband whispered. The mother squeezed his hand and smiled as the starlight shone on the smooth and the sturdy wood. "This manger is beautiful," she said. And suddenly the first tree knew he was holding the greatest treasure in the world.

One evening a tired traveler and his friends crowded into the old fishing boat. The traveler fell asleep as the second tree quietly sailed out into the lake. Soon a thundering and thrashing storm arose. The little tree shuddered. She knew she did not have the strength to carry so many passengers safely through with the wind and the rain. The tired man awakened. He stood up, stretched out his hand, and said, "Peace." The storm stopped as quickly as it had begun. And suddenly the second tree knew he was carrying the king of heaven and earth.

One morning, the third tree was startled when her beams were yanked from the forgotten woodpile. She flinched as she was carried through an angry jeering crowd. She shuddered when soldiers nailed a man's hands to her. She felt ugly and harsh and cruel. But on Sunday morning, when the sun rose and the earth tremble with joy beneath her, the third tree knew that God's love had changed everything. It had made the third tree strong. And every time people thought of the third tree, they would think of God. That was better than being the tallest tree in the world.

So next time you feel down because you didn't get what you want, just sit tight and be happy because God is thinking of something better to give you.

January 4

Classic Tangram Puzzle
Craft/Activity

MATERIALS

Fun Foam Sheets - assorted colors
scissors or craft knife
Marking pen
ruler

DIRECTIONS

1. While you can make this puzzle out of 1/4-inch plywood. I find it is more fun to use fun foam, even card stock will work and make several so you can mix and match the colors.
2. Cut your fun foam into an 8-inch square.
3. The pattern on the next page is reduced by 30%. If you use it as it is it creates a 6-inch tangram.
4. Here are the steps to create your own. Start with a square piece of paper. I will show you how to fold it and then mark it or you can draw it out by starting with a 2-inch grid (16 squares) following the directions below just drawing the lines instead of folding.
5. Step one: Fold your paper diagonally. Then fold it again diagonally. When you unfold it you will see a large X in the middle. Draw from one corner to the other with a ruler.

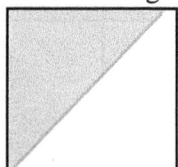 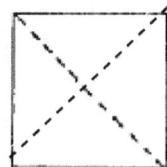 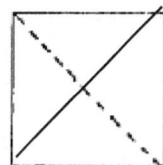

6. Step two: fold one corner to the middle. Fold corner back and draw across that line.

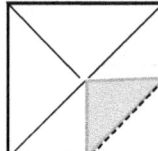 

7. Step three: draw from the corner across the center to the center of the small corner triangle along the folded line.

 Crazy About Christmas

8. Step four: turn paper to the left and fold corner to the center, unfold and draw line from center line to bottom triangle.

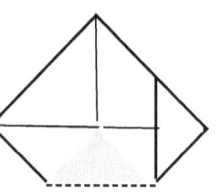

9. Step five: turn to the left and fold top edge to the middle, unfold and draw remaining small triangle from center line to bottom triangle.

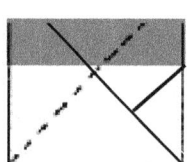

10. Place pattern on fun foam and cut out pattern. I suggest you use a ruler and a craft knife on a cutting mat. Another option is to cut the pattern apart and trace on foam.

11. Now the fun begins. Make up your own designs or follow a few of the patterns below. You can also find lots of patterns on the web by just searching under tangram patterns.

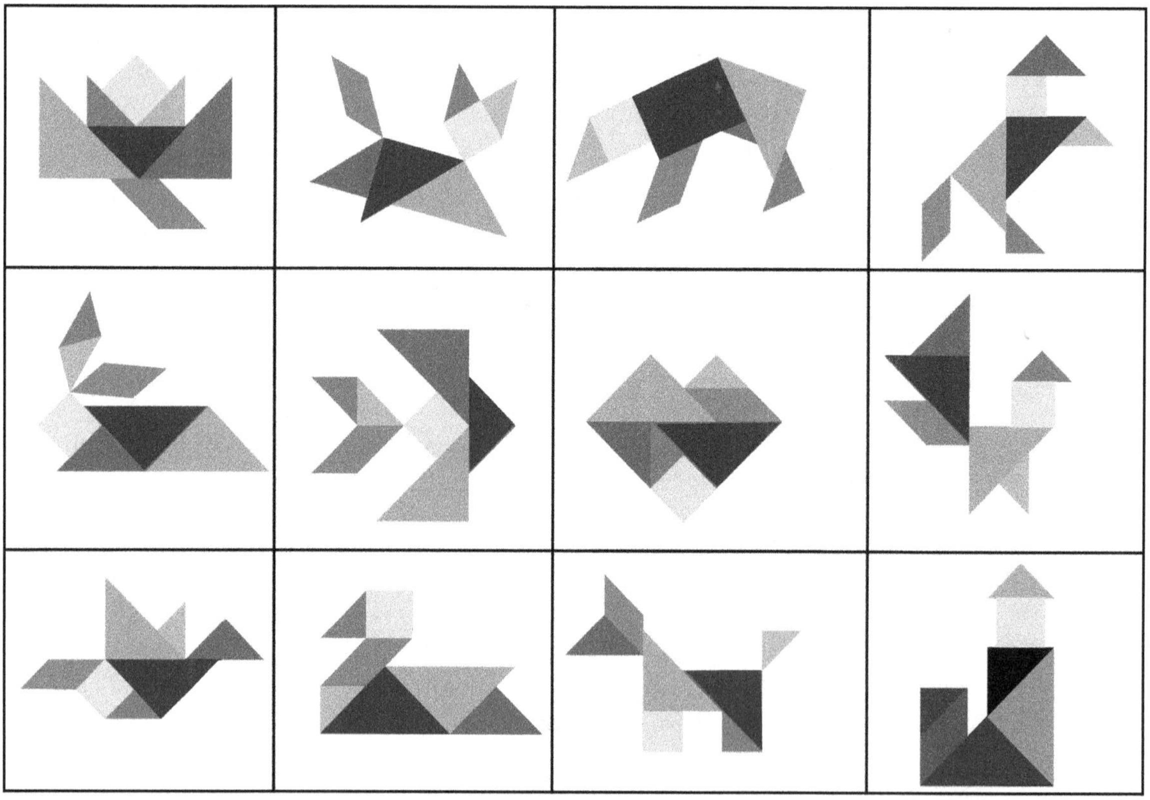

January 4

This pattern has been reduced by 30% to fit in this book.

281

Appetizer Tree Board

SUGGESTED INGREDIENTS

Assorted olives
Cherry Tomatoes
Assorted cubed cheese
Cubed ham
Red and Green Grapes
Fruit in season
Cubed Pineapple
Celery Sticks
Carrot Sticks ...

INSTRUCTIONS

1. Wash your fruits and vegetables set aside to dry.
2. If your cheeses are not already cubed, Cut into 1-inch cubes
3. If your ham is not already cubed. Cut into 1-inch cubes
4. Take a slice of cheese or pineapple and using a sharp knife or a cookie cutter cut out a star.
5. Cover a large cutting board in aluminum foil or place on a nice tray.
6. The size of your tree is only limited by the size of the board/tray you put it on. Starting at the bottom to set the base for your tree. I start with a layer of cheese because it doesn't move or roll away.
7. For your next layer add a row of fruit or ham. Keep building one layer at a time paying attention to the shape of your tree. Each row should be just a little smaller than the previous row. Use celery or carrot sticks for your tree trunk.
8. When you get to the top add the star you cut out. Don't forget to set out some crackers and some toothpicks when you serve your appetizer tree.

Note: Make more than one tree so that you can have one that is vegetables and the other fruits and cheese or make one with meat and cheese there no end to the possibilities.

January 5

Le Befana the Giver of Gifts
A Tale of Italy
as told by MyLinda Butterworth

Herod was king of Jerusalem when my story begins. My friend Strenae, lived on a hilltop in Italy where she lived by herself. Living alone was not her choice, her husband was a soldier who died in battle and her only son died as young boy. You would think this would make her a bitter old woman, but that was not true, she had a big heart, she had many vegetable gardens she cared for along with a garden full of herbs. The herbs she bundled and made into tinctures or remedies for all kinds of ailments or to clear the air. The vegetables she used to feed herself and when there was an abundance she always shared with those who had less than her. Her shawl was tattered and her shoes were worn, her dress was patched but it used to be dyed in bright colors. In the village where she lived the people new Strenae for her healing, baking, cooking, sweeping and cleaning. Her home was always clean. Why does all this matter? Let me tell you her story.

In three very far away countries lived some very learned men who study the stars, some people called them astrologers, some Magi, and some just wise men. Their names were Melchior, Balthasar, and Gaspar and for many years they searched the sky for a new star that would verify the prophesy that the Holy Child, the King of the Jews had been born and each of them had vowed when that new star appeared that they would follow it to where this special babe had been born. One night while they were gazing into the skies a star burst upon the clear sky and shown brighter than any star they had ever seen. They knew at that moment that the child of prophesy had been born. Each one of them packed up provisions for the trip, along with a gift fit for a king. One brought a box of gold, one the gift of myrrh a holy oil, and the third one brought frankincense, the finest of all incense.

They each traveled from their own country and one day as they were all approaching the great city of Jerusalem they met each other. They did not speak the same language, dress alike, or even look alike but they all had one thing in common, they were all searching for the star that would show over the dwelling of the new born king. It was at that moment that nothing else mattered and they decided to travel together, these three wise men.

Later that day as they approached the top of hill they saw a woman outside sweeping and humming to herself. Gaspar got off his great horse and said, "Shalom, my dear woman. Would you allow us to stop and water our animals? It has been a long trip and we are tired."

Strenae immediately put down her broom, "Why of course." She leads them to a trough where they could care for their animals. "I see that you are tired as well, please sit and I will feed you if you will share the story of what brings you to my humble home."

The three wise men nodded their heads and sat at her table and began to tell Strenae about the new star in the east that they were following and how it would lead them to the child of the prophecy. The story was fascinating to Strenae since she too had noticed the new star which had just appeared in the sky and had noticed how bright it was.

Balthasar stood to leave and said, "Strenae, we thank-you for your hospitality but we must continue our journey to find the Holy Child before the stars light fades away. Will you not join us on our quest?"

Strenae blushed like a new bride thinking about the chance to meet this special child, but then busied herself by clearing the table. "I thank you for your offer but I have too many chores to do right now."

The Magi bowed deeply to their hostess and gathered their animals to leave. Once more Balthasar turned to Strenae and said, "Are you sure you would not like to travel with us?"

Once again Strenae hung her head and began to sweep saying, "No, no I am much too busy to make such a long journey with you, but I thank you again for your offer and the good news. May your journey be successful." She watched as they mounted their animals and headed towards the east following the star. Melchior turned and waved at her as they left.

Strenae watched as they rode out of site and began to wonder why she could not have put aside her chores just this time and gone on this once in a lifetime adventure to see the child of the prophesy. She began to have an aching in her heart as she thought of her own son and how she loved little children. Before long she was chiding herself for always putting work before doing something for herself and without even thinking she had grabbed her largest basket and filled it with food and all her son's belongings. As she closed the door she grabbed her broom and swept away the dirt from in front of her door, because she just could not bear the thought of leaving her house dirty.

Once out the door Strenae followed the path of the Magi in hopes of catching up with them. She ran for miles, but soon became so exhausted that she had to sit down to catch her breath. As she sat she leaned against tall tree thinking to herself that she would stop for just a few moments but soon her eyelids fluttered and before long she was asleep. As she slumbered a light from the new star descended upon her and she woke up. What she saw in front of her was a heavenly being who leaned over and sprinkled stardust on Strenae's broom and basket and then gone as quickly as they had appeared.

Strenae sat straight up and rubbed her eyes, she wasn't sure if what she had seen was a dream or real but she knew that she must hurry if she was to have any chance of seeing the Holy Child. When she stood up she was full of energy. She picked up her broom and basket and they felt as if she was lifting a feather. She began to run when she noticed that she was being lifted off the ground by her broom and so she sat down and hung her basket

January 5

on the broom. What magic was this or maybe it was a gift Strenae thought to herself, no matter she was in a hurry and this would help her.

As Strenae traveled that night every time she saw a baby or child she stopped and gave them some food and a gift for she never knew which child would be the Holy One. As hard as she searched she never did find those Three Wise Men but she did eventually find the child, Jesus. She gave him the gifts she had brought to make him happy. The infant child, Jesus was so delighted that he bestowed a gift on her as well. In her mind she heard these words, "Strenae because thou hast been valiant in your efforts to find me I will bless you to be the mother of all the children of Italy for one night each year, you will give small gifts to the children as a reminder that God loves them. Finally, from this day forth you shall be known as La Befana. "

La Befana literally means giver of gifts, so if you are lucky enough to be in Italy the eve of Epiphany, look to the sky and to see if you can see her flying overhead on her broom bringing joy to good children, for it brings a smile to her face to know that she serves the King of Kings.

Canadian Postage Stamp, 1992.
Designed by Louis Fishauf

Note: This legend began in the late 12th to early 13th century so you can imagine that there are many versions of this story. In some stories Befana never finds the Christ Child and still searches. Although she has been unsuccessful in her search, she still leaves gifts for good young children because the Christ Child can be found in all children. Some times Befana sweeps the floor before she leaves. Sweeping meant the sweeping away of the problems of the year. Epiphany marks the official end of the Christmas season, commemorating the day when the Three Wise men arrive at the manger bearing gifts.

Aroma Therapy Candles
Craft

MATERIALS

Beeswax
Essential Oils
Cotton wicks
Clean can to melt wax
container to hold candle - mason jars, tins, glass votives, etc.
pot
Decorative paper (optional)

DIRECTIONS

1. Create a double boiler by placing water into a pot and bring to a boil.
2. Place beeswax into clean can (I like a large tomato can because it has a wide opening - clean it well) and place into water until it melts.
3. While your waiting cut wicks to fit clean mason jars, tins, glass votive and tape around pencil. Place over top of container.
4. When wax is melted take out of water and stir in essential oils. *Hint*: Don't add the oil to the wax when it is very hot or it will burn off the scent. The amount of essential oil you use depends on the scent strength of the oil, if your mixing them, and the amount of wax you use. My rule of thumb is to add essential oil until I can smell it and then add a few more drops. .
5. Pour into melted wax into prepared containers. Reset your wick position if necessary.
6. Allow to cool completely.
7. To adorn your candle cut a decorative piece of paper to fit around your container and attach with double stick tape. If you are giving it as a gift you can either make a label to attach to the front or add a hanging gift tag.

Herbes de Provence
Makes about 2/3 cup

INGREDIENTS

- 3 tablespoons marjoram, dried
- 3 tablespoons thyme, dried
- 3 tablespoons savory, dried
- 1 tablespoon basil, dried
- 1½ teaspoons rosemary, dried and crumbled
- ½ teaspoon sage, dried
- ½ teaspoon fennel seed, optional

INSTRUCTIONS

1. Combine herbs and mix well.
2. Place in air tight container. To keep fresh for a long time store in refrigerator.
3. Use any place you might use Italian seasoning. It is great with soups and sauces or over fresh vegetables. Makes a great gift for giving.

Season Salt
Makes about ½ cup (serving size is a pinch)

INGREDIENTS

- 6 tablespoons sea salt
- ½ teaspoon marjoram
- ¼ teaspoon onion powder
- ½ teaspoon thyme
- ½ teaspoon curry powder
- ½ teaspoon celery seed
- 2¼ teaspoons paprika
- ⅛ teaspoon dill seed
- ½ teaspoon garlic salt
- 1 teaspoon dry mustard

INSTRUCTIONS

1. Mix all of the above ingredients together until evenly distributed.
2. Place in and airtight container. Use wherever you want to spice things up.
3. This is a good all around seasoning.

We Three Kings of Orient are,
Bearing gifts we traverse afar,
Field and fountain,
Moor and mountain,
Following yonder Star.

O star of wonder, star of light,
star with royal beauty bright,
westward leading, still proceeding,
guide us to thy perfect light.

—John Henry Hopkins

January 6 - Epiphany

The Magi in the West and Their Search for the Christ
A Tale for the Christmas Tide
By Frederick E. Dewhurst

Now, it happened a long time ago, in the year ——, but the exact year does not matter, because you will not find this story written in the history of any of the nations of the world. But in one of the countries of Europe bordering on the Mediterranean Sea was a lofty mountain, which, to the dwellers in the plains below, seemed to reach to the very sky. At times its summit was covered with clouds, so that it could not be seen; at other times it stood out fair and clear, as though silently asking the people to look up and not down. The lower slopes of the mountain were covered with olive trees, with groves of oranges and lemons, and with vineyards, and they were dotted here and there with the little white cottages of the peasants who made their living from these groves and vineyards, the fruit of which they sold in the city not far away.

Along the mountain-side wound a foot-trail even to the summit, and nowhere, in all the region, was there a finer view of the Mediterranean than from the summit of this mountain. In the long summer afternoons the peasants and children would climb to the top and look off on the lovely picture of land and sea. Then they would eat their simple lunch of bread and dates and olives and quench their thirst from the spring on the mountain-side, which they called "Dew-of-heaven," so clear and fresh and sparkling was it; and when the sun began to touch the western sky with his pencils of gold and carmine and purple, they hastened down, that they might reach their cottages before the night shut in.

On the day when this story begins a man was standing on the summit of the mountain looking across the sea in the direction where you will find Tyre and Joppa on the map. He was, very plainly, not one of the peasants who lived on the mountain-side. He looked about sixty years of age; he was tall and erect, though he carried a staff in his hand. His hair and beard were long and flowing, and almost gray, but his eye was clear and penetrating, and he was looking across the sea as though he expected some one to appear.

And while he stood there gazing seaward, there appeared a second man on the summit, helping himself up with his staff, and panting with the effort of the long climb. From his dress and manner it was plain that this man, too, was not one of the peasants, for, like the first comer, he seemed to belong to another age and clime. The two men glanced at each other and gave such greeting as strangers might who should meet in so solitary a spot as a mountain summit. Then both lapsed into silence and looked off across the sea.

Presently the last comer seemed to awake from his reverie. He walked over to the place where the other man was sitting, still gazing off toward Joppa, and touched him on the shoulder: "A thousand pardons, my friend," he said, "but my mind is haunted with some far-off recollection, as though in some other land and some far-off time I had seen thy face. Wilt thou have the kindness to tell me thy name?"

Without lifting his eyes from the sea, and in a tone which seemed regretful and sad, the stranger replied: "My name is Gaspard."

"Gaspard! Indeed, then have I seen thee! Look at me, my friend; dost thou not remember me? My name is Melchoir. Dost thou not recall that time, how long I know not, when thou and I and Balthazar followed a star which led us to a little Jewish hamlet, thou bearing gold and I frankincense, and Balthazar myrrh? Dost thou not remember how, on the long journey thither, we talked about the young Prince, whom we expected to find in a royal palace, and how at last when we reached the village, following the star, we were led not to a palace but to a little inn, and not even to a room within the inn, but to the stable-yard, where we found a sweet-faced woman bending over a babe cradled in a manger; and standing near, a sturdy peasant, proud and happy, whose name was Joseph? Dost thou not remember, too, that when we had recovered from our surprise, we left our gifts and greetings, and went our way as men who had been dreaming? Gaspard, dost thou not remember?"

And Gaspard, looking now intently in the other's face, replied: "Yes, Melchoir, I remember thee, and I remember the journey of which thou hast spoken better than I remember aught else. Neither have I forgotten the surprise and disappointment with which we came to the place whither the star led us; nor how, after leaving our gifts, we went away as in a dream; and, Melchoir, I have been dreaming ever since. Even here hast thou found me in a dream of perplexity. I am still Gaspard, the wandering magician; for how many years I know not, I have wandered up and down these lands of Europe. I have crossed the seas; in every place I have sought to find the kingdom over which we were told this young prince was one day to reign. Dost thou not remember that we were told His kingdom was to last forever, that He would reign in it himself forever and would never die? Alas! I have lost the old power of the magician's art. I can summon no star to guide me to the place where I shall find this kingdom and its king."

"Truly, Gaspard," answered Melchoir, "the story of your wanderings is but the repetition of my own; and even now was I drawn to this mountain summit on the self-same errand that brought you here,—to see if I could not discover in the direction of yonder land, where Bethlehem was, some star which might prove to be His star, and which might guide me in the new quest. If only our old companion, Balthazar, were with us now, he might give us the clew to our search, for not only was he more skillful in the magician's art, but he was braver and more courageous, and withal more serene in spirit."

January 6 - Epiphany

Now, even while Melchoir was speaking, a voice was heard a little way down the mountain. Gaspard and Melchoir stopped to listen. The voice was singing, and the words of the song floated up to them distinctly:

> If the sun has hid its light,
> If the day has turned to night,
> If the heavens are not benign,
> If the stars refuse to shine—
>
>> Heart of man lose not thy hope;
>> Door, there's none that shall not ope;
>> Path, there's none that shall not clear;
>> Heart of man! Why shouldest thou fear?
>
> If for years should be thy quest,
> If for years thou hast no rest,
> If thou circlest earth and sea,
> If thou worn and weary be—
>
>> Heart of man, lose not thy hope;
>> Door, there's none that shall not ope;
>> Path, there's none that shall not clear;
>> Heart of man! Why shouldest thou fear?

"That," exclaimed Gaspard and Melchoir together, "is the voice of Balthazar," and they hastened to meet him, for he was now almost at the summit, and the refrain of his song was still upon his lips. At that moment Balthazar sprang up from the sloping path into full view of the two men, and, giving each a hand, exclaimed: "Gaspard, Melchoir, beloved companions, I have found you at last. The peasants below were not mistaken. From their description, I was certain I should find you here. And you, too, have been searching these long years for the kingdom of the Christ! and, like me, you have met with disappointment; but, comrades, be not of faint heart:

> Door, there's none that shall not open;
> Path, there's none that shall not clear.

Let us hasten down the mountain, for see! The sky is already growing gold and crimson beyond the pillars of Hercules. Let us seek the wayfarer's lodging with the hospitable peasants in the valley, and tomorrow let us begin our search for the Christ anew. We have wandered alone; let us invoke now the star to guide us together."

That night, therefore, the three strangers lodged with the simple peasant people in the valley, partaking with thankfulness of the coarse bread, the dates and the red wine—the common fare of their daily life. Nor did they fail to notice a motto inscribed above the fireplace in rude Greek letters:

On the morrow they were ready to begin their search together for the Christ, and they hoped not to wander far before they should find at least the outskirts of His kingdom. But whither should they go? In what direction should they first turn their steps?

While they were thus wondering and debating, Balthazar suddenly exclaimed: "I see the star!" And behold, a little way before them, and at no great distance above their heads, they discerned in the gray of the early morning a star of pale, opal light, which seemed to move forward as the men moved toward it.

"We must follow the star!" Balthazar said in a whisper. Silently and breathlessly his companions followed on.

Now, so intently did the three men keep their eyes fixed upon the star, and so eagerly did they follow in the direction where it seemed to lead, that it was only after a considerable time they discovered that they had become separated from each other, and that their paths were getting farther and farther apart. Yet, there before each of them was the star, shining with its soft, opalescent light, and still ringing in their ears were the words of Balthazar—"we must follow the star."

So each followed the star, each by himself alone. Gaspard's path wound along near the shore of the gulfs and bays of the Mediterranean, until at last the star turned southward and drew him nearer and nearer to a great city, and finally stood still over the dome of a vast cathedral. "It must be," thought Gaspard, "that I have come to the end of my search. This must be the capital and palace of the eternal king."

The square in front of the cathedral was thronged with people; multitudes were pouring in through the great portals. Gaspard joined the throngs, and at last found himself under the mighty dome, which seemed to him as far away as the sky itself. Everything in this wonderful place appealed to his imagination. There were great rows of massive columns, symbol of a strength eternal, and they seemed like wide-open arms holding out a welcome to the human race. There were statues and paintings by great masters in art. The light of the sun poured in through many-colored windows, on which were blazoned the deeds of heroes and saints. Strains of music from the great organ in the distance floated out upon the air. Touched and thrilled by all he saw, Gaspard exclaimed to himself: "The place on which I stand is holy ground."

Soon, however, he perceived that the throngs of people were not lingering, like himself, in awe and wonder over the great columns and the dome, and the statues, and the paintings, and the windows. Their eyes were fixed intently upon something that was going on

January 6 - Epiphany

in the far end of the cathedral. An altar was there, and priests in white robes passing up and down before it, and tall tapers burning around it. Near the altar was the image of a man hanging from a cross; his hands and feet were pierced with nails, and a cruel wound was in his side. The people were gazing at this altar, and at the image, and at what the white-robed priests were doing. The strains of solemn music from the organ blended with the voices of priests chanting the service. Clouds of incense rose from censers, swung with solemn motion by the altar-boys, and the fragrance of the incense was wafted down the long aisles. At last, the tinkling of a bell. The organ became silent for an instant, as though it felt within its heart the awful solemnity of the moment; and then it burst forth into new rapture, and the people began pouring out through the great doors.

Gaspard went forth with the throng into the cathedral square. "And this," he said, "is the end of my search. I have found the Christ. His kingdom is in the imagination of man. How beautiful, how wonderful, how strange it was! 'Dominus vobiscum,' did not the priests say? Here, then, at last I have found the city of the great King."

But as he lingered, behold! The star which had stood over the dome of the cathedral was now before him, as at first, and seemed to waver and tremble, as if beckoning him on. So, although his feet seemed bound to the spot, and his heart was still throbbing with the deep feelings the cathedral service had created in him, remembering the words of Balthazar, "we must follow the star," he slowly and reluctantly walked on.

In the meantime Melchoir also had followed faithfully the path along which the star seemed to lead. Through forests in which he almost lost his way, across rivers difficult and dangerous to ford—still he followed on. At length Melchoir's star seemed to tarry over the spire of a Gothic church, into which the people were going in throngs. Waiting a moment, to be sure that the star was actually standing still, Melchoir went in with the rest. In this place was no altar, such as Gaspard saw; no image on the cross; no white-robed priests; no swinging censers. But, as Melchoir entered he heard strains from the organ, and a chorus of voices was singing an anthem beginning with the words, "Te Deum Laudamus." And when the anthem came to a close, a man clothed in a black robe, such as scholars were wont to wear, rose in his place upon a platform elevated above the people, and began to speak to them about the kingdom of Christ. Melchoir listened in eager expectancy. The Truth Shall Make You Free "The kingdom of the Christ," the preacher said, "is the kingdom of the truth, and the truth is to be continued and kept alive by the strength of man's belief. Those things which have been handed down by holy men and sacred oracles since Christ was here upon the earth, are the truths by which we live. How can Christ live except He live in our beliefs? Why did the Father of all entrust us with our reasons, unless it were that we should make them the instruments of our faith and our salvation? Let us therefore stand in our places, while we recite together the articles of our holy faith."

Crazy About Christmas

These and many such words did the scholar-preacher declare. And as he sat there with the people, Melchoir felt the weight of the solemn and earnest words, and he said: "So at last have I come to the end of my search. The kingdom of Christ is in the mind of man. His kingdom is the kingdom of the truth."

Then he followed the throngs as they went forth from the church; but the star which had tarried over the lofty spire was now before him, and the opal light wavered and trembled, as if beckoning him on; and the words of the preacher, "we must believe," seemed to blend with the words of Balthazar, "we must follow the star." So, reluctantly and slowly he followed on.

But Balthazar—whither went he, following the star? Over many a rugged way, through many a tangled thicket, through valleys and over hills. His star tarried over no cathedrals; it lingered over no Gothic spires. It seemed capricious and restless and tireless. At times it seemed intent on coming to a pause over the head of some human being, but perhaps it was because these human beings themselves were so restless and so busy that the star could not accomplish its intent. For Balthazar saw these men and women hurrying hither and thither on errands of mercy, or deeds of justice; he saw them ferreting out great wrongs, laying heavy blows on the backs of men who oppressed and defrauded their fellow men.

At length Balthazar seemed to understand the movements of the star, and, drawing nearer, he would seem to hear these men repeating cheering and encouraging words to one another. "Pure religion and undefiled," he heard one exclaiming, "is to visit the fatherless and widows in their affliction, and to keep himself unspotted from the world." And another echoed, "Inasmuch as we do it to the least of these, we do it unto Christ."

Ah! thought Balthazar as he listened, I see the meaning of it now; I am coming to the end of my search. The kingdom of Christ—I have found it. It is in the deeds of men; it is in the conscience and the serving will. Devotion to right, this is the law of the kingdom of Christ."

Then Balthazar turned to go in search of his comrades again; but behold! The opal star was trembling, as if beckoning him on. So, still doubting if he had reached the end of his search, he followed the star.

Thus Gaspard, Melchoir and Balthazar, each following the star, at last approached each other. The star of each seemed to melt and blend into the star of the others, and the opal light stood at last in the center of the group. Gaspard exclaimed: "I have found that which we all were seeking. The kingdom of Christ is in the imagination; Christ lives in what man feels."

"Nay," said Melchoir, "I have followed the star, and I have found what we sought. The kingdom of Christ is in the reason of man. Christ lives in what man believes."

"But," cried Balthazar, "my star has led me to a different end. The kingdom of Christ is in the will of man. Christ lives in what man does."

"The truth," once more exclaimed Melchoir, "is the law of the kingdom."

January 6 - Epiphany

"Not truth," declared Balthazar, "but justice, righteousness, goodness and purity—these are its laws and its marks."

"Nay, comrades beloved, hearken to me," answered Gaspard, "it is the miracle of the divine presence. It is God among men, realized in the holy mass. I beheld it all in yonder cathedral."

But lo once more the star began to tremble and to change its place.

"Let us follow the star!" Balthazar whispered. "We will follow it," echoed the other two.

Then the star led them on, and they followed together until they came at length to the doorway of a little cottage; and within the cottage they saw a woman bending over a cradle, and in the cradle a little child lay sleeping. She was a peasant woman; her clothing was not rich; the furnishing of the cottage was humble and scanty. The cradle itself was rude, as if put together by hands unskilful in tasks like that. But when the mother looked at her babe a sweet smile played about her lips, and a light was in her eyes. Then all suddenly the three men remembered another scene long before, when they were bearers of gold and frankincense and myrrh to another babe.

And while they stood and wondered by the door, there came a strong and sturdy peasant, broad-shouldered, roughly clad, his face browned in the sun, his hands hardened with toil. He came and stood beside the woman, and they bent together over the cradle of the sleeping child, and the man drew the woman tenderly toward him and kissed her brow.

And still the three men lingered; for behold the star stood still above the child, and they dared not speak. But the heart of Gaspard was saying in silence, "There is something greater than the repeated miracle of the mass."

And Melchoir was thinking, "There is something mightier even than the mind; something superior to naked truth."

And Balthazar was confessing to himself that he had found something more potent even than the righteous deed. For here they all beheld how life was made sweet and blessed and holy by the power of love; and by love for a little child, in whom was all weakness and helplessness, whose only voice was a cry, but who was all strong and mighty with the power of God, because he could transform roughness into tenderness, and selfishness into loving care, and poverty itself into gifts of gold and fragrant myrrh.

"Truly, my comrades," Balthazar said, "love is the greatest of all."

"And now I understand," said Gaspard, "how the weak things of the world can confound the mighty."

"And I," added Melchoir, "see what it means for God to come to earth in the form of a little child."

And so they turned away, and the radiance of the star was round about them, and they were saying to each other: "Our search at last is ended."

from *"The Sketching Club,"* Indianapolis, IN. 1903

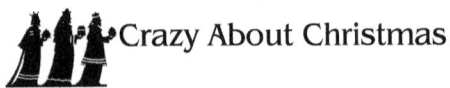
Crazy About Christmas

Fizzy Bath Bombs
Craft/Gift

MATERIALS

- 1/2 cup Citric Acid*
- 1/2 cup Corn Starch
- 1/2 cup Epsom Salts
- 1 cup Baking Soda
- 1 teaspoon water
- 2 teaspoons Essential Oils for scent
- 2-3 tablespoons Coconut oil, Almond oil or Vegetable oil
- 1 tablespoon water
- Natural food coloring (optional)

DIRECTIONS

1. Mix citric acid, baking soda, Epsom salt, and corn starch together in a large bow. Use a whisk to make sure the mixture is clump free.
2. Mix oil, water, essential oil and food coloring together in small bowl or shake in a jar.
3. Slowly add the liquid to the dry mixture. Really slowly like a teaspoon at a time. Whisk as you go, and slow down if it starts to fizzy. The result should look like damp sand.
4. Stuff into molds. Your molds can be silicone, plastic ornaments, metal tart or muffin tins, or you can purchase molds online specifically for making bath bombs. Press the mixture down very firmly.
5. Let the bath bombs dry completely then pop them out.
6. Throw one into your tub and enjoy the fizzy goodness of a soft and relaxing bath. Take the rest of them and place cellophane gift bags to share with your friends and family.

Scent Combinations:
Spa Scents: eucalyptus and lavender, lavender with a drop of peppermint or vanilla.
Energizing/ mind clearing: lemon and wild orange or lemongrass, rosemary and thyme
Balancing: sage, mint and tea tree
Calming: geranium, lavender and rose, lavender
Uplifting/Stress Relief: orange and clove, cedarwood and lemon

*Citirc Acid is found in citrus fruit and is used as a natural preservative in foods.

January 6 - Epiphany

Quick and Easy King Cake
Serves 12 - 16

INGREDIENTS

1 dozen frozen cinnamon rolls
   icing packets from cinnamon rolls
   sugar crystals in purple, gold, and green

INSTRUCTIONS

1. Spray a Bundt or Tube pan with cooking spray.
2. Place frozen rolls on their sides in the pan. There may not be much space between them. If you cannot get all of them in the pan put the rest back into the freezer for later. Cover pan with plastic wrap and put in refrigerator to rise over night or on the counter to rise for 3-5 hours till doubled, depending on the temperature of your kitchen.
3. Preheat your oven to 350 degrees.
4. Bake for 20 - 25 minutes or until the cinnamon rolls are lightly brown.
5. Remove from oven and let rest for 5 minutes before turning out onto platter.
6. In the meantime, knead the frosting packets gently before opening.
7. Before icing the cooled cake make a small slit somewhere in the cake and insert the small plastic baby pushing it far enough inside so it cannot be seen.
8. Spread the icing and decorate with alternating sugar colors in purple, gold and green. *Hint* if you don't have decorating sugar crystals you can make your own by putting a small amount of sugar in a ziplock bag and add a drop of two of food coloring to the sugar and shake well. If you want a darker color add a drop and shake until you get the desired color.

Tradition holds that the cake is "to draw the kings" to the Epiphany. A figurine, generally a baby to represent the Christ Child is hidden in the cake and the person who finds the trinket in his or her slice will have good luck, become king for the day and will have to bring next year's cake. The colors used to decorate the cake have meanings; purple to symbolize justice, green to symbolize faith, and gold to symbolize power.

Works Cited

Baum, L. F. (1904, December). A Letter from Santa Claus. The Delineator.

Bosworth, Frederick N., (1982) The Young King and the Stones

Browne, F. (1916). Granny's Wonderful Chair and its Tales of Fairy Times. New York: E.P. Dutton.

Butterworth, M. (1997). Just 24 Days Till Christmas. Oviedo, FL: Day to Day Enterprises.

Clemens, S. (1931). A Letter from Santa Claus. In C. Clemens, My Father, Mark Twain.

Curtiss, P. A. (1916). Christmas Stories and Legends. Indianapolis, IN: Meigs Publishing Co.

Dewhurst, F. E. (1903). The Magi in the West and Their Search for the Christ: A Tale for the Christmas Tide. Chicago: The Abbey Company.

Forrester, F. (1856, January). A Happy New Year. Woodworth's Youth's Cabinet, pp. 1-3.

Hoffman, E. (1853). Nutcracker and Mouse-King. (M. S. Simon, Trans.) New York: D. Appleton & Company.

Olcott, F.J. (1914) Great Stories for Great Holidays. Boston & New York: Houghton Mifflin Company.

Picthall, M. L. (1914). The Worker in Sandalwood. New York: Everyland.

Pocci, C. F. (1920). The Stranger Child A Legend. In S. S. Harriman, Stories for Little Children. Boston & New York: Houghton Mifflin Co.

Potter, B. (1903). The Tailor of Gloucester. England: Frederick Warne & Co.

Smith, N. A. (1891). The Story of Christmas. In K. D. Smith, The Story Hour. Houghton, Mifflin and Company.

Tolstoy, L. (1885). Where Love is There God is Also. Worth While Booklet Series.

Index

Symbols
90 Minute Dinner Rolls 215

A
ABC's of Christmas 51
A Christmas Orange 187
ACTIVITES
   Christmas Carol Game II 202
   Classic Tangram Puzzle 279
   Handprint Reindeer Shirt 26
   Jigsaw Puzzle 3
   Musical Chairs 13
   Quest for Stories 234, 235
   White Elephant Exchange 165
A Different Kind of Christmas 191
A Happy New Year 249
A Kidnapped Santa Claus 63
Alden, Raymond Macdonald 55
   In the Great Walled Country 55
A Letter from Santa Claus 73
   Twain, Mark 73
Amazing Crustless Quiche 168
APPETIZERS
   Amazing Crustless Quiche 168
   Appetizer Tree Board 282
   Chicken Nut Puffs 169
   Ham Pinwheels 167
   Herb and Garlic Cheese 167
Appetizer Tree Board 282
Aroma Therapy Candles 286
A Sweet Reminder 125

B
Bacon Baklava 196
Bacon Cheddar Potato Pancakes 276
Barley Cream with Fruit 230
Baum, L. Frank 63
   A Kidnapped Santa Claus 63

BEVERAGE
   Mistletoe Punch 166
Bird Bath/Feeder 108
Bosworth, Frederick N. 45
   Young King and the Stones, The 45
BRAZIL
   Brigadeiro 14
   Violin's Song, The 11
BREAD
   90 Minute Dinner Rolls 215
   Gingerbread Muffins 186
   Idaho Style Cinnamon Rolls 84
   Ontbijtkoek 21
   Overnight Eggnog French Toast 211
   Savory Cheese Coins 50
   Soft Pretzels 271
Brigadeiro 14
Broccoli Salad 214
Browne, Frances 37
   Christmas Cuckoo, The 223
   Story of Childe Charity, The 37
Butterworth, MyLinda
   A Sweet Reminder 125
   Elves and the Shoemaker, The 273
   Le Befana the Giver of Gifts 283
   Legend of the Snow Maiden, The 239
   Luda, The Reindeer Maiden 23
   Mullah Nasreddin and the Feast 1
   Why the Evergreens are Forever Green 93

C
CAKE & FROSTING
   Carrot-Apple Cake 78
   Cream Cheese Frosting 109
   Hot Fudge Pudding Cake 155
   Hummingbird Cake 109

Crazy About Christmas

Irish Dairy Cake 9
Pecan Cream Cheese Frosting 78
Pumpkin Pie Crunch Cake 216
Quick and Easy King Cake 297
CANDY
  Brigadeiro 14
  Chocolate Cherry Mice 104
  Pumpkin Pie Fudge 150
  Spiced Candied Pecans 142
  Winter-Mint Crunch 130
Candy Cane Mice 102
Candy Cane Vase 129
Caramelized Orange Flan 190
Carrot-Apple Cake 78
Cascading Star Mobile 247
CELTIC
  Clever Baker, The 5
  Irish Dairy Cake 9
Cheesy Potatoes 213
CHEROKEE LEGEND
  Why the Evergreens are Forever Green 93
Chicken Nut Puffs 169
Chief Cookie Baker Apron 33
Chocolate Cherry Mice 104
Christmas Card Boxes 148
Christmas Carol Game II 202
Christmas Cuckoo, The 223
Christmas Fairy 134
Christmas Fairy of Strasburg, The 131
Christmas Feast 212
CHRISTMAS FEAST
  90 Minute Dinner Rolls 213
  Broccoli Salad 213
  Cheesy Potatoes 213
  Pumpkin Pie Crunch Cake 213
  Sweet Potato Casserole 213
Christmas Humor 157
Cinnamon Stick Santa 90

Classic Tangram Puzzle 279
Clay Pot Santa 82
Clever Baker, The 5
Cookie Cutter Gift Bags 161
COOKIES & BROWNIES
  Gingerbread Cookies 35
  Gingerdoodles 123
  Lebkuchen Bars 86, 91
  Sand Art Brownies 176
  Streusel Linzer Squares 170
Coppée, François 119
  Wooden Shoes of Little Wolff, The 119
Coyne, J. Stirling 131
  Christmas Fairy of Strasburg 131
CRAFTS
  Aroma Therapy Candles 286
  Bird Bath/Feeder 108
  Candy Cane Mice 102
  Candy Cane Vase 129
  Cascading Star Mobile 247
  Chief Cookie Baker Apron 33
  Christmas Card Boxes 148
  Christmas Fairy 134
  Cinnamon Stick Santa 90
  Classic Tangram Puzzle 279
  Clay Pot Santa 82
  Cookie Cutter Gift Bags 161
  Crystal Coal Garden 71
  Dishtowel Angel 180
  Embossed Foil Art 229
  Fizzy Bath Bombs 296
  Fruity Playdough 185
  Gift Tags 60
  Handprint Reindeer Shirt 26
  Handsy Santa 75
  Holiday Coasters 113
  Holiday Cone Boxes 140
  Holiday Pillow Cases 117
  Jigsaw Puzzle 3

Index

Kissmas Trees 153
Ojo de Dios or God's Eye 269
Personalized Calendar 251
Personalized Journal 255
Pine Cone Elves 275
Pomander Ball 189
Quest for Stories 234
Rustic Wood Slat Tree 94
Scrabble Ornaments 53
Snowflake 241
Sock Snowman 20
Spinning Whirligig Toy 122
Stained Glass Jars 174
Stained Glass Manger 194
Thank-You Cards 221
Tug Dog Toy 43
Word Rocks 49
Cranberry Raspberry Jam 135
Cream Cheese Frosting 109
Cream Puffs 181
Creamy Coconut Curry 4
Crystal Coal Garden 71
Curtiss, Phebe A. 163
   Legend Of The White Gifts, The 163
   Little Piccola 87

D
Day, Linda S. 105
   Legend of the Christmas Robin, The 105
DECORATION
   Candy Cane Mice 102
   Candy Cane Vase 129
   Cascading Star Mobile 247
   Christmas Fairy 134
   Cinnamon Stick Santa 90
   Clay Pot Santa 82
   Dishtowel Angel 180
   Embossed Foil Art 229

Handsy Santa 75
Kissmas Trees 153
Ojo de Dios or God's Eye 269
Snowflake 241
Stained Glass Manger 194
DESSERT
   Bacon Baklava 196
   Barley Cream with Fruit 230
   Caramelized Orange Flan 190
   Cream Puffs 181
   Homemade Marshmallows 243
   Strawberry Santa 72
Dewhurst, Frederick E.
   The Magi in the West and their Search for the Christ 289
Dishtowel Angel 180

E
Elves and the Shoemaker, The 273
Embossed Foil Art 229

F
Fairy's New Year Gift, The 253
   Poulsson, Emilie 253
Finger Food Party Night
   Amazing Crustless Quiche 168
   Chicken Nut Puffs 169
   Ham Pinwheels 167
   Herb and Garlic Cheese 167
   Mistletoe Punch 166
   Streusel Linzer Squares 170
First Christmas Rose, The 171
Fizzy Bath Bombs 296
Forrester, Francis 249
   A Happy New Year 249
Fruity Playdough 185

G
GAMES
   Christmas Carol Game II 202
   Musical Chairs 13

Crazy About Christmas

    White Elephant Exchange 165
GERMANY
    Christmas Fairy of Strasburg, The 131
    Elves and the Shoemaker 273
    Soft Pretzels 271
GIFT
    Candy Cane Mice 102
    Dishtowel Angel 180
    Embossed Foil Art 229
    Fizzy Bath Bombs 296
    Glazed Popcorn 162
    Holiday Coasters 113
    Holiday Cone Boxes 140
    Holiday Pillow Cases 117
    Hot Chocolate Sticks 61
    Personalized Calendar 251
    Sand Art Brownies 176
    Stained Glass Jars 174
    Word Rocks 49
Gift Tags 60
Gingerbread Bees, The 29
Gingerbread Cookies 35
Gingerbread Muffins 186
Gingerdoodles 123
Glazed Popcorn 162
God's Eye. *See also* Ojo de Dios
Golden Legend, The
    Offero, The Legend of St. Christopher 231

H
Ham Pinwheels 167
Handprint Reindeer Shirt 26
Handsy Santa 75
Harvest-Nut Granola 28
Herb and Garlic Cheese 167
Herbes de Provence 287
Hoffman, E.T.A. 137
    The Nutcracker and the Mouse King 137
Holiday Coasters 113
Holiday Cone Boxes 140
Holiday Pillow Cases 117
HOLLAND
    Ontbijtkoek 21
    Three Skaters, The 15
Homemade Marshmallows 243
Hot Chocolate Sticks 61
Hot Fudge Pudding Cake 155
Humble Pie 237
Hummingbird Cake 109

I
Idaho Style Cinnamon Rolls 84
Indoor Fairy Garden 7
In the Great Walled Country 55
Irish Dairy Cake 9
ITALY
    Le Befana the Giver of Gifts 283

J
JAMS & JELLIES
    Cranberry Raspberry Jam 135
Jigsaw Puzzle 3

K
Kingsley, Florence M.
    The Star 177
Kissmas Trees 153

L
Le Befana the Giver of Gifts 283
Lebkuchen Bars 91
Legend of the Christmas Robin, The 105
Legend of the Snow Maiden, The 239
Lentil, Kielbasa, and Garlic Stew 258
Letter of Thanks 217
Little Piccola 87
Luda, The Reindeer Maiden 23

M
Macaroni and Cheese. *See* Savory Toasted

Index

Cheese with Noodles
Magi in the West and their Search for the Christ, The 289
MAIN DISH
  Amazing Crustless Quiche 168
  Creamy Coconut Curry 4
  Humble Pie 237
  Savory Toasted Cheese with Noodles 114
  Taco Stack-Ups 54
  Turkey Pot Pie 222
  White Christmas Chili 95
MIDDLE EAST
  Mullah Nasreddin and the Feast 1
Miracle, The 111
Mistletoe Punch 166
MIXES
  Herbes de Provence 287
  Season Salt 287
Most Beautiful Thing, The 151
Mullah Nasreddin and the Feast 1
Musical Chairs 13

N
Nutcracker and the Mouse King, The 137
  Hoffman, E.T.A. 137

O
Offero, The Legend of St. Christopher 231
Ojo de Dios or God's Eye 269. *See also* God's Eye
Ontbijtkoek 21
ORNAMENT
  Cinnamon Stick Santa 90
  Handsy Santa 75
  Holiday Cone Boxes 140
  Kissmas Trees 153
  Scrabble Ornaments 53
Overnight Eggnog French Toast 211

P
PAPER CRAFTS
  Christmas Card Boxes 148
  Christmas Fairy 134
  Cookie Cutter Gift Bags 161
  Gift Tags 60
  Handsy Santa 75
  Holiday Cone Boxes 140
  Kissmas Trees 153
  Snowflake 241
Party Chow Snack Mix 252
Pecan Cream Cheese Frosting 78
Personalized Calendar 251
Personalized Journal 255
Pickthall, Marjorie L. C.
  Worker in Sandalwood, The 143
PIE
  Snowdrop Pecan Pie 248
Pine Cone Elves 275
Pocci, Count Franz 115
  Stranger Child, The 115
POLAND
  Gingerbread Bees, The 29
Pomander Ball 189
Potter, Beatrix 97
  Tailor Of Gloucester, The 97
Poulsson, Emilie 253
  Fairy's New Year Gift, The 253
Pumpkin Pie Crunch Cake 216
Pumpkin Pie Fudge 150

Q
Quest for Stories 234
Quick and Easy King Cake 297
QUOTES
  Dreams- M. Scott Peck 244,
  Kindness-Kahlil Gibrar 238
  Magical dust of Christmas-Max Lucado 182
  Make a difference-Lindsey Stirling 10

Crazy About Christmas

Messes-Andy Rooney 156
Miracles-Albert Einstein 110
Santa Claus-Truman Capote 62
This Christmas-Howard W. Hunter 198
We Three Kings-John Henry Hopkins 288

R
RECIPES
90 Minute Dinner Rolls 215
Amazing Crustless Quiche 168
Appetizer Tree Board 282
Bacon Baklava 196
Bacon Cheddar Potato Pancakes 276
Barley Cream with Fruit 230
Brigadeiro 14
Broccoli Salad 214
Caramelized Orange Flan 190
Carrot-Apple Cake 78
Chicken Nut Puffs 169
Chocolate Cherry Mice 104
Cranberry Raspberry Jam 135
Cream Puffs 181
Creamy Coconut Turkey Curry 4
Gingerbread Muffins 186
Gingerdoodles 123
Glazed Popcorn 162
Ham Pinwheels 167
Harvest-Nut Granola 28
Herb and Garlic Cheese 167
Herbes de Provence 287
Homemade Marshmallows 243
Hot Chocolate Sticks 61
Hot Fudge Pudding Cake 155
Humble Pie 237
Hummingbird Cake 109
Idaho Style Cinnamon Rolls 84
Irish Dairy Cake 9
Lebkuchen Bars 91
Lentil, Kielbasa, and Garlic Stew 258

Mistletoe Punch 166
Ontbijtkoek 21
Overnight Eggnog French Toast 211
Party Chow Snack Mix 252
Pecan Cream Cheese Frosting 78
Pumpkin Pie Crunch Cake 216
Pumpkin Pie Fudge 150
Quick and Easy King Cake 297
Sand Art Brownies 176
Savory Cheese Coins 50
Savory Toasted Cheese with Noodles 114
Season Salt 287
Snowdrop Pecan Pie 248
Soft Pretzels 271
Spiced Candied Pecans 142
Spicy Sausage and Bean Soup 118
Strawberry Santa 72
Streusel Linzer Squares 170
Sweet Potato Casserole 212
Taco Stack-Ups 54
Tasty Dog Treats 44
Turkey Pot Pie 222
White Christmas Chili 95
Winter-Mint Crunch 130
RECYCLE PROJECT
Christmas Card Boxes 148
Gift Tags 60
Tug Dog Toy 43
Roberts, Lynne 15
Three Skaters, The 15
RUSSIA
Legend of the Snow Maiden 239
Rustic Wood Slat Tree 94

S
SALADS
Broccoli Salad 214
Sand Art Brownies 176
Santa Claus-Truman Capote 62

Index

Savory Cheese Coins 50
Savory Toasted Cheese with Noodles 114
Scrabble Ornaments 53
Season Salt 287
SEWING
  Holiday Pillow Cases 117
SIBERIA
  Luda, The Reindeer Maiden 23
Smith, Nora A.
  Story of Christmas, The 199
SNACKS
  Glazed Popcorn 162
  Party Chow Snack Mix 252
Snowdrop Pecan Pie 248
Snowflake 241
Sock Snowman 20
Soft Pretzels 271
SOUPS
  Lentil, Kielbasa, and Garlic Stew 258
  Spicy Sausage and Bean Soup 118
Spiced Candied Pecans 142
Spicy Sausage and Bean Soup 118
Spinning Whirligig Toy 122
Stained Glass Jars 174
Stained Glass Manger 194
St. Nicholas Day 86
STORIES
  ABC's of Christmas 51
  A Christmas Orange 187
  A Different Kind of Christmas 191
  A Happy New Year 249
  A Kidnapped Santa Claus 63
  A Letter from Santa Claus 73
  A Sweet Reminder 125
  Christmas Cuckoo, The 223
  Christmas Fairy of Strasburg, The 131
  Christmas Humor 157
  Clever Baker, The 5
  Curtiss, Phebe A. 163

  Elves and the Shoemaker, The 273
  Fairy's New Year Gift, The 253
  First Christmas Rose, The 171
  Gingerbread Bees, The 29
  In the Great Walled Country 55
  Le Befana the Giver of Gifts 283
  Legend of the Christmas Robin 105
  Legend of the Snow Maiden, The 239
  Legend Of The White Gifts, The 163
  Letter of Thanks 217
  Little Piccola 87
  Luda, The Reindeer Maiden 23
  Magi in the West and their Search for Christ, The 289
  Miracle, The 111
  Most Beautiful Thing, The 151
  Nutcracker and the Mouse King, The 137
  Offero, The Legend of St. Christopher 231
  Story of Childe Charity, The 37
  Story of Christmas, The 199
  Tailor Of Gloucester, The 97
  Teach the Children 79
  The Star 177
  The Stranger Child, The 115
  Three Skaters, The 15
  Three Trees 277
  Two Babes in a Manger 183
  Where Love Is, There God Is Also 259
  White Dwarf, The 245
  Why the Evergreens are Forever Green 93
  Wooden Shoes of Little Wolff, The 119
  Worker in Sandalwood, The 143
  Young King and the Stones, The 45
Story of Childe Charity, The 37
Story of Christmas, The 199
Stranger Child, The 115

Strawberry Santa 72
Streusel Linzer Squares 170
Sweet Potato Casserole 212

T
Taco Stack-Ups 54
Tailor Of Gloucester, The 97
Tasty Dog Treats 44
Teach the Children 79
Thank-You Cards 221
Thaxter, Celia. *See* Curtiss, Phebe A
The Star 177
Three Skaters, The 15
Three Trees 277
Tolstoy, Count Lev Nikolaevich.
    See Tolstoy, Leo
Tolstoy, Leo
  Where Love Is, There God Is Also 259
Tug Dog Toy 43
Turkey Pot Pie 222
Twain, Mark 73
  A Letter from Santa Claus 73
Two Babes in a Manger 183

V
VEGETABLES
  Bacon Cheddar Potato Pancakes 276
  Broccoli Salad 214
  Cheesy Potatoes 213
  Sweet Potato Casserole 212
Violin's Song, The 11

W
WEARABLE ART
  Chief Cookie Baker Apron 33
  Handprint Reindeer Shirt 26
Where Love Is, There God Is Also 259
White Christmas Chili 95
White Dwarf, The 245
White Elephant Exchange 165

Why the Evergreens are Forever Green 93
Winter-Mint Crunch 130
Wooden Shoes of Little Wolff, The 119
Word Rocks 49
Worker in Sandalwood, The 143

Y
Young King and the Stones, The 45

About the Author

MyLinda Butterworth is the owner and Creative Director of Day to Day Enterprises an independent publishing house since 1997. She is the award-winning author of *For Health's Sake: A Cancer Survivors Cookbook* and *The Monster Run*. Other books to her credit are *Just 24 Days Till Christmas,* plus **the With Magic Scissors Series which includes**: *Springtime, Summer Sizzles, Autumn Adventures and Winter Fun* as well as *Frogazoom* all of which she wrote with her mother, Linda S. Day. MyLinda is a performing artist with Totally Stories where she tours schools and stages across the country. MyLinda has a BFA in theatre education and communications from Brigham Young University, graduate studies in costuming from Arizona State University, and has a Masters Degree in Storytelling from East Tennessee State University. She currently carries the title of Dean of the College of Performing Arts with the The Society for Creative Anachronism (SCA) where she is known as Scholastica Joycors.

Since the beginning of Covid19 MyLinda has been performing alliterations, tongue twisters, and stories on her YouTube channel - Totally Stories. A month after the pandemic started she launched Alliteration Adventure for a daily dose of tongue twisters and alliteration, then she started performing dramatic narrations of *A Thousand Nights and a Night* (1001 Arabian Nights) and then went to the next set of epic tales.

Besides writing, storytelling ,or keeping up her websites MyLinda can be found in the kitchen trying out new recipes (she is a real Mrs. Butterworth after all), in her sewing room piecing quilts, creating crafts, practicing calligraphy and illumination or participating in historical re-enactments with the SCA. But she says her best role in life is being a mom to her two grown children and hanging out with her husband.

Coming 2026
45th Anniversary Edition

Books by Award-Winning Author MyLinda Butterworth

Available from AMAZON.COM and Other Bookstores

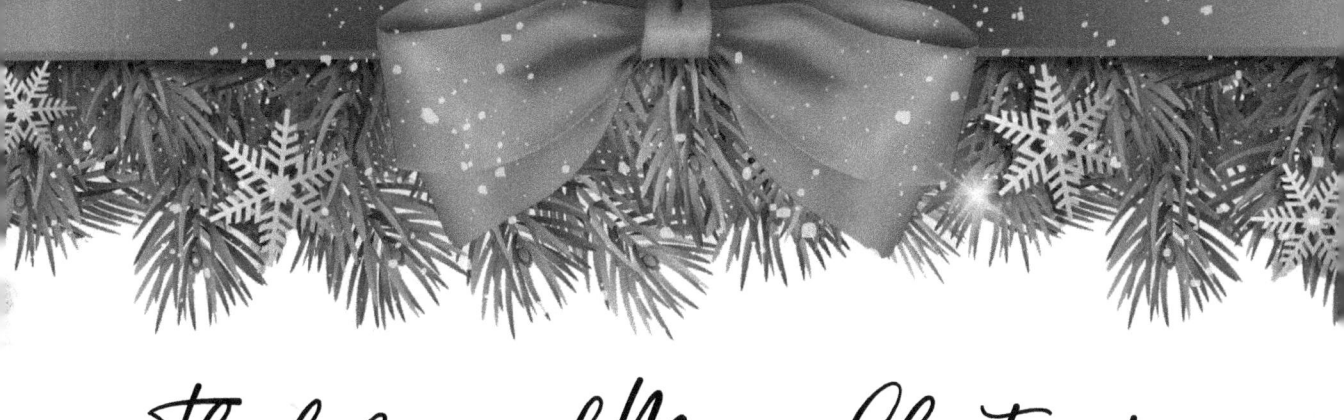

Thank You and Merry Christmas!

I just wanted to say thank you for taking the time to read my book. I hope you enjoyed it.

I love hearing your reaction as it helps me as I create my next book.

Please leave me a helpful review at Amazon, Barnes and Nobles, or Good Reads letting me know what you thought of this book. Your comments help me in creating better books for you.

As my way of saying thanks I will send you my *Embracing Togetherness for the Holidays Journal* if you email me a screen shot of your review to CrazyAboutChristmasBook@gmail.com

Thanks Again!

My Linda Butterworth

www.ingramcontent.com/pod-product-compliance
Lightning Source LLC
Chambersburg PA
CBHW062126160426
43191CB00013B/2205